HARLAN ELLISON'S

THE CITY ON THE EDGE OF FOREVER

The Original Teleplay That Became The Classic Star Trek® Episode

WITH AN EXPANDED INTRODUCTORY ESSAY BY HARLAN ELLISON

Books by Harlan Elliso

NOVELS:
WEB OF THE CITY [1958]   THE SOUND OF A SCYTHE [1960]
SPIDER KISS [1961]

SHORT NOVELS:
DOOMSMAN [1967]   ALL THE LIES THAT ARE MY LIFE [1980]
RUN FOR THE STARS [1991]   MEFISTO IN ONYX [1993]

GRAPHIC NOVELS:
DEMON WITH A GLASS HAND
(*Adaptation with Marshall Rogers*) [1986]
NIGHT AND THE ENEMY (*Adaptation with Ken Steacy*) [1987]
VIC AND BLOOD: THE CHRONICLES OF A BOY AND HIS DOG
(*Adaptation with Richard Corben*) [1989]

SHORT STORY COLLECTIONS:
THE DEADLY STREETS [1958]   SEX GANG (*as Paul Merchant*) [1959]
A TOUCH OF INFINITY [1960]   CHILDREN OF THE STREETS [1961]
GENTLEMAN JUNKIE AND OTHER STORIES OF THE HUNG-UP GENERATION [1961]
ELLISON WONDERLAND [1962]
PAINGOD AND OTHER DELUSIONS [1965]
I HAVE NO MOUTH & I MUST SCREAM [1967]
FROM THE LAND OF FEAR [1967]
LOVE AIN'T NOTHING BUT SEX MISSPELLED [1968]
THE BEAST THAT SHOUTED LOVE AT THE HEART OF THE WORLD [1969]
OVER THE EDGE [1970]
DE HELDEN VAN DE HIGHWAY (*Dutch publication only*) [1973]
ALL THE SOUNDS OF FEAR (*British publication only*) [1973]
THE TIME OF THE EYE (*British publication only*) [1974]
APPROACHING OBLIVION [1974]   DEATHBIRD STORIES [1975]
NO DOORS, NO WINDOWS [1975]
HOE KAN IK SCHREEUWEN ZONDER MOND (*Dutch publication only*) [1977
STRANGE WINE [1978]   SHATTERDAY [1980]
STALKING THE NIGHTMARE [1982]   ANGRY CANDY [1988]
ENSAMVÄRK (*Swedish publication only*) [1992]
JOKES WITHOUT PUNCHLINES [1995]
ROUGH BEASTS [1996]   SLIPPAGE [1996]

COLLABORATIONS:
PARTNERS IN WONDER COLLABORATIONS WITH 14 OTHER WILD TALENTS [1971]
THE STARLOST: PHOENIX WITHOUT ASHES (*with Edward Bryant*) [1975]
MIND FIELDS 33 STORIES INSPIRED BY THE ART OF JACEK YERKA [1994]

White Wolf Publishing
780 Park North Blvd, Suite 100
Clarkston, GA 30021
www.white-wolf.com

Printed in Canada

White Wolf Edition: September 1996

Cover and Book Design by Michael Scott Cohen

Acknowledgments

Only time will tell. Those who deserve thanks in the Hard Times of one year, turn out to be somewhat less deserving in the Harsh Glare of three decades later. We live and learn. Sometimes we live and learn and get so damned angry we forget earlier kindnesses blunted by the ache of betrayal. Which is about as Zen as I care to get.

Back then, when the series was just debuting and I was writing the teleplay you'll be reading here, both Herb Solow and Bobby Justman were extraordinarily kind to me. Time has passed away, and maybe memory has dimmed, and I ain't very happy about some of the things these two pals of days-gone have written and said about events covered in this book . . . but I remember with clarity how they befriended me back then, and I would rather dwell on those times than these. So, I thank Herb and Bob.

Steadfast from the git-go, David Gerrold and John D. F. Black and Dorothy Fontana, whom you know as D. C. Fontana. Years have slipped behind us, the four of us, and Johnny's beard has grown to truly Moseslike proportions; and David just got around to writing the best story of his career ("The Martian Child") and they gave him a Hugo and a Nebula for it, and he's finally managed to shuck off that cloaca of being "just a *Star Trek* tv writer"; and Dorothy, well, despite a truly recent stunning revelation included in her Afterword to this volume, I confess to deep and unassailable admiration and affection. These are four from the old days (and from this four-year agony of putting *City* between covers). It took four years because it was the hardest, probably nastiest, job of writing I've ever had to do, and when it was almost finished, Gene Roddenberry screwed me up yet one more time by dying.

Here are the soldiers and scavengers and hustlers and shotgun-riders who helped get this book into your hands. Please kindly do not forget this list. Commit it to memory. When those of you who will get demented at what I'll be saying in these pages run amuck and come with blazing torches to *schlep* me out of my bed for crucifixion, I'd like to think all these aiders and abetters will likewise dot the landscape with their anguished bodies. No one likes to be the only yotz at the party.

In no particular order:

Mark Evanier; David S. Rosenbaum at Paramount legal; Richard Curtis; Larry Closs, Executive Editor at *TV Guide;* Kevin Ryan at Pocket Books, who served as amenuensis; Sharon Buck; Bill Amend, creator of the wonderful cartoon strip, *Fox Trot*, for allowing me to reprint the gag on page 46; and to a decent and honorable investigative journalist who cannot be named, and to employees of NBC and Paramount who cannot be named, and to divers correspondents, informants, moles and insiders who cannot be named . . . my secret thanks to you all. Have no fear: they could pound my balls flat with a steel-stamping press, and they'll never get your names from me; not even yours, Arthur.

It's been a killer of a preproduction procedure. Months. Snarls. Immaturity, rudeness, earthquakes, medical problems, idiot computer programs that required us to proof these pages over and over till we nearly lost our eyesight and our minds, heart attacks, quadruple bypass surgery, poverty, lies, blasphemy, perfidious behavior, tainted foods, strange alien creatures from foreign lands, senility, uncontrolled flatulence, impending death or disfigurement. Months. Snarls.

But we got through it, and we're still alive, so what the hell. Thank you to Scott Cohen, our fecund and idefatigable designer, right up to the blue line additions. Thank you. Thank you particularly to the remarkable Laura Perkinson, White Wolf's demon editrix on this project. Her attention to detail, her delicious punctiliousness, her dogged commitment to producing an error-free text, cannot be praised highly enough. Thank you. Now go put a cold compress on your brow.

The good friends who wrote the Afterwords. Each a star, each with better things on which to spend time than writing a coda to this book. But they did it. Because they're stand-up. I am in the debt of each of you. (Not to mention Stewart Wieck.)

Last of all, Susan. My wife. Yeah, you.

If it were not for Susan, trust me on this, I would long-since have taken to the streets with an assault rifle. You can all thank your lucky stars she's here on my behalf—because frankly, it's been *decades* since I was a responsible person.

Not once, but many times.

Not just in private chats,
but in print, on the air,
and where it counted.

For thirty years he knew
the truth and wasn't afraid
to tell it. He was there.

In friendship,
this one is for

ALAN BRENNERT

The author with Leonard Nimoy and William Shatner, in 1966, on the set of
STAR TREK® with the inscriptions, "Who's the kid in the middle—Bill
Shatner" and "Harlan—love you and your great credits—Leonard Nimoy."

Photo from the author's personal collection.

Contents

"It's not the vision I had."
Gully Jimson

The Horse's Mouth
by Joyce Cary

WOULD YOU BUY A USED GALAXY FROM THIS MAN?

30 March 1988

Museum of Broadcasting, 5th Annual TelevisionFest held at the Los Angeles County Museum of Art's Leo S. Bing Theater

---

Gene Roddenberry Speaks To The Crowd. In answer to a question about the writers on the original *Star Trek* series: "Most of those I don't want in the same room with me. I've given all of them a chance. Harlan got a chance on the first show and wrote a $350,000 estimate budget show in those days when we only had $186,000. And when I told him to cut the budget, he sent me back a note that said, 'Do it with special effects.' He then submitted his original script for a Writers Guild Award, and when he won the prize, which he deserved for the script ... except that many people would get prizes if they wrote scripts that were budgeted out at three times the show's cost. I rewrote that script for Harlan, and it won the Nebula Award, which he rushed up on stage and took credit for, too . . . David Gerrold has been condemning the show constantly, although I had him on staff for many months. He never wrote an episode we could shoot. So beware of these people that are loud voices. Give your attention to people who quietly do good work." (Thunderous applause.)

CAN YOU SPOT THE DEMENTED LIES IN THE ABOVE TRANSCRIPT?

(*Clue*: "The City on the Edge of Forever" never won a Nebula Award. It won a Hugo. In a letter to Harlan Ellison only two months after "City" aired, Gene Roddenberry stated the episode had only been $6,000 over budget. When Ellison accepted the Hugo Award—only one of the 8 ½ he has won—he clearly noted to the vast audience that this honor was being bestowed on a crippled, eviscerated, fucked-up version of his original dream. David Gerrold never wrote an episode that Gene thought was shootable ... then how do we account for something titled "The Trouble with Tribbles"?)

NOW READ "Perils of the 'City'" AND LEARN THE TRUTH!

INTRODUCTORY ESSAY

AUTHOR'S NOTE

There was a 1000-copy limited edition of this book published in late October of last year. Due to arbitrary technical limits set on the size of the volume, two years before the book was actually written, the introductory essay that follows had to be truncated. Additional material already at hand could not be included, and a number of egregious errors were introduced into the introductory text. This edition includes all of that additional material, addresses the glitches and inconsistencies of the earlier essay, and speaks to subsequent assertions about "City" and the Author made in several books published since last year. I don't expect *ever* to be free of the endless gossip, surmises, misstatements, uninformed theories and "Chinese Whispers" attendant on "City," but as best I can tell it, and with truthfulness as best I can practice it (the poet Olin Miller has written "Of all liars, the smoothest and most convincing is memory"), this is the corrected, full story.

Perils of the "City"

Speak no ill of the dead?

Oh, really? Then let's forget about writing a true introductory essay to this book. Let's give a pass to setting the record straight. Let's just shrug and say, ah, what the hell, it's been more than thirty years and the bullshit has been slathered on with a trowel for so damned long, and so many greedy little pig-snouts have made so much money off those lies, and so many inimical forces *continue* to dip their pig-snouts in that *Star Trek* trough of bullshit that no one wants to hear your miserable bleats of "unfair! unfair!" . . . that it ain't worth the price of admission, Ellison. So shine it on, and let the keepers of the holy flame of *Star Trek* and the preservers of the bullshit myth of Roddenberry have the field to themselves. The field, *and* the exchequer.

Oh, yeah, that's what lies at the core of it. The money.

What is it Deep Throat said: *Follow the money.*

If it weren't for the money, for that overflowing *Star Trek* trough in which the pig-snouts are dipped every day, no one would give a rat's-ass if the truth about Roddenberry and the show got told. But if you follow the money, you see that river of gold flowing straight off the Paramount lot in boring sequel-series after clone-show, and you see the merchandisers and the franchisers and the publicists and the QVC hustlers and bought critics like *TV Guide*'s Jeff Jarvis, and you see the fanmagazine fanatics and the convention-throwers and the endless weary biographies and the huge pseudo-book franchise of useless *Star Trek* novels written by a great many writers who ought to take up fly-speck analysis instead of littering the bestseller lists with their poor excuses for creative effort (not to mention the few really excellent writers who ought to know better, but have gulled themselves into believing they're writing those awful turd-tomes out of adolescent affection for nothing nobler than a goddamn *tv show*, when the truth is they're doing it for the money, they follow the money, just like all the other *Star Trek* barnacles attached to that lumbering behemoth); and you see the venal liars and adulterers and con-artists and charlatans and deluded fan-fools who have a vested interest in keeping *Star Trek* sailing along, and all the innocent but naive tv absorbers, and you figure, Ah what the hell, Ellison, let it go! Just forget about it!

And, pretty much, except when my anger got too intense, or my gorge got too buoyant, or when one of the little piss-ants got within arm's reach, I *have* let it slide for thirty years.

Thirty years. That is a piece of time.

Probably more years than are owned by most of the people who will buy this book. And with the historical soapbox *Star Trek* stands upon, to insure its posterity (not to mention its view of "how things happened"), the story those under-30 readers will have had to swallow by the time they *get* to this book . . . well, Ellison's somewhat jaundiced and politically unkempt telling of that history has about as much chance as a snowball in a cyclotron.

So. Speak no ill of the dead. And let it go, pal. Give it a rest. As my wife says, belt up.

And I have. For thirty years, more or less. I won't dissemble and pretend that I haven't tried to refute some of the most widely-held canards-cum-mythology that have circulated through the *Star Trek* world, at conventions, or in private conversations. But in the main, for the most part, partially out of dismay and partially out of weariness, I've let most of it pass. To attempt to stem the tide of fannish folderol and gossip would mean I'd have to devote every waking hour to an essentially pointless task. And it would be as likely to do any good as trying to sweep the beach clean of sand.

As for that "speak no ill of the dead" admonition, I only wish the same Christian Charity was visited on the living. Yet I never said anything about Roddenberry in private or public that I didn't (or wouldn't have) said to his face.

But trying to present another viewpoint of Roddenberry—and we're talking now about all those years prior to his death, before the tell-all books by virtually every member of the cast, before the scathing revelations in GENE RODDENBERRY: *The Myth and the Man Behind Star Trek* (Hyperion, 1994) by investigative journalist Joel Engel, before even the whitewash biography by David Alexander—a man who was in Roddenberry's hip pocket when Gene was alive, and managed to get to the task of grave-robbing Roddenberry's life faster than the speed of blight—titled *The*

Authorized Biography of Gene Roddenberry: STAR TREK CREATOR (ROC, 1994)—trying to portray Roddenberry as anything approaching a fallible human being would bring down the tsunami of Trekkie wrath. To them, he was a bright and shining light, and they would eviscerate anyone who said otherwise. This is a degenerative process called "heroification."

(As James W. Loewen writes in his 1995 book LIES MY TEACHER TOLD ME: *Everything Your American History Textbook Got Wrong,* "Heroification . . . much like calcification . . . makes people over into heroes. The media turn flesh-and-blood individuals into pious, perfect creatures without conflicts, pain, credibility, or human interest. . . . authors selectively omit blemishes in order to make certain historical figures sympathetic to as many people as possible. . . . A certain etiquette coerces us all into speaking in respectful tones about the past. . . . It perpetuates what might be called a Disney version of history."

(As Washington Irving wrote in his heavily-heroificated biography of Christopher Columbus, "Care should be taken to vindicate great names from pernicious erudition.")

By wildly extravagant heroification of Gene Roddenberry, all the untruths, all the false credit, all the betrayal and perfidious behavior he wallowed in, has been permitted to be flensed. . . . leaving only this glowing icon who wouldn't tell a lie or hurt a fly. Yeah, and there are actually schmucks who think Adolf Hitler made the trains run on time.

So I tried to let it all pass, without comment most of the time. But thirty years is a piece of change. It is much longer to keep getting kicked in the ass than anyone should have to put up with.

So I let myself get talked into writing this book.

Yeah, yeah, I know: "You *let* yourself get talked into writing this book? Come on, Ellison! Who the hell's supposed to believe *that?* Ain't this the same world we went to bed in last night? Isn't the reason for doing a *Star Trek* book of *any* kind—picayune biography, sharecropping derivative novel, moron quiz book, obsessional trivia book, adolescent episode guide—for the money? Follow the money? We're not fools, Ellison! Yeah, we might swallow any crap the Paramount p.r. mill cares to throw out, and all pre-production inside-secrets desiderata, but we ain't naive enough to believe you're doing this book for any other reason than money."

So okay, all right, all you little cynical television goobers, believe what the hell you choose. *I* say I was talked into doing this book, that left to my own devices I'd have spent my time on more worthwhile projects, and if I make money off this thing, well, since I've never seen more than a pittance from "The City on the Edge of Forever," while every thug and studio putz and semiliterate bandwagon-jumper and merchandiser has grown fat as a maggot in a corpse off what *I* created, then you can chalk it up to achieving something not even close to balance in the Unjust Universe. But if you *want* the truth, here it is.

There is only one reason I'm doing this book:

FYODOR DOSTOEVSKY

"It is not at all to justify myself that I've been doing all this talking. . . . But no! That's a lie! I precisely wanted to justify myself. I make this little note for myself, gentlemen. I don't want to lie. I've given my word."

— from NOTES FROM UNDERGROUND

For thirty years I've had to listen to others shoot off their faces about how *they* saved "City." How *they* rewrote this and trimmed that and suffered oh so awfully with the irresponsible Ellison.• For thirty

---

• Before we get too far along, let me offer you a sample of the kind of bullshit I've had to put up with for three decades. *This* little gem comes out of a volume titled CAPTAIN'S LOGS: *The Complete Trek Voyages* by Edward Gross & Mark A. Altman (Image Publishing 1993).

On page 41, in a section dealing with "City," here is what we find:

"City on the Edge of Forever" *is generally considered the best episode of* Star Trek *ever produced. At the same time, it is perhaps the most controversial, due to the fact that Gene Roddenberry supposedly rewrote Harlan Ellison's original teleplay and Ellison was not happy about the rewrite.*

For over two decades fans have accepted the fact that Roddenberry did the rewrite of Ellison's script, however [schlock tv producer] Glen Larson disputes this point, stating that it was actually Gene L. Coon who was responsible. This startling revelation came to Larson's attention during a Writers Guild award ceremony in which the script was a nominated entry.

"That night," Larson reflects, "I knew that something was troubling Gene and I asked him what was wrong. And he said, 'There are two scripts up tonight for the Writers Guild award, and I wrote them both.' One of them was by Harlan Ellison, and he said, 'If Harlan wins, I'm going to die.'

"Coon had a great respect for writers . . . . Nevertheless, if you knew a guy was going to stand up and accept an award for what you did, that was more painful than the money. The mere fact that somebody was going to get credit for his thoughts and actual words, because they were so important to him, was almost too much to bear. He shared that with me."

As far as Roddenberry's taking credit for the rewrite, Larson offers, "Gene Coon was there . . . "

Yeah, and pandas will fly out of Glen Larson's ass! Every sentence of that crap is laughable, and Larson knows it. Even if the late Gene Coon *said* all that—and I doubt that it ever happened—then he was also full of shit. Because, as everyone in Hollywood knows (but apparently the gullible Messrs. Gross and Altman don't), the writer has the option which version of the script to submit. The work is blind-judged by many levels of unidentified (but color-coded) writers, and the aired version of the show is not only never seen, it's never considered. I submitted the version of "City" that you will read in this book. Exactly as you find it here. Even if Roddenberry, or Coon, or any one of the half

years I've slapped back only when they got me too angry to lay back
. . . or when they got within arm's reach. And now, with Shatner's
pinheaded memoir, and that laughable "biography" by David
Alexander that tried to make Roddenberry look like fuckin'
Prometheus . . . well . . . I let myself get talked into doing the
original, unexpurgated, you-read-it-and-judge-for-yourself teleplay,
with additional material, and alternate versions and various
treatments . . . and this is my final word on the matter. If it makes
money, that's terrific: I deserve it. (A lot more than the creeps
who've fed off my work for three decades.) And if it doesn't . . .
yeah, well, what are the odds all the brain-damaged Trekkies wanted
to hear the truth anyhow?

Here's the way this Rosetta Stone will be revealed to you. The script
you are about to read is the original version. It is *not* the teleplay as
presented by NBC on April 6th, 1967. The episode of *Star Trek*
broadcast on that evening was rewritten. Many times. Some of those

---

dozen or so others who've claimed credit for my work, had "saved my ass" as they were so
fond of saying, it wouldn't have meant diddly-squat in terms of winning a WGAw award,
because the one and only script that was ever submitted, the one and only script that
made it through all those levels of judges, the one and only script that beat out every
other script in the Dramatic Category . . . was *mine*. All mine. The one this idiot Larson
doesn't seem to understand was the one that was judged. Not some half-assed rewrite by
Coon or some quarter-assed re-rewrite by Roddenberry, or anyone else. So here's the guy
we fondly refer to in Hollywood as "Glen Larceny" playing his violin and breaking our
hearts with this tragic tale of the goodhearted producer who bought karma points by not
stealing script credit the way Larson did regularly on *his* shows. So here is just the first of
many such bullshit stories you will encounter in this introductory essay, in which poor
dumb Ellison can't find his own ass in a windstorm, but every other cosmically talented
tv hack who never won an award on his own, bleats about how he "saved" my wretched
script from the clutches of *my* Olympian ineptitude.
     In fact, there's yet another claimant, in that same section of Gross and Altman's
unsubstantiated fantasy. Listen to *this* flight of overweening ego, that makes my hubris
seem like virginal innocence.

          Director Joseph Pevney is someone who doesn't agree with Ellison's view of
          his own script. "This was the end of the first season," he says. Harlan was very
          happy to get his story on *Star Trek*. He was down on the set thanking me. It's
          great that Gene rewrote it, though, because Harlan had no sense of theater . . .
          It was a well conceived and written show. But in the original script's dramatic
          moments, it missed badly. "It was a motion picture," he continues. "I treated
          it as a movie . . . "

     Blah blah blah. All righty, now. Here we are only a few pages into this little historical
diatribe, and already we've got three literary birth-mothers for my script. (And don't forget:
you can read the script, in its entirety, right after this essay. In fact, just so you can make
your own decisions about how "the dramatic moments missed badly," why not skip right
over to "City" itself and try on the original, so when you come back here, you'll know
whether guys like Pevney—who must have been talking to my astral projection on the
set of "City" because I never went *near* the set, never thanked Pevney, never set foot
back on *Star Trek* territory after they got done rewriting me—whether guys like Pevney
and Larson and others you will soon meet in these pages, are stuffed full of wild blueberry
muffins. Gee, folks, I wish I had a sense of theater. Just even a *teensy* sense of theatuh.)

times by me. Some of those times by others. For the first time in thirty years, right here in this book, you will discover—as I did only when *preparing* this manuscript—who it was that had a hand in the rewrites of my script besides Coon and Roddenberry and Carabatsos. You may be mildly startled to learn the name of that person, but I guarantee you will not be *nearly* as astonished as *I* was. Because I never had a suspicion for three decades that there had been anyone but the "usual suspects" involved. I knew it wasn't Roddenberry, even though I was certain he had fiddled around with the final version. How did I know? Because as one well-known tv writer (an award-winner himself) has said, "There are chunks of dialogue speech Edith Keeler gives about how in the future everything will be wonderful because we'll have spaceships to feed hungry people—which is precisely the kind of dopey Utopian bullshit Roddenberry loved." So I knew Gene had screwed around, because that's how he was able to lie to himself (and everyone else) that he was the Great Guiding Intelligence. But I also knew he hadn't done the massive restructuring that was done to my story, although that expert liar told people from lecture platforms for the better part of a quarter century that it was *he* who rescued that brilliant script from the inept paws of the Slacker Ellison . . . when, in truth, Roddenberry had about as much writing ability as the lowest industry hack. A fact. Do with it what you will.

Oh, and when those I savage here decide they will punish me for my impetuous impertinence in muddying the great and golden icon *Star Trek*, let me advise you of something salient:

Though, indeed, I have a letter of permission from Paramount permitting me to publish this teleplay, I never needed it. (I sought out such a letter only because the publisher of the limited edition of this book, in the wholly premature announcements four years ago, sought to strike a deal with Paramount for some sort of commercial tie-in. By the time I learned of the letter, it was clear to me that I had better get Paramount "placed" before they decided to play lawyer with me. So I finessed a "release" that permitted me and White Wolf to do this book.) But in truth, I never needed such a letter. Because this is not the script that is the property of Desilu-Paramount.

It is the *original* version. The version they returned to me. It is also the version that was copyrighted by me in 1975. It is the version that was mine from the git-go by the "separation of rights" clause in the Writers Guild of America contract we lovingly call the Minimum Basic Agreement. And it is the version that was published in January of 1976 in the Washington Square Press paperback volume, SIX SCIENCE FICTION PLAYS. Had Paramount wished to do anything about my claims to this property, they should have (and certainly *would* have) done so more than twenty years ago. But since they didn't, even the dullest attorney over at Paramount Legal would have to represent to anyone intent on "punishing" me, that you can't make a case when you haven't done shit about the matter in two decades. Statute of limitations, that sort of thing. It's why the Pope exonerated the Jews for allegedly nailing up Christ. Statute of limitations. Only two thousand years. But, sadly, in the case of Paramount, it was twenty. So.

First, I'll reprint the introductory essay I did for the original anthology appearance, back in 1976. That one's copyright in my name, too. Then I'll come back and lay out a few anecdotes, show you a few pictures, reveal some evidence, name some names, write some long footnotes, expose myself, expose Roddenberry, piss off the faithful, give you your money's worth, and tell you the truth as best I know it.

Remember, as you read this next section:

It was written in 1975, only eight years after the initial airing of "City." If you find inconsistencies in my manner or my tone of voice, or specifics, well, Roddenberry was still alive, I was still working in the same industry, I had been getting buffeted and banged around pretty good by fanatical Trekoids, and I suppose I may have been looking to put a peaceful paw on the matter. But time passed, and Roddenberry never stopped shitting in my consommé, and as you will see in later sections of this introduction, I grew less and less ready to accommodate.

Leading us, finally, to the ravening beast before you.

It is mealtime. The repast is steaming. If you need some ketchup with your raw meat, just ask.

Here is what the editor of SIX SCIENCE FICTION PLAYS wrote in the 1976 edition:

> "Trek" has become, in many respects, more popular since its cancellation than it was before. Now in reruns throughout the country, it has grown into a cult object, a rallying point for "trekkies." One convention of fans in New York City had an attendance of 16,000!
>
> Harlan Ellison was one of the most talented scriptwriters for the series. A novelist, award-winning short

story writer and anthologist of note (the *Dangerous Visions* books), he was contacted by the creator of *Star Trek*, Gene Roddenberry, even before the series had its network slot finalized. Through Ellison, *Star Trek* employed many well-known science fiction writers for its first year's scripts. But even Harlan Ellison had problems with changes in his original teleplay, changes which he discusses in the special introduction he has written for this Washington Square Press edition.

The author of this remarkable script has fought production company and network censorship with virtually every teleplay he has done in Hollywood (and they now number well over two dozen, for the top shows on all three networks); the things he has to say about working conditions for writers in TV, therefore, are from the inside, and they come from the only writer in the twenty-six year history of the Writers Guild of America awards for Most Outstanding Teleplay to win that honor *three* • times. His ethics are beyond reproach, incidentally: he walked away from $93,000 in profits when a series he created, *The Starlost,* was creatively butchered.

"The City on the Edge of Forever" is one of those three award winners and appears here for the first time anywhere in its original, uncut—first draft—version.

And here's what *I* wrote in 1975, twenty years ago, and ten years after the eviscerated version of "City" was aired. I had not spoken to Roddenberry during those ten years. But Gene did me a small kindness shortly before I reached my deadline on this introduction, and we more-or-less buried the hatchet. It was a rapprochement that did not last very long.

It's almost ten years since the day Gene Roddenberry called me to say he had sold a series to NBC called *Star*

• Make that *four.* I picked up another one in 1986 for my *Twilight Zone* script, "Paladin of the Lost Hour." It should be noted that the superlative scenarist Christopher Knopf also won three times, *after* this was published. I'm the only writer in the now-nearly-50-year history of the WGAw awards, to win this prestigious honor *four* times for solo work. I make a big deal point of mentioning this, not so much to pound my chest, as to establish right at the outset that I have solid credentials for asserting that *I know what the fuck I'm doing when I write a script.*

Trek. "It's going to be a sophisticated Wagon Train to the Stars," Gene said; and we both laughed. • We both laughed because Gene was making fun of the tunnel-vision thinking of many television network programming clowns who cannot perceive of any new property in an original way, but must tag it in as being "just like *The Fugitive,* except the guy is running to keep people from taking his blood, which makes people immortal" *(The Immortal),* or "similar to *Bonanza,* except the father is married to a beautiful Mexican woman" *(High Chapparal),* or "it's *Mannix* with a fat detective" *(Cannon),* "an old, thin detective" *(Barnaby Jones),* "a blind detective" *(Longstreet),* "a crippled detective" *(Ironside).*

Star Trek went on the air in September of 1967 and despite the wild enthusiasm of science fiction aficionados, it had a rough go its first year, due mainly to that purblind arrogance of the nameless decision-makers on their skyscraper mountaintops.

(As an aside: I was asked to do a magazine piece on the show, in 1968, and in researching the subject, from an intimate knowledge of what went on behind the scenes because of my personal involvement, I discovered that at

---

• In fact, though Roddenberry claimed that phrase as original with him—as the shorthand log-line he had dreamed up to penetrate the regimented thinking of network executives who ideate only in clone images of previous tv "successes"—I learned some years later that the phrase had been spoken off-the-top-of-the-head by Samuel Anthony Peeples at a dinner party where Roddenberry announced he was going in to see the NBC programmers. Sam, who also came up with the phrase "to boldly go" (and, yes, I cringe every time I hear that split infinitive), was brought in to save *Star Trek* the first time, when Roddenberry's windy script of "The Cage" was rejected by the network. Sam then wrote "Where No Man Has Gone Before," the teleplay that made NBC smile and got Roddenberry on the air. I have no idea if this particular nugget of truth has ever been published in the miles-high stack of books, pamphlets, fanzines, magazines, and assorted incunabula of the *Trek* industry. I'd tend to doubt it. Anything that casts shadow on the papal infallibility of the Great Bird of the Galaxy tends to get lost very fast. I'll talk more about that a little later, but for the nonce, let it suffice that Peeple's authorship of the phrase was conveyed to me not once, or twice, but on three separate occasions by three different people who were also seated at that dinner table on that evening. For his part, Sam Peeples is a fine and honorable gentlemen, and his loyalty to those who have employed him is legendary. Sam remains, if not precisely silent on the point, sedulously circumspect. I mention it, more than a trifle grimly, as a side-note to contentions I will assert later as to Gene's need to abscond with others' ideas and words, and to convince himself in very short order that they sprang fullblown from his own well of genius.

one point, early in the show's existence, NBC wanted to make Mr. Spock more "human." He wasn't going to be that jaundiced shade of yellow, he wasn't going to have the arched eyebrows that always made Leonard Nimoy look as though he'd just been caught in the act of doing something unspeakable, he wasn't going to have the pointy hobbit ears. He was going to be a more human-style extraterrestrial. NBC even went so far as to have photos of Nimoy in the Spock regalia retouched, and those air-brushed photos were included in promotional flyers. I managed to get hold of one, long after the series had become a hit, and when I started following up the chain-of-command that had ordered the alterations [what Trekkies would term] a desecration, I found no one would cop the rap for it. Every network official I spoke to said it had never happened . . . until I whipped the actual flyer on him. Then he'd go fumfuh-fumfuh and aim me in the direction of the next higher-up. Till finally I confronted the then-president of NBC—I can't remember his name nearly a decade later; they change scapegoats at the networks more regularly than normal people change their socks—and he feigned an attitude of *horror* that such a thing could even have been considered; an attitude so convincing he should have been nominated for an Emmy in the category of Executive Dissembling. With all the ethic of a Nixon throwing a Mitchell to the dogs, he picked up his phone and demanded his staff find out exactly *who* had been responsible for such a cataclysmic awfulness. Naturally, all the well-creased and dryer-blown dudes who had second-guessed the alien makeup were covered, and the only martyr they could serve up was some poor *schlepper* in the art department who, they assured me, had taken it upon himself to make the changes. Now, *you* know and *I* know there isn't any rational way in which a 32nd art assistant down in the advertising department at NBC is going to presume to alter one of the major elements of a prime-time series, but they actually thought I'd go for it. And they fired the poor slob. To prove they were upright and conscientious. I must confess I felt considerable guilt about that chain of events, even though I was innocently the catalyst that caused the reaction. But it solidified for me, for all time, the reality of just how far, and how low, television executives will go to cover up their mistakes and avoid even the faintest scintilla of bad press.)

World's longest aside.

Anyhow, I went in to work on *Star Trek* and devised a story I was anxious to tell. I called it "The City on the Edge of Forever." I wrote it carefully, with considerable love, and with enthusiasm at being part of what looked to be the most faithful translation of pure science fiction to the television medium since the second year of *The Outer Limits*. (Not the first year: that was all bogeymen and monsters; but the second year was frequently identifiable science fiction that did not induce projectile vomiting, and some bloody fine shows they were. Now *that* was a series I dug working on; I'll tell you about it some time.)

I handed in my script to rave comments by Gene, Dorothy Fontana—who was, herself, writing scripts for the show, even while she was serving as Roddenberry's assistant—and the then-story editor, John D. F. Black.•

• Writers, no less than sculptors, ballerinas, workers in origami, have a way of deluding themselves as to the value of their work. To quote John Steinbeck: "The writer must believe that what he is doing is the most important thing in the world. And he must hold to this illusion even when he knows it is not true."

Writers, no less than professional race car drivers, scientists experimenting at the furthest edges of their specialty, strippers, all believe what they're doing is sensational. When it doesn't go down as sweetly as they think it should, they delude themselves that the work was great, just great, absolutely great; and the boneheaded masses (or critics) (or fans) are simply not noble enough to appreciate the grandeur of their creation.

I wrote, back in 1976, "I handed in my script to rave comments by Gene, Dorothy Fontana . . . and the then-story editor, John D.F. Black." I wrote that in 1976, but all through this essay you will find examples of statements from Roddenberry, Coon, Pevney, and any passerby who cared to dump a load of rat-puke on my abilities, attesting to how impossible the script was.

But I wrote that my submission was greeted by raves. Am I deluding myself? Am I trying to save face by saying everyone else is misremembering, lying, altering the past to protect the memory of Roddenberry? Am I simply a writer who wrote a bad script and can't admit it?

Well, in 1976 I never contemplated writing this book. In 1976 none of the *Star Trek* memorabilia books had come out. In 1976 none of the cast members or the Paramount staff, or those who worked on *Star Trek* had spoken out. And in 1976 I had no access to the *Star Trek* archive of papers—letters, memos, schedules, and on and on—housed at UCLA's Theatre Arts/Media Library (University Reference Library, 2nd floor).

They all said it was dynamite and that they'd be "putting it up on the boards" at once, for early shooting. But then, peculiar things began happening.

The script was put aside for several months and scripts I'd been told were "lesser in quality" began to slip into the progressively later slots "City" had been intended to fill. I kept checking back, to see what was going down—I was writing a segment for another series at that time, I don't remember which one•—but kept getting the runaround.

Now, understand something: for many years after the period I'm talking about here, Gene Roddenberry and I didn't speak to each other. Considerable bad vibes and poisoned blood between us. I felt I'd been badly used; Gene felt I was being unfair and unnecessarily condemnatory

---

• It was "Knife in the Darkness" for the 90-minute CBS western series, *Cimarron Strip*, created by that same Christopher Knopf I mentioned a minute ago, starring Stuart Whitman. (Aired on Thursday 25 January 1968.)

But it is 1996 as I write this, and all of those sources have been revealed. I wrote in 1976 that I got rave reviews. At that time I was just saying it. Now I have the proof. Here are some examples:

Robert H. Justman was the Co-Producer of *Star Trek*. He is co-author with Desilu-Paramount's Executive in Charge of Production for *Star Trek*, Herbert F. Solow, of the large recently-published volume INSIDE STAR TREK: *The Real Story* (Pocket Books, 1976). When I handed in the script he wrote a memo that said:

"Without a doubt, this is the best and most beautifully written screenplay we have gotten to date and possibly we'll ever get this season. If you tell this to Harlan, I'll kill you." (INSIDE STAR TREK, page 278)

William Shatner: "'City' is my favorite of the original *Star Trek* series because of the fact that it is a beautiful love story, well told." (Direct quote, 9/28/91)

Oh, screw it! I don't have to justify the quality of the goddam script in footnotes! Go read the damned thing and make up your own mind. But remember, we go in very short order from "this is a brilliant script" to "we can't shoot this damned thing."

But Justman—with whom I worked on *The Outer Limits* prior to *Star Trek*—on page 277 of the same book describes how we had a similar problem of budgeting a script I had written for *The Outer Limits*, and how easily we solved it, how amenable I was to suggestions from the very same Justman who later wrote so many memos saying "we can't shoot this, it's too expensive."

I had written "Demon with a Glass Hand" as a cross-country chase. *The Outer Limits* had the stingiest budget ABC could come up with. Bobby Justman took me one lunchtime to a magnificent building in downtown L.A. called the Bradbury Building. He asked if there was any way I could rewrite the script to be shot there, permitting the production company a way of producing the show within the budget.

Were I the intractable, primadonna pinhead Roddenberry and these other clowns have tried to paint me, I doubt seriously that I would have had the acumen to rethink "Demon" on the spot, and say to Justman, "A chase can be linear . . . horizontally . . .

(not to mention loudmouthed) about my treatment on the series. Those days are past. Gene and I have reached rapprochement and he has done a number of very gentlemanly, wholly unsolicited good deeds in my behalf. I choose, and so does Gene, to forget the hassles of that period. So I won't lay them out here like dismembered corpses. Suffice to say, Gene's contention was that I had written a script that cost too much to film on the budget NBC had allowed (a budget that kept getting smaller as the season wore on and one segment after another ran over cost); I contended that unnamed parties had leached all the humanity from the story and had turned it into just another melodramatic, implausible action-adventure hour. Those who have read the original version of the script assure me my teleplay has greater depth, emotionalism and quality than that which finally was aired. But of course they would tell *me* that. They don't want to go through life without a nose. Even so . . . the original version

---

or vertically! If I postulate a force bubble around the building, invisible but impenetrable, then when the protagonist is lured to the building, and trapped inside, the chase becomes *vertical!*" And we shot it, and it won a Writers Guild award, and no one claimed they'd rewritten me, to save my ass.

Same Justman. Same situation.

If I had written it too expensive, if I had written it over budget, why were all these wise heads, all these sage intellects incapable of doing what Justman had done: treat me like a professional, stop running around like hysterical loonies throwing their hands in the air screaming "it's too expensive!" and just tell me where it needed to be brought back into budget.

I did it with the use of McCoy (Dorothy Fontana's suggestion) when it was considered by Roddenberry to be imprudent that there could be a corrupt officer on board the *Enterprise*. Oh, yeah, it was D.C. who suggested McCoy replace Beckwith. Not Coon. Not Roddenberry. Not Justman. Not Solow. It was the woman whose Afterword on page 257 of this book told me thirty-year-old secrets that astonished me. (But it was *not* she who altered the interesting, sensible way in which McCoy is infected—see one of the revisions that follows the script—and had him make an asshole of himself by injecting himself with his own hypodermic. Caramba!)

I wrote to order. If I'd written it too expensive, just sit down with me and explain why. There were set and cast and budget considerations of which I (as well as most other writers) was unaware. One would have to be on staff to know such things.

But if Justman, on page 277 of his book relates how professionally I behaved, turning my own script inside out without a murmur, then why could not such a situation have reprised itself on *Star Trek*? Or is it possible the show was a maelstrom of petty politics, with Roddenberry constantly having to create a "boogieman" threatening us—Paramount or NBC or censors or some Nameless Menace—with petty bickering and egos even larger than mine having to be succored? Is it possible the *real* reason that script "needed" to be overhauled has yet to be revealed in this essay? Yeah, fer sure, it's possible.

won the Writers Guild award as the best dramatic-episodic teleplay of the 1967-68 season. But *Star Trek* fans swear by the aired version, awarded it a Hugo at the World SF Convention and a George Méliès Fantasy award at the International Film Festival in Los Angeles in 1973. I like to think the latter awards were given because that which I bled into the script could not be totally drained off, even by several rewrites by other people. But, who's to know? It could be that I was, and maybe still am, too close to the material to know when it's been bettered by other hands.

But even though I have reached peace with myself about the script, I continue to maintain the belief that art-by-committee is *never* great, or even good art. It is cobbled-up like Frankenstein's monster, with bits and pieces from different minds.

The solitary creator, dreaming his or her dream, unaided, seems to me to be the only artist we can trust.

However, that's a judgment you'll have to make yourself. I'm permitting the script in its original version to be published here for the first time anywhere, because it has come to my attention that copies of the shooting script, the rewritten version, have sold hundreds of copies in high-priced mimeographed editions; and everywhere I go . . . to conventions, to colleges where I lecture, to autograph parties in bookstores when my books are published . . . invariably I'm asked, "Where can I get a copy of the original version of 'City'?"

Till now, my answer has always been: nowhere.

James Blish attempted to turn it into a short story, using the best elements of both versions for the first *Star Trek* paperback. It didn't really satisfy. Not even Jim, who admitted same, even though he did as good a job as he could trying to meld two disparate scripts into a coherent whole. But here it is, unedited, intact, just as I wrote it back in 1966.

Naturally, I hope *you* think it's dyn-o-mite, but even if you *still* prefer the aired version (which shows up regularly on syndicated reruns of the *Star Trek* series all over the country), I have the personal satisfaction that all creators retain when they know they've brought a dream to life with what Balzac called "clean hands and composure."

• • •

Now a few words about the form in which a teleplay is written, and then a few words about some elements of the plot that were pivotal in my writing the script the way I did.

Television terminology is more complex than that used for either radio plays or stage productions, naturally. A scenarist writes not only the plot, dialogue and sequences, he or she also writes the camera angles, the description of characters, the sets, sometimes—if it's important—even the music for a certain mood.

When you see O.S. it means "offstage," as when someone is speaking but isn't on camera. POV means "point of view" and refers to that which the character in question sees, through his or her eyes. An ARRIFLEX shot is one made with a hand-held camera. The Arriflex, or "arri" as it's usually called, used to be the basic hand-held implement for such work—useful in getting around quickly with that jerky, documentary feel that's so important for scenes of rapid movement or personal combat—but these days they use a French-made camera, the Eclair.• When you see (beat), as in some character's speech, it merely means taking-a-beat, a pause. A SMASH-CUT is a sharp, dramatic cut from one scene to another, and is scenarists' mickeymouse, because a cut is a cut, and that's the long and short of it, but a HARD CUT or a SMASH-CUT means that the action preceding and following the cut should be very slambang, the way they used to do it on Mission: Impossible or The Man from U.N.C.L.E. An ESTABLISHING SHOT is a full frame shot that is used to orient the viewer as to where the coming action will take place, a street, a ballroom, a vast plain with armies poised to battle. A LAP-DISSOLVE is a very slow dissolve in which one scene is superimposed over another for a few beats, one fading, the other coming in stronger, so we have a sense of passage of time.

Beyond those few technical details, I don't think

• That was the state of the art in 1975. These days, with the new computer technology and the universal use of Steadicam™ and its other refinements, the term HAND-HELD is used. I've made that change from the original script. But I've retained the name "Arriflex" in the body-copy of the stage directions, just for old times' sake.

you'll have any trouble deciphering the jabberwocky of
the tv medium. Just sorta kinda picture what's going on
as if it were playing on a screen in your head. Get visual.
That's what we have to do when we write the stuff.

Now. There are things in this script that were taken
out entirely. The first is the character of Beckwith. I was
advised by NBC network continuity, at the time of the
turn-in of the first draft of this teleplay, that drugs—even
something as clearly a fantasy construct as the Jewels of
Sound—could not be permitted on a show that was airing
so early in the evening. Further, there is a killing on board:
one crew member kills another. I was told that was nixed
because no one onboard the starship *Enterprise* could be a
bad guy. I railed at that concept. It always struck me as
nonsense that the network could try to pass off a space
battlecruiser of that size, with a complement of many
hundreds of people, without a few rotten apples in the
barrel. Just the rigors of space exploration and tight
confinement should have made *some*body go bananas. But,
no, they didn't want to shatter that silly myth that all tv
heroes are just that: heroes. I was going for some reality,
but the network gets inordinately uptight about such stuff.
In the televised version, the entire Jewels of Sound/
Beckwith/LeBeque situation was replaced by the ship's
doctor injecting himself with some drug that made him
go loonie, and *he* became the Beckwith character, going
back in time.

The entire alternate universe thing with the space
marauders was excised.● Much of the relationship between
Kirk and Edith Keeler was watered down, to my way of
thinking. But the two most significant changes, the ones

● Which was the ultimate irony. When Gene insisted that I "put the ship in jeopardy,"
a perennial pain-in-the-plot that Roddenberry adored, and one he shoehorned into
almost every script (and then blamed on NBC, which was bullshit), I resisted like a
man in chains. But I did it, finally, because Roddenberry said if *I* didn't do it, *he* would.
So I wrote the space pirate element—and when you read the script, notice that Mr.
Spendthrift Ellison, who wrote too expensive a script, did it in a way that cost *nothing*,
shot as it would have been in one already-standing set—and it was the first thing NBC
demanded be dropped.

I resented most bitterly, were these:

The joy of writing television is small. Once having written a script, once having poured one's hours and emotions into a story, the script is passed into the hands of others, who alter the dream to fit their own interpretations and their own need to put their mark on something someone else has created. They have to justify their own jobs, even their existences in some cases.

To hear directors tell it—with that moronic "auteur theory" by which they bamboozle audiences into believing it is *they* who have the vision—nothing comes to life without them. If the truth be told, were it not for the writer, who has the idea, orders it sequentially and logically, builds the characters and gives them their words, the directors would be standing around with their fingers in their mouths waiting for divine guidance. Producers, network continuity people, production personnel, every advertising executive who has bought time on the show, and his or her spouse, and mother-in-law . . . all of them take credit for the script. But it is the writer who starts it all rolling. Without the writer you would turn on your television set tonight and be dazzled by uninterrupted hours of test patterns or, at best, recorded organ music.

So the primacy of a writer's investment in the work is frequently ignored. He or she is never consulted about the script, never invited to sit in on the shooting, seldom even asked to rewrite if such becomes necessary. Ham-handed assistants, all of whom know in their secret heart of hearts that they could write "if they only had the time la-de-dah," these are the ones who dumb down a script. With working conditions like that, is it any wonder any writers who care move on to other mediums? Films, books, quiet evenings around the campfire. And for those of us who *do* care, who make nuisances of ourselves by sticking with a script despite the baleful stares of producers and studio personnel, it becomes a matter of inserting those small things in a script that enrich us as creators.

For me, in this script, the personal, secret things I planted were the character of Trooper, and what happens to him, and the characterization of Kirk that said he was willing to sacrifice the ship, the crew, himself, Spock, all time itself if need be, for love. In the end, he would allow time to be warped and never returned to its original state, just to keep Edith alive. It was Spock, logical and rational, who held Kirk back from saving Edith's life.

I was told: "Our character wouldn't act like that."

Bull. Who *knows* how someone will act when pressed to the final, ineluctable confrontation with himself? I felt it vastly deepened the one-dimensional character of Kirk-the-rock-jawed, and made a point about mortality and the necessity for love that television seldom considers. And it was to be topped off by the first (and perhaps only) time in the series when Spock spoke to Kirk calling him by his first name. It was supposed to be a pair of scenes filled with genuine emotion and some kernel of human anguish, not the counterfeit emotion which tv usually substitutes for genuine pain, thereby dulling and diminishing all of us who watch the little box.

Trooper was removed entirely. I think he is the best character I've ever written into a script. I would have liked to've seen him come to life. His death in the show says, I think, something fearful and important about the passage of our lives on this tiny grain of dust we call the Earth.

I am sad he never had the breath of life blown into him by the magicians of the coaxial cable.

Perhaps some other time, in some other script.

Well. That about logs it closed. Had I but world enough and time, I would go through the months and events of this script and what happened to it, in much greater detail. But that's the past, and as has been said, past is merely prologue. Here is the script. I've just reread it, after almost ten years, just to see if it needed any touching up. I still like it. My hope is that you feel similarly. And it was nice visiting with you.

HARLAN ELLISON
NEW YORK CITY
6 DECEMBER 1974

• • •

So it didn't end there. It *should* have, but Roddenberry's character flaws included one that continued to get his ass in trouble year after year. And that flaw—oddly enough omitted from the "authorized" biography as written by David Alexander—was his need to subsume into his self-perpetuating mythos of being El Supremo, every witticism, cleverly-turned phrase, story-concept, deed of derring-do, noble thought or selfless action of anyone he met.• If something was clever, or successful,

---

•When I wrote those lines in August of 1995, INSIDE STAR TREK: *The Real Story* by Solow and Justman (studio executive on *Trek* and co-producer, respectively) had not yet been published by Pocket Books. But now it has, and my assertions are verified that Roddenberry was a pathological credit-grabber, a man who made up his past and his credits to aggrandize himself, a guy who could not bear to admit that no matter how he and others fiddled with it, that "City" was the best of the original series, and that it was I, not he, who conceived the story that made it so memorable.

Throughout the Solow-Justman book—filled with authentication that is irrefutable—those two men who worked closest with Gene during the years of the original pilot and then the series state again and again that Roddenberry was a glory-hog, taking credit for everyone else's contributions to the show. Not once or twice, do they state that position, in clear and forceful language, but again and again.

And that is why the evidence of Roddenberry's need to claim "City" credit is so blatant. As, for instance, the following:

In a letter to me from Roddenberry dated June 20, 1967, Gene wrote: "Next, never outside this office and particularly nowhere in S.F. or television circles have I ever mentioned that the script was anything but entirely yours."

In the March 1987 issue of *Video Review* magazine, in a candid interview with Gene, we find the following, referring to "City":

VR: That was a great episode.
RODDENBERRY: It was a fun episode to do.
VR: Who wrote that one?
RODDENBERRY: Well, it was a strange thing. Harlan Ellison wrote the first draft of it, but then he wouldn't change it.
VR: That's Harlan Ellison.
RODDENBERRY: Yeah. He had Scotty dealing drugs and it would have cost $200,000 more than I had to spend for an episode.
VR: That's like E.T. wearing a coke spoon.
RODDENBERRY: When I called these things to Harlan's attention, he said, "You've sold out, haven't you?" I said, "No, I haven't sold out. I only have $180,000 to spend on an episode." So I rewrote the episode. And his original won a Writers Guild award, but my rewrite won the Nebula award for actually being filmed.

So much for Roddenberry never telling anyone outside the office that the script had been written by anyone but me.

(And though I deal with it elsewhere in this essay, let me point out that Gene didn't *do* the rewrite, he only fiddled with it after it had been through three other hands. Let me also point out, yet again, for the nine millionth fucking time, that nowhere in my teleplay does Scotty even *appear*, much less deal drugs. Read the script, it's here, in your hands; read it and see if Roddenberry wasn't a glory-hog who had to invent idiot conversations about "selling out" so he could look like the Last Model of

June 20, 1967

Mr. Harlan Ellison

Dear Harlan:

Despite the cuts in sets and cast, the final budget figures on
"City" were close to $257,000, or about 56,000 over our show
budget of $191,000. We might have made it for around $20,000
less if I had not insisted on quality in casting, set constructions,
special effects and so on.

The point of this is, despite enormous criticism from studio business
men, I would not have done it any differently. I felt under an
obligation to you to produce as good a show as possible within
the limits of the re-write we thought necessary. Although we
have a disagreement over that re-write, every evidence is that the
show was highly successful both from the mass audience aspect necessary
to maintaining a show on the air, and from the critical audience
as well. I note that every fanzine received has commented warmly
on that Harlan Ellison episode. And our mail, including letters
from S.F. writers and fans, say the same.

Next, never outside this office and particularly nowhere in S.F.
or television circles have I ever mentioned that the script was
anything but entirely yours. As you know, I have recommended you
to fellow producers a number of times.

Which brings me to the point of this letter. Whether true or not,
I have heard from a number of sources that you have been less than
faithful to your side of this arrangement. I am told you do not
hesitate to accept full praise and responsibility for the show
but on the other hand go out of your way to say or suggest that I
treated you badly, was dishonest in my dealings with you, and
showed a lack of efficiency in my tasks which only your superior

$\mathcal{D}esilu$ STUDIOS · 780 NORTH GOWER STREET, HOLLYWOOD, CALIFORNIA 90038 · PHONE (213) HO 9-5911

writing overcame. I further understand that you have stated you intend to say or intimate something of the same at Westercon 20 and possibly at the World Science Fiction Convention in New York.

I hope this isn't true. While you are entitled to any honest opinion of me personally or professionally, you must understand that I will not permit any lies or misinformation to be circulated. At the risk of turning our currently honest disagreement into something more serious, I will fight such a thing with every weapon at my disposal. I never like to hurt a man but no man should feel he can back me into a corner where my reputation, and therefore my livelihood and therefore my family is imperiled.

I trust this letter isn't necessary. As a matter of fact, I was thinking warmly of you just the other day while in Morro Bay with Eileen and discussed you at some length. My thought at that time was attempting to find a resolution involving a problem with someone I wanted to respect. This is the course I would like to take. I sincerely hope it is yours.

Sincerely yours,

Gene Roddenberry

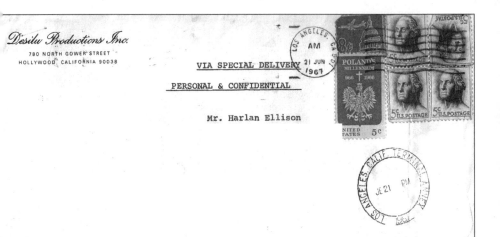

or artful, it was his. If it was shit, it was ours. If something went wrong, it wasn't *his* fault, it was the Conspiracy Theory machinations of the invisible men in black who *actually* ran the Network; or it was evil, ungrateful, penny-pinching Paramount that was out to get him; or it was the fault of those unruly, temperamental writers who acted like cranky babies and who needed the stern—but Solomonically fair and kindly—hand of El Supremo to set them back on the path of righteousness: the path of fulfilling Gene's dream and vision of himself as the incarnation of his wearyingly repetitive god-surrogates (Adonis, V'Ger, Charlie X, The Squire of Gothos, Nomad and Q, just to reprise a mere half-dozen of the Deity-as-Demento that Roddenberry either wrote himself

---

Rectitude in the Universe, who *had* to keep repeating the "Scotty sold drugs" delusion, who *had* to keep insisting how much over budget my show would have been . . . rather than admitting that the high-water mark of his claim to fame was conceived not by him, but by someone else.)

The evidence of Roddenberry's duplicity and determination to convince the gullible that his giant brain had been capable of the originality and depth of passion that were the hallmarks of "City"—even those snatches of originality and passion that remained after everyone had a whack at it—exists in brief and clarity.

Elsewhere in this essay (if you've been paying attention) you read Roddenberry's March 1987 *Video Review* interview, with its assertions that mine was a deeply flawed script, and that one of my dumbest goofs was having Scotty sell drugs.

Well, in the May 1987 *Video Review*—just two issues later—that same award-winning Alan Brennert I've mentioned before, wrote a letter. (See *Video Review* art.)

And on 25 March 1987 Brennert received a letter from Gene Roddenberry. (See Roddenberry letter.)

I urge you to riffle back through and up ahead in this long self-defense, and log in the number of times Roddenberry repeated these canards, though he admitted he was wrong in the Brennert letter. When it served his ego, he always conveniently "misremembered"—and most times he was called on it by someone in an audience or in print. But it didn't stop the myth from continuing in fandom.

As for that miserable lie he told *Video Review* about how I "only wrote the first draft," well, you'll find several sections of later rewrites off my second and third drafts, published right here in these pages. As they say in Latin, *res ipsa loquitur*, "the matter speaks for itself," which makes Roddenberry's endless repetitions of the lie, as they say in Latin, *res judicata*, "a matter already settled."

Yet . . .

I am driven, compelled, maddened, to bombard you with the evidence, so no smallest rat-hole is left through which a rabid apologist for the way Roddenberry dealt with me—as he did so many others—can scuttle, to cobble up some rationalization for his remarks. To that end, here is an inventory sheet from the previously-noted UCLA archive of Roddenberry's papers.

Kindly note how many *different* versions of the script, as written by Harlan Ellison, appear in this log.

"Harlan Ellison wrote the first draft of it, but then he wouldn't change it."

Speak no ill of the dead. But it seems the dead, in this case, goes right on speaking, repeating the same lies enjoyed in his life.

or forced into the work of others); or it was the evil ineptitude of Lurkers Within, the Iago or Brutus or Judas figures inside his own studio or production unit, whose smiling faces masked their true intent to thwart his Great Plan to show the less-perfect human race that they could be Starswept and Galactic, if only they would pay heed to Gene Roddenberry's immaculate view of human perfectibility. Flaws could not be permitted in the rest of the human monkeymass, but El Supremo was never to be confronted with his *own* teensy imperfections—such as plagiarizing John Meredyth Lucas's "Nomad" and Alan Dean Foster's teleplay, to create the script for the first feature film (Foster had to go to the Guild to get his credit, and to the end Roddenberry kept insisting the work was original)• . . . betraying his most loving colleague, David Gerrold, by hiring him to write the bible for *The Next Generation*, then merchandising it ruthlessly, and denying Gerrold had ever written a useable word (Gerrold won his suit against Roddenberry for back wages to the tune of something close to seventy thousand dollars) . . . and doesn't that story have an interesting resonance with the "unuseable script" of yet another sweet young writer named Ellison? . . . exploiting Bjo and John Trimble, who had set up Roddenberry's merchandising arm, Lincoln Enterprises, by having them work their asses off independently until the divorce was finalized with Eileen Roddenberry, and thus avoiding the ex-Mrs. R's claim to half those profits, and then freezing them out and giving it to his girlfriend Majel Barrett.

As one disillusioned ex-*Trek* official recently said, "You know why they cremated Gene? They were afraid people would come to piss on the grave."

So it didn't end there. Roddenberry continued to rewrite history in his head and spew out the revisions at conventions everywhere. And the vast monkeymass of Trekkie fans who have trouble differentiating between the fiction of television shows and the reality of those who *created* the shows, rewarded Gene with bouquets of gullible acceptance. Whatever Roddenberry said became canonical. And right up there in

---

• That Source of All Wisdom, the recently-married Alan Brennert, has apprised me—subsequent to my having written those lines about Roddenberry plagiarizing Lucas and Foster—that Roddenberry's claim about the origin of "In Thy Image" is at least partially correct. Alan's belief is that it originated as a story idea called "Robot's Return" in the bible Gene did for the *Star Trek II* series. Alan Dean Foster picked that as the episode he wanted to write, which became "In Thy Image." But Roddenberry *still* stole it from John Lucas's Nomad. This attempt at being punctilious about the facts comes to you through the courtesy of the Auctorial Honesty Network. At the tone, the time will be ten forty-two, and thirty seconds.

GENE RODDENBERRY COLLECTION (#062)

(March, 1975, inventory called it STAR TREK COLLECTION (#118);
July, 1988, inventory called it STAR TREK COLLECTION (#062).)

Donated by Gene Roddenberry to the UCLA Theater Arts Library
(second floor of the University Research Library), which became
the Arts, Architecture and Urban Planning Library (AAULP).
Circa November 1990-1991 it was made a special collection
(AAULP/Special Collection), to be viewed by appointment only. It
is now called the Arts Library/Special Collection. Brigitte Kueppers
has been head of the collection for the last 5 years. Her assistant
is Paul Camp. (Open Mon-Fri, 9-5; 310/825-7253.)

Inventory of "City on the Edge of Forever" material as of March, 1975:

1 NBC Broadcast Standards Department memo
Credits (3 copies)
4 research sheets
32 miscellaneous memos and correspondence
Treatment (3/21/66)
Treatment (5/1/66)
Treatment (5/13/66)
Draft teleplay (1/27/67, 3 copies)
Revised final draft teleplay (8/12/66)
Draft teleplay (1/23/66)
Draft teleplay (6/3/66)
Shooting script (1/27/67)
Final draft teleplay (2/1/67)
Undated first draft teleplay (2 copies)
Revised pages

Inventory of "City on the Edge of Forever" material as of July, 1988:

File 1:   Treatment (3/21/66; 16 pp.; 2 copies)
          Treatment (5/13/66; 22 pp.)
          Treatment (12/29/66; 13 pp.)
          Treatment (1/18/67; 13 pp.; 2 copies)
          Treatment (undated)
File 2:   Undated first draft teleplay (2 copies)
File 3:   Draft teleplay (6/31/66)
File 4:   Revised final draft teleplay (8/12/66; 2 copies)
File 5:   Unrevised undated pages and revised pages (2/2/67)
File 6:   Production materials; shooting script (1/27/67);
          2 call sheets

Inventory of "City on the Edge of Forever" material as of July 23-24, 199

File 1:   Script (3/21/66; 2 copies; "Cordwainer Bird")
          Script (6/3/66; "red cover"; "Harlan Ellison")--on loan to
                National Air & Space Museum
          Script (5/13/66; "Harlan Ellison")-- on loan to National
                Air & Space Museum
          Script (1/18/67; 13 pp.; 2 copies; "Harlan Ellison")
          Teaser (5 pp.)
File 2:   Undated script (67 pp.; red cover; "Steve Corabatsos")--
                probably May 1966
File 3:   Empty

```
File 4:   Revised final draft (8/12/66; "Harlan Ellison")
          Second copy (blue cover; no title page)
File 5:   Script (2/8/67; 19 pp.) --on loan to National Air &
              Space Museum
          Script (no date; 61 pp.;  "Harlan Ellison")--on loan to
              National Air & Space Museum
          Pages 7-13 (undated)
          Pages T-1 to T-6 (undated)
          Photocopy script (undated; "Harlan Ellison")
          Script (5/13/66; 24 pp.; "Harlan Ellison")
          Script (1/23/67; 71 pp.; "Harlan Ellison")
          Schedule and end credits ("written by Harlan Ellison")
              (2 copies)
          Revised pages IV-52, IV-53, IV-54A, IV-54B, IV54-C
              (2 copies)
File 6:   Shooting script (32 pp.)--on loan to National air & Space
              Museum
          Call sheet (2 copies)
          Concept (13 pages)--on loan to National Air & Space Museum
```

'Trek' Trips, More Depth And Viewers View Reviews

'BEAM ME HIGHER, SCOTTY'

In his interview in your March issue, Gene Roddenberry states—not for the first time—that in Harlan Ellison's "City on the Edge of Forever" Harlan "had Scotty dealing drugs" in his original draft of the script. Either Gene is seriously misremembering the script—it was, after all, 20 years ago—or he is deliberately perpetuating an untruth.

Scotty was not, for God's sake, "dealing drugs." In Harlan's draft there was, in fact, a subsidiary character named Beckwith aboard the *Enterprise* who dealt in "dream narcotics" called Jewels of Sound. In this version it is Beckwith, not McCoy, who goes back in time and changes history. Beckwith was no more an integral character than any of the nameless ensigns who were routinely bumped off in the first act of almost every *Star Trek* episode.

I happen to like the version of "City on the Edge of Forever" that aired, but I also like and admire the original script; it was a poetic and brilliantly written piece. It may well, as Gene says, have been too expensive

Spock, Kirk and Scotty: misty, watercolored memories?

to shoot. But Harlan cannot be maligned for making wholesale changes in the show's characters when those changes exist solely in Mr. Roddenberry's flawed recollection.

Alan Brennert
Marina del Rey, CA

•Alan Brennert is executive story consultant for CBS's The Twilight Zone.—*Ed.*

3-D DELIGHT

I believe that Robert Gerson's article on 3-D ("Looking Ahead," March '87 *VR*) missed some big points. He claims that "3-D adds almost nothing to the viewing experience." On the contrary, since real life has three dimensions, this process is capable

of adding a key element to motion pictures. I can clearly recall seeing some good movies (*House of Wax, It Came From Outer Space*) transformed into truly magical experiences by the addition of depth.

There are two problems with 3-D. First, sloppy photography or projection are responsible for the blurs and headaches, since focus and alignment are absolutely critical. If it is properly presented, there are no technical problems with 3-D. Second, this process is murdered over and over again every time it pops up by unscrupulous producers, who use it as a gimmick to foist shoddy pictures and pointless sequels upon us. At the end of the first 3-D cycle, some fine middle-of-the-road pictures (*Kiss Me, Kate, Dial M For Murder*) were shot in 3-D, and they've been shown that way lately. They had been originally released flat, not because of technical problems, but because by that time the process had been associated with trashy movies.

Rob Rosen
Tujunga, CA

WORD DU JOUR

Let's have a little fun here. In your next issue forbid your critics to use the word "angst" in their reviews. It will be interesting to see what grand attempts at creativity and originality are made by your reviewers when such an insignificant word is removed from their vocabulary.

Ronald G. Sheridan Jr.
Columbia, SC

ALLY OOPS!

I was cheerfully flipping through your December '86 issue when I spotted a very important name: Ally Sheedy. I was glad to see that she was listed under the "What's Hot/What's Not" column, but was both

Vincent Price waxes hysteric in 3-D.

shocked and dismayed when I realized that she was under the "What's Not" portion. Miss Sheedy is one of the most talented, vivacious actresses of our time. I admit that *Short Circuit* was no masterpiece and *Blue City* was less than magnificent, but Miss Sheedy always displays her capabilities as a marvelous actress. Also in this issue I found a full-page advertisement for *Blue City*. By looking at this ad, anyone can see that Miss Sheedy is definitely "hot."

Ally Sheedy may not be as big as Molly Ringwald or as sexy as Demi Moore, but she certainly does not belong in the same column as wired remote controls and receding hemlines. Are you sure this wasn't simply a misprint?

Jay W. Owens
Enid, OK

•Positive. —*Ed.*

REVIEWS REVIEWED

In the "Video Reviews" section of your February issue, you identified an actress in the *Desert Hearts* photograph as Helen Shaver when, in fact, it is Andra Akers.

Mary Anne Bollen
New York, NY

I enjoyed Clive Barnes' review of *The Gods Must Be Crazy* (January '87 *VR*). I'd

Selected correspondence addressed to **Video Review,** *902 Broadway, New York, NY 10010, is printed in the "Letters" section, space permitting.* **VR** *reserves the right to edit and condense selections for publication. Sorry, no personal replies.*

March 25, 1987

Mr. Alan Brennert

Dear Mr. Brennert:

Re your letter to "Video Review", 10 February, subject
Scotty dealing drugs in The City on the Edge of Forever,
you are quite right in pointing out that I misremembered
the script.

Harlan and I have since talked about it and I believe he
understands that I remembered a drug dealing crewman in
his script and over the years erroneously thought of him
as "Scotty". As you must certainly realize, I had 78
other shows also on my mind during those three years.

Thank you for calling this to my attention.

Best wishes,

Gene Rodddenberry

GR:ss

the forefront of his lies-made-history was that *he* had saved "City" from the drooling jaws and clubby hands of Spendthrift Ellison.

He never stopped retelling that story.

And I kept seeking the definitive rebuttal to that lie, for thirty years.

Well, all else in this essay notwithstanding, I *finally* found that single definitive bit of evidentiary support.

It came into my hands only as this book was going to press in its White Wolf edition. It can be found on page 31 of a large, coffee-table-style trade paperback titled WHERE NO ONE HAS GONE BEFORE: *A History in Pictures* (Pocket Books, 1994, and updated 1996) by J.M. Dillard.

The rebuttal comes from a source so unimpeachable, that standing alone it should consign to outer darkness the last echo of Roddenberry's wretched untruths about the creation of "City."

The rebuttal comes from the man who truly first conceived *Star Trek*, who had his "Wagon train to the stars" line filched by Roddenberry, who wrote "Where No Man Has Gone Before" as the successful pilot when NBC rejected Roddenberry's first pilot script, "The Cage." The rebuttal comes from Samuel A. Peeples.

Here is what appears on that page 31:

> However, Roddenberry massively rewrote the original script, much to Ellison's consternation. In an interview with Tom Snyder on the *Tomorrow* program, Ellison commented, ". . . they had mucked it up badly. It took six or seven years before Gene Roddenberry and I even spoke to each other again."
>
> Writer Sam Peeples concurred. "I thought Harlan's version of his script that won the Writers Guild award was far better than the script that was shot . . ."

And then J.M. Dillard proceeds to repeat Roddenberry's bullshit assertions that *he* rewrote me, and that "City" won a Nebula, and that I "rushed up on stage" and took credit for his aborted, stunted, thalidomide-baby script-by-committee. But since it was a Hugo, and it was at a World SF Convention, and since Roddenberry *wasn't even there*, he didn't know if I rushed up and took credit or not.

In truth, as you will find it reported in *Locus*, the newspaper of the science fiction world, I made it very clear to those at the ceremony—

and anyone who cared to read of my remarks in their many published reincarnations—that it was a wretched, half-witted, abortive version of my lovely script that they had seen on television, and I accepted the Hugo for Best Dramatic Presentation "in memory of the script they butchered, and in respect to those parts of it that had the vitality to shine through the evisceration." I *never* took credit for what they had done to my work, only to what they could not kill, though it took a gang-bang of them to do it!

But now, back to the original time-line.

Even after repeated phone conversations between us in which I reminded him that I was hardly the sort of guy who would take these endless canards with a smile and an aw-shucks. And every time Gene would figuratively slap his forehead and laugh and say something like, "Oh, gee whiz, Harlan, yes, now I remember that it wasn't like that at all! It must be my memory! Gee whiz, Harlan, I must be getting old and senile! I promise it won't happen again."

And it happened again. And it happened *again*. And it happened again and again and again. He never stopped. And after a while I decided, fuckit, he's screwed everyone I love on that show, and he's lied about me for decades, and now the time has come to feed him a mealy diet of his own mendacity.

What's that? You think I'm just a meanspirited guy? Well, how about someone *else* commenting on Gene's way with other writers' scripts? How about this excerpt from the latest ghost-written Shatner memoir, STAR TREK MOVIE MEMORIES, a remembrance by "creative producer" Harold Livingston of how well he was treated by Roddenberry when he, Livingston, saved Roddenberry's ass by writing the screenplay for what turned out to be the first feature film. I quote from the HarperPrism paperback edition, pp. 74-76:

> "In Thy Image," having now been abandoned by William Norton and due to be finished in less than three months, was stuck in a no-win situation. A round of inquiries found that the best writers in town were all simply too busy to jump into the task at this late date, and those who *were* available were ultimately deemed unsuitable by Livingston and/or Roddenberry. Still, *somebody* had to write this thing . . . and fast.
>
> With that in mind, Livingston, under enormous time pressure and lacking confidence in Roddenberry's abilities,

took the task upon himself. He turned the bulk of the series' story editing duties over to Jon Povill, locked himself into his office, and spent the next month pounding "In Thy Image" into a complete first-draft screenplay . . . .

Livingston's first-draft script was really quite close to the one that would ultimately become *Star Trek: The Motion Picture*. The only real difference was the ending . . . .

"I brought in my script on a Friday afternoon. I gave it to Gene and he said, 'Okay, now you've done your job. Let me do mine.' He then goes home, and rewrites the whole goddamn thing over the weekend. Monday morning, he hands out copies of his revised version to Goodwin, Bob Collins, Jon Povill and me, and at first glance, I immediately notice that the cover page now reads '*In Thy Image* by Gene Roddenberry and Harold Livingston.' He'd put his name on top of mine.

"So now we all go into our offices, we all start reading this thing and maybe an hour or so later, we'd all finished. At that point, everybody congregated in my office, saying 'What are we gonna tell him? WHO's gonna tell him?'

"So I picked up his script, walked into his office, and while he was sitting there with this expectant grin on his face, I said 'Gene, this is SHIT!' Just like that. And the grin remained frozen on his face, so I got myself excited, and I asked him, 'Why'd you do this? When something works, you don't piss in it to make it better!'"

That was Gene. Couldn't write for sour owl poop, but strutted around for the benefit of the gullible Trekkie Nation, explaining how every failure was someone else's fault, and every success was due to his fecund imagination, vast literary ability, and CEO-level organizational skills. Do I strike you as vicious in my presentation of these facts? Yeah, well, just so, gentle reader, just so. I put up with this crap for the better part of three decades, and now it's my turn. Do not expect from me a nobility that was not possessed by the late, great Bird of the Galaxy, who spent more than a few hours of those years dropping bird-shit on me and my version of "City."

• • •

Now we come to the section of this Introductory essay that was excerpted in a recent *TV Guide* Special on the *Trek* phenomenon. I was asked to write the piece by Larry Closs, senior editor at *TV Guide*. He contacted me (if I recall accurately) late in December of 1994, and he asked me if I was now ready, after all those years of the Roddenberry version, to tell the Ellison version of how "City" came to be. I was extremely reluctant. Ask Closs, he'll tell you. I said no a few times, capping the refusal with the phrase, *"TV Guide* hasn't got enough money to get me to write this sordid little epic." He asked how much money that would be. Now, since I know that *TV Guide*, for all its enormous circulation and ocean-swallowing advertising revenues, pays some of the worst rates in magazine writing, I named a figure about five times what their best pay-out had been in my experience. Closs called back later that day and said, "You got it."

Well, 'pon mah soul! What an epiphany, folks! There was actual rowrbazzle size money to be made from this kind of thing. Not just everyone else with their pig-snouts in the trough, but li'l ole me, too! So I wrote it. And Closs even reproduced some of the photographic evidence that proves I'm not just makin' this shit up as I go along. (And there's all of that stuff, plus more, here in the full-length book version. We want you should get your money's worth. Also, we want the winged monkeys who'll come to carry me off should have a hard time saying I'm a big fat liar, when you can see the actual documents here reproduced.)

So I wrote the article.

And the first phone call on my answering machine after the issue hit the newsstands, was the hysterically tearful voice of a woman who—in properly Roddenberry perfect-humanity manner— left no name, but in heart-rendingly (albeit cowardly) fashion excoriated me. "You rotten person," she screamed, "you should die and burn in hell forever! You aren't fit to speak Gene Roddenberry's name, you lying sonofabitch bastard!" And on and on, without much originality or innovative use of defamatory verbiage. (Don't you just hate it when some plucky little pustule summons up the sneaky strength to give you an anonymous call, and the best they can come up with is *fuck you*? If you're going to go at it, do try to heed H. L. Mencken's admonitions about the pallid nature of American cursing.)

But, astonishingly, thereafter, every single letter or phone call or InterNet message passed along to me (I have no computer or modem or interest in wasting my life on these electronic *yenta* boards) congratulated me for having the (what one reader called) "ethical muscle" to tell it "like it was." Well, gee whillikers, folks, how swell that you thought I was an icon of rectitude and justified moral indignation. I just have one question to ask:

Where the fuck were you for thirty years while Roddenberry and his running-dogs dissed me and smeared my rep?

But, then, I shouldn't be rude to you. After all, didn't you pay good money to buy my book? So let me just get on with it, and reprint my article from *TV Guide.* And when I return, New Horrors! New Horrors!

Last fall, *Entertainment Weekly* did one of these special *Star Trek* issues and they ranked all 79 episodes of the original series. Number one, all-time best, most popular episode was "The City on the Edge of Forever." Undisputedly the best episode of *Star Trek.*

I wrote that episode. The words didn't spring unbidden from Spock and Kirk's mouths, they were written. By me. The tragic love story in which the principal protagonists of the *Enterprise* went back in time to New York City during the Great Depression of 1930, and Kirk watched as the woman he loved—Sister Edith Keeler—was killed . . . I spent most of 1966 writing and rewriting and re-rewriting.

I watched it once, only once—when it originally aired over NBC on April 6, 1967—and have been unable to bring myself to look at it again since that evening. One would think the anger and the punch in the heart would abate after more than thirty years. But *Star Trek* has become as anally retentive a cult as the most obsessive True Believer could wish, and the urban myths that have been cobbled up about "City," and my script, march on tirelessly. They are horse puckey, but on they trudge.

In the film *The Man Who Shot Liberty Valance,* there is a line that has become famous. It is this: "When the legend becomes fact, print the legend."

TREK

THE GOOD, THE BAD & THE DORKY:

We know, we know—there are already enough *Trek* episode guides to fill a Ferengi freighter. But ours is the first to actually *rank* all 303 episodes from best to worst. How'd we do it? Our crack *Trek*-ologists devised a formula so sophisticated (plot + F/X - cheesy costumes ÷ number of times Bones says "He's dead, Jim!") not even supercomputer M-5 could figure it out. In the end, though, there's only one thing to remember: *Trek* is a little like sex—even when it's bad, it's pretty good.

ranking the episodes

CLASSIC TREK

1 THE CITY ON THE EDGE OF FOREVER
Comedy, pathos, drama, Joan Collins—who could ask for anything more? Bones accidentally time-travels to 1930s New York and saves social worker Collins' life, thus drastically altering history; Kirk and Spock set things right. Cosmic themes, effective acting, and a heart-wrenching ending make this the undisputed Über-Trek. (Episode 28)

2 SPACE SEED
An episode so good they made it into a movie (*Star Trek II: The Wrath of Khan*). As Khan, a defrosted egomaniacal dictator from 20th-century Earth's Eugenics Wars of the 1990s, Ri-

cardo Montalban out-emotes even the mighty Shatner. (Episode 24)

3 MIRROR, MIRROR
A transporter malfunction sends Kirk and pals into a parallel universe, where the Federation is an evil empire, the *Enterprise* an imperial warship, and its crew a band of cutthroats. Worth repeat viewings if only to see Spock's goatee. (Episode 39)

4 THE DOOMSDAY MACHINE
A giant ice cream cone from another galaxy goes on a planet-killing spree. Goofy F/X, but William Windom's bugged-out performance as a captain who loses his starship earns him a special spot in *Trek*'s pantheon of scenery chewers. (Episode 35)

5 AMOK TIME
A don't-miss episode in which Spock gets the Vulcan seven-

year itch and must return to his home planet for the Pon farr mating ritual—or die. You know what they say about guys with big ears... (Episode 34)

6 THE DEVIL IN THE DARK
Miners on Janus VI are deep-fried by a Horta, a rock-munching life-form. Classic scene: Spock's mind-blowing mind-meld with Mother Horta. (Episode 26)

7 THE TROUBLE WITH TRIBBLES
Things get hairy on the command bridge when the *Enterprise* has a brush with a bushel of fuzzy critters. Silly, but a real crowd-pleaser. (Episode 42)

8 THIS SIDE OF PARADISE
So cool it was immortalized in a

skit on *MST3K*. Spock gets socked by a love-spore and goes gaga for Jill Ireland. Best bit: Ireland asks Spock his first name; he replies, "You couldn't pronounce it." (Episode 25)

9 THE *ENTERPRISE* INCIDENT
Slick *Mission: Impossible* send-up: Kirk poses as a Romulan while Spock charms a cloaking device out of a female Romulan commander. Bonus points: Fake Vulcan "death grip." (Episode 59)

10 JOURNEY TO BABEL
Spock's Vulcan dad (Mark Lenard) and his Earthling mother (Jane Wyatt) drop in for a visit. Spock's deadpan description of Vulcan teddy bears—"[They're] alive and have six-inch fangs"—is a high point of the series. (Episode 44)

GREATEST *TREK* ON EARTH: Joan Collins in the ultimate episode, "The City on the Edge of Forever"

That is to say, why bother with the truth when horse puckey allows the True Believers to enjoy their obsession in a state of blissful ignorance?

I cannot tell you the truth. You would not want it, or believe it, or honor me in any way for having told it to you. Crybabies whine for the truth.

What you want is myth and half-truth. Okay, I can do that. But what follows is only that part of the truth that will not curdle your milk. The snail on the rose remains hidden.

Roddenberry and I sat in a booth at Oblath's. The restaurant was nearly empty, only a few gaffers and extras sipping coffee or dumping down a late breakfast. It was sometime between ten in the morning and noon. I was working on a meat loaf sandwich, and Gene had a drink in front of him. He looked at me and said, "They're conspiring to cancel the show."

Gene had called me at home and asked me to come down for "a private talk." He didn't want to meet at the *Star Trek* offices in the "E" building of Desilu Studios, which adjoined Paramount. He asked me to meet him at Oblath's, the now-vanished luncheon joint that stood just across the narrow street from the Marathon gate of Paramount. It was always crammed with people from the studios, but not till coffee break or lunchtime. Now, we were alone, and Gene was telling me that dark and inimical forces inside NBC were plotting the demise of this new space adventure series to which I'd been devoted since Gene had invited me to be a writer for the series in late 1965.

It was November of 1966, and they were getting ready to shoot "City" after ten months of my slow writing of the script, and after much duplicity and aggravation, and after Gene had given my work to others to rewrite—betraying the promise to me that if changes were needed, I'd be the one to make them. It was November, "City" was in preproduction, Gene and I hadn't spoken in many weeks, and he had asked me to come to a meeting so he could confide that the network was out to kill the show.

"I need your help," he said.

I wasn't a kid. I was 32 years old, I'd already won the first of four Writers Guild awards for Most Outstanding Teleplay for my *Outer Limits* script, "Demon with a Glass Hand" starring Robert Culp. I'd been a professional for a decade and had already published 11 of my 62 books; I'd been on my own since I'd run away from Ohio at age thirteen. I wasn't a kid. But I went for it. What they used to call in the carny, the *okeydoke*. The hustle. The con.

Gene had an astonishing ability to tell people what they wanted to hear, to charm them into doing his bidding, all the time thinking the chores had been self-generated. I went for the okeydoke and believed (what is generally acknowledged now to be utterly untrue) that there were idiot monsters at NBC who were trying to scuttle *Star Trek*.

Despite my lingering animosity at what Gene had done, and had allowed to be done, to my script, I volunteered to help save the show. And I came back to the Studio and Gene set me up in one of the vacant offices, and I created The Committee.

THE COMMITTEE

Poul Anderson • Robert Bloch • Lester del Rey • Harlan Ellison
Philip José Farmer • Frank Herbert • Richard Matheson • Theodore Sturgeon
A. E. Van Vogt

Dear   ,

It's finally happened. You've been in the know for a long time, you've known the worth of mature science fiction, and you've squirmed at the adolescent manner with which it has generally been presented on television. Now, finally, we've lucked-out, we've gotten a show on prime time that is attempting to do the missionary job for the field of speculative fiction. The show is STAR TREK, of course, and its aims have been lofty. STAR TREK has been carrying the good word out to the boondocks. Those who have seen the show know it is frequently written by authentic science fiction writers, it is made with enormous difficulty and with considerable pride. If you were at the World Science Fiction Convention in Cleveland you know it received standing ovations and was awarded a special citation by the Convention. STAR TREK has finally showed the mass audience that science fiction need not be situation comedy in space suits. The reason for this letter -- and frankly, its appeal for help -- is that we've learned this show, despite its healthy growth, could face trouble soon. The Nielsen Roulette game is being played. They say, "If mature science fiction is so hot, howzacome that kiddie space show on the other network is doing so much better?" There is no sense explaining it's the second year for the competition and the first year for STAR TREK; all they understand are the decimal places. And the sound of voices raised. Which is where you come in.

STAR TREK's cancellation or a change to a less adult format would be tragic, seeming to demonstrate that real science fiction cannot attract a mass audience.

We need letters! Yours and ours, plus every science fiction fan and TV viewer we can reach through our publications and personal contacts. Important: Not form letters, not using our phrases here; They should be the fan's own words and honest attitudes. They should go to: (a) local television stations which carry STAR TREK; (b) to sponsors who advertise on STAR TREK; (c) local and syndicated television columnists; and (d) TV GUIDE and other television magazines.

The situation is critical; it has to happen now or it will be too late. We're giving it all our efforts; we hope we can count on yours.

Sincerely,

Harlan Ellison

Harlan Ellison
for The Committee

December 1, 1966

I got hold of all the membership lists of the World Science Fiction Conventions from recent years, fan clubs across the country, mailing lists from antiquarian sf booksellers, a huge Rolodex of names. Then I enlisted eight of the biggest names in the world of speculative fiction— from the author of *Dune*, Frank Herbert, to the legendary author of *Slan*, A. E. van Vogt—and under a letterhead declaring us The Committee, I sent out thousands of letters asking for the help of fans and viewers, help in persuading NBC to keep the show on the air.

I worked night and day in that little office. I cut the stencil, and took it to the mimeograph room at Desilu where scripts were run off on an old Gestetner mimeograph, and I actually cranked that handle for hours to create the letters of S.O.S. on the reams of light green paper Gene had provided for the purpose.

When I hear all the toots and bleats from those who came later, that *they* saved *Star Trek*, my jaw muscles get tense.

But I did it, nonetheless. I went for the okeydoke because I had no idea what was about to happen to me and "City."

I was no kid. I should have heard the sounds of lies in the night.

Yeah, it took me an impossible ten months to get that script written. I don't cop out on that. But I've written scripts as quickly as over a three-day weekend. I've got 50 scripts to my credit; it doesn't take all that much time. So I have no excuse. But I *do* have an explanation.

In a dopey book called Captain's Logs: *The Complete Trek Voyages* (1993), in a section devoted to "City," the authors quote my old pal John D. F. Black, who was the story editor on *Star Trek* during my writing months. He wrote, "Harlan always had 40 things going. He was doing a book and he had this short story he had to get in, or whatever…"

Johnny doesn't seem to remember what the working situation for freelance writers was like in the '60s. How it went, was this: the new season began in September; every show got an order for 28 to 32 segments from the networks; but they got those purchase orders earlier, in May or June. And then they would start showing the pilot episode to every writer in town. They had "cattle calls" in which you'd be sitting with twenty or thirty other scenarists, in a screening room at the studio. And after you'd seen the pilot episode they'd shot the year before, everyone would trample his gramma to get to the producer or story editor, to pitch an idea.

And it all happened during a couple of weeks in the spring. What you would have to live on for the rest of the year was predicated on how fast, and how many, gigs you could smash'n'grab during the cattle-call fortnight. (And in them thar days, kids, the pay was a lot less. For a half hour script, it was something like fifteen hundred bucks, and for an hour-long segment, like *Trek*, it was maybe three grand.) So if you wanted to live above the poverty line in expensive L.A., you glommed onto three or four assignments all at the same time.

No excuse, just the way it was.

And I had a couple of assignments on *The Man from U.N.C.L.E.* as well as completing the last of a feature film assignment (coincidentally, also at Paramount). Gene came on the scene after I was committed to those jobs, but he wanted me on *Trek* so much, and I was so enamored of the idea of working on the first really big-time sf space adventure show . . . I accepted the contract.

So it is true. I was slow. I was riding three horses at the same time. But early on, I fell in love with my story of Kirk and Spock trying to set time right, of Kirk's great, tragic love affair, of the immutability of time and the human spirit. I threw myself into writing "City" as I had done with no other story save "Demon with a Glass Hand." And I wrote treatment after treatment to keep up with Roddenberry's ever-changing "script direction" and "input"—most of which came as a result of either Desilu or NBC suggesting this nitwit idea or that bonehead concept, I wrote and wrote and wrote. More than the Writers Guild regs permitted, more than I was ever paid for, more than was required. What sort of imbecile demands?

Well, Gene called me up one day and said, "The *Enterprise* has to be in danger. *Big* danger."

I replied that the focus of the show was not on the *Enterprise*, which existed in a timeless place frozen in the chrono-stream till Kirk and Spock could either set time in the past back the way it was supposed to be . . . or change the future, in which the ship might not even exist.

"No, no," Gene said, getting troubled that I was arguing with him, as if I knew what I was doing, "we *have* to have a great threat to the ship in every episode. The network is asking for it."

"But it's beside the point, Gene! It only wastes time and takes the viewer's focus off the love story, which is what this is all about."

"You'll have to do it!"

So I did it. To Gene's order, I created a sub-plot about the *Enterprise* being thrown into an alternate future where they had become, gulp!, space pirates. It was an unnecessary, foolish, redundant distraction . . . but Gene thought it would placate the suits over at NBC. (Eventually, of course, it was dropped. But it helped contribute to the myth that I had written this unshootable, incredibly expensive teleplay. Horse puckey.)

And there was, of course, the opening, in which I had one of the ship's complement getting a weak-willed officer to do something crooked, by tempting him with Jewels of Sound, a kind of futuristic hallucinogenic narcotic. Oh no, I was told, we can't *possibly* have anyone on the *Enterprise* doing anything as scummy as that. Our people wouldn't act that way.

That was the first time I ever heard that miserable excuse for hackneyed formula writing. Our hero wouldn't act that way. Our lead won't allow her character to act that way. Our people wouldn't act that way.

No, indeed not. What they *can* do is act the same damned predictable way each and every week, in each and every new situation. Never mind that human beings are irrational and unpredictable and an amalgam of good and bad and smart and dumb, never mind that the most universal reason that most of us do *anything*, even if it gets us in trouble or messes us up, is that It Seemed Like a Good Idea at the Time. Never mind that making these characters unchanging gave them about as much depth as a saucer of oatmeal. Never mind that common sense tells us that if you jam a mixed crew of approximately 450 people into an interstellar tunafish tin, for extended periods, that maybe, possibly, whaddaya think *someone* might get just a touch cranky with someone else? You mean to tell me, I said to whomever would listen, including Gene and John and Herb Solow (then head of the studio), and Bobby Justman, who was, at the time, associate producer—all of whom tell wonderful stories about how I didn't know what the hell I was doing, and how *each* of them, according to them, saved this script—that all 450 of these spacefaring men and women are saints, without flaw or natural human instincts or crankiness or rotten spots in their nature? No, I was told, Gene believes in the ultimate perfectibility of the human race. (Yeah, but all them third world aliens, who were nothing more than surrogates for ghetto minorities, *they* could be miserable rotten sonsabitches. Talk about your White Man's Burden.)

Yet, with all of that in there, Gene okayed the treatment finally, and I set about the long chore of writing the script.

So you know who it was that *really* sandbagged me?

It was Shatner.

I wasn't a kid. I should have heard the sound of creeping actors in the night.

Shatner had been sucking up. No, let me correct that, heaven forbid any of the True Believers get the impression that Bill wasn't absolutely and strictly the kindest, least self-serving entity in the universe. Bill had been solicitous of my friendship. I won't talk about that afternoon at the Hamburger Hamlet in Beverly Hills. All I'll say is that Bill was a sharp listener, and he knew that I had won the Writers Guild award, plus all these science fiction Hugos and Nebulas, and I was coming off a feature film that (until the wretched thing, in fact, opened) gossip was predicting would make a fabulous film . . . and he made me his little pal, his little chum. Leonard Nimoy wasn't like that. He was simply a good guy, and never hustled me, and we have remained friends for a quarter of a century.

But Shatner had me conned. Butter wouldn't melt . . . well, you know the rest. And I was going for the okeydoke again, silly me.

Bill had made it clear that the moment I finished that *great* script everyone on the show said I was writing, he wanted to see it, wanted to hold it in his hands still warm and pulsing from the typewriter.

I finished the script on Saturday the 28th of May, the day after my thirty-second birthday. I wrote FADE OUT and THE END and sat back and smiled and felt great compassion for Captain James T. Kirk, who would have sacrificed the entire universe, all of time and space, for the woman he loved. And I was filled with pride at having created the character of Trooper, a legless veteran of World War I, whose bravery meant nothing in the infinite flow of merciless time. Boy, I *loved* that damned script!

And like the Mt. Everest of schmucks, instead of going and playing a game of miniature golf or swimming the Hellespont, I made one of the great idiot mistakes of my life. I took an actor's disingenuous camaraderie as true friendship, and I called Shatner at his home.

"I'll be there in 20 minutes," Bill said.

I wasn't a kid. I hadn't just taken a dive off the turnip truck. OhBoy, if Time really *could* be called back!

I heard his Harley coming down the mountain road toward my house long before he shot halfway past the driveway, decided to course-correct doing 35 on a steep slope, and laid his bike down in the tarmac with a hideous wounded-beast screech.

The scar from his wheelie remains to this day in my driveway, though the 1994 Northridge earthquake splintered it some.

He came limping up to the door, I opened it, and in came The Great Actor, to peruse my humble offering.

Shatner sat on the sofa in the living room, and read the script front to back, top to bottom, page after page. I went off around the house to tend to

other matters—everything having gone to hell while I'd obsessed over
the dawn-to-dusk writing of "City"—and every once in a while I'd cruise
past and offer him a cuppa coffee or ask if everything was cool. He was
abstracted, but he indicated everything was peachykeen. It took him some
time to read it. He read it close, bro, *very* close.

Then, when he had finished it, he sat there for a few minutes,
staring out through the sliding doors of the living room toward the
watershed land behind my house. Contemplative. Then he picked up
"City" and started reading it all over again.

This went on for a couple of hours.

And after he completed the second pass, I saw him slowly turning
the pages, studying the script for something . . . I knew not what.

Talk about being a Mt. Everest capacity jerk, that was me, that
was I, that was the both of the not-a-kid.

He was line-counting. The Great Actor was weighing the freight
of lines spoken by his publicity nemesis on *Star Trek*, the enigmatic
Mr. Spock, the excellent Leonard Nimoy, against how many Kirk shots
there were. And let me not suggest that the ego of Bill Shatner
influenced his opinion, but when he toted up the numbers in his head,
and found that Lenny had, what, maybe half a dozen more lines . . . I
was on my way to an anger and a heartpunch that has lasted for thirty-
five years.

He told me how great the script was, how he couldn't wait to play
it, how he was going to tell Gene it was the best script they'd ever had
for the show . . . and I battened on the banana oil flattery like a bad
dresser buying a cheap suit. (I'm sixty-one years old. Shatner calls me
"a surly young man.")

Shatner, of course, still limping from his flameout, went straight
to Roddenberry and said he'd seen the script and it was swell, just
perfectly swell, *but he had a few problems with it.*

(A small digression. MY STAR TREK MEMORIES "written by"
William Shatner—which is to accuracy as *Le Sacre du Printemps*
"danced by" Harlan Ellison at the Bolshoi is to reality—had an
initial printing of 250,000 copies. And though I don't follow
Shatner's business dealings with even minuscule attention, I do
know that in December of 1993 HarperCollins went back to press
for another 25,000 copies.

(That means that yet another quarter of a million gullible readers read the following fanciful interpretation of Shatner's one and only visit to my home, as I've just described it to you. This is from page 219 of STAR TREK MEMORIES:

("Finally, when it got to the point where Justman and Roddenberry felt they were going to have to give up on the script, Gene sent me up to Harlan's house, hoping that I might be able to reason with him, and I have to admit, I failed miserably. At the time I was rather friendly with Harlan, and I'm sure that Gene felt like maybe he'd listen to me if I went up there and told him why his script wasn't usable. And I can remember driving up to Harlan's house on my motorcycle, getting inside the house and being yelled at throughout my visit. Harlan was very irate and within a rather short period of time he'd thrown me off his property, insane with anger at Justman, Roddenberry and Coon. I was just the messenger, but he was out to kill me, too."

(I've told you what really happened.

(That this is complete codswallop, the delusionary attempt to insert oneself into a game being played by others, that it bears absolutely no relation to the facts, is not startling. Mr. Shatner's memory, and the accuracy of that implement, has been called into public question before. Take for instance, in the 4 December 1993 edition of *TV Guide*, in the "Grapevine" section, a pullquote insert box called "Sound Bite." Shatner, during an interview, was asked about the U.S.S. *Enterprise*'s "five year mission" on *Star Trek*, one of the most familiar lines in the pantheon of American Pop Culture Babble, if I'm not mistaken. And, in the words of *TV Guide*, Shatner "drew a blank" and finally had to have the lines repeated to him, at which point this Paragon of Infallible Recollection responded . . .

("Seek out new civilizations, oh, yeah, I remember."

(Using this anecdote as trope, as metaphor, as touchstone, as anydamnthing you choose, kindly explain how it was that Shatner was sent to explain to me why my script was unusable, when actors and writers on tv series barely *meet* each other, much less get these Mission: Impossible assignments by the Executive Producer to intercede when all else has failed. In fact, Shatner was the first to see the script, as I've said, before *anyone* read it, Justman, Roddenberry, Coon, *anyone!* Shatner was at my home once. Only once. And I've described what happened. But here we go again, for thirty years, yet *another* minion of Star Trek Memories advising a quarter of a million strangers that I was—and likely still am—no-price, a bum, a dawdler, an incompetent.

(Do I seem to get angrier and angrier as I write this introductory essay? Yeah, well, as I said, thirty years is much too long to keep getting kicked in the ass before one does something about it.)

After all that time it had taken me to write it, Roddenberry now had been put on notice by his leading man that if the script wasn't substantially altered, there would be, er, uh, some hesitation on Bill's part when it came time to shoot the story.

Oh, hell, why belabor it . . . I rewrote the script, I rewrote it again, I worked on it at home and on a packing crate in Bill Theiss's wardrobe room in Building "E" and when Gene kept insisting on more and more changes, and when I saw the script being dumbed up, I couldn't take much more, and I went on to do a 90-minute script for *Cimarron Strip*.

And Gene gave it to a guy named Steve Carabatsos, who'd been brought on staff after Johnny Black had his falling out with Gene and righteously walked off the show; and Carabatsos took a chain-saw to it, and screwed it up so badly that Gene asked me to come back and do yet *another* rewrite (for no money, of course); and then it was rewritten by yet another hand (whose name I'll not reveal here, but it wasn't Roddenberry, who for years afterward told everyone that *he* had been the great talent who had "saved" poor inept Ellison's script), and I hated it; and I tried to take my name off it, and put on my pseudonym *Cordwainer Bird*—which everyone in the industry knew was Ellison standing behind this crippled thing saying *it ain't my work* and sort of giving the Bird to those who had mucked up the words—but Gene called me and made it clear he'd blackball me in the industry if I tried to humiliate him like that; and I went for the okeydoke. I let my name stay on it.

And then he called me in to save his damned show.

In Shatner's STAR TREK MEMORIES, on page 220, he writes, "Believe it or not, Harlan Ellison, who had become so thoroughly disenchanted with Gene Roddenberry and his *Star Trek* creation, can actually be held directly responsible for saving the show when it appeared headed for cancellation at the end of our first season," and then he goes on to get the story I've told you here all wrong in his charmingly Shatnerian way. But he verifies what I've written here, and concludes with this:

"It is truly one of the show's greatest ironies that *Star Trek* may have owed its continued existence in large part to Harlan Ellison, a man who would shortly become one of the show's greatest detractors."

And then they shot it. And I hated it. And I wept for Trooper, who never got to exist, and for the really lovely way I wrote that ending in which Spock, for the first time in the series, called Kirk Jim and not "Captain."

And then the original version—the one published in this book—the unabridged, unchanged, unscrewed version—won the Writers Guild Award as Most Outstanding Teleplay. Not the aired version; not the many-hands-in-the-soup version; but my own original story that John Black and Gene Roddenberry and director Joe Pevney and Solow and Justman and Shatner and *Trek* zombies who write dopey books like THE CAPTAIN'S LOGS have been telling people was too expensive, too lacking in drama, too inept to shoot as I wrote it. My story won the most prestigious award a Hollywood screenwriter can win from his peers, an award given only after blind voting based on hundreds of scripts submitted. Me, not Gene Coon or Roddenberry or any of the people who have said, as Roddenberry said in a 1987 interview in *Cinefantastique*, "I think Harlan's a genius but he's not exactly the most disciplined writer in the world. He had my Scotty dealing in interplanetary drugs and things like that!"

I gotcher Scotty right here, Gene.

Anybody who ever read that script *knows* there's no Scotty selling drugs. Or any of the other horse puckey that has been spread for more than twenty-five years.

Do I still burn? Gee, gang, sorry about that. Am I less than slobberingly attentive to the myths and the upheld torches of historical revisionism that make me look like a jerk and mythologize Roddenberry as a high-flying interplanetary *rara avis*? Does my manner offend thee? Yeah, I'm always getting complaints about that.

But when it comes to the end of the day, it was I, no one but the guy who created and developed and wrote about "The City on the Edge of Forever" who dreamed that dream for the rest of you to call the best of the best. You should have gotten better, though. You should have gotten the original.

But, sadly, to quote one last time, from the 19th Century French essayist Jules Renard: "Writing is an occupation in which you have to keep proving your talent to people who have none."

Think how interesting this screed would've been if I'd been permitted to tell you the *whole* truth.

Have a nice day. Have just a *real* nice day. And thank your mother for the chicken soup.

Bill Amend, 5 October 1993.

THE CITY ON THE EDGE OF FOREVER will bring a bold new dimension wherever it is displayed in your home.

THE CITY ON THE EDGE OF FOREVER

Season: 1st
Episode: 28
Air Date: April 25, 1967
Awards: Hugo Award, 1967
Author: Harlan Ellison
Director: Joseph Pevney

Available only on Planet Earth from
The Franklin Mint

A

So now we come to that portion of the *TV Guide* source material I was unable to use in such a limited venue. Remember: the article I wrote was more than 4000 words in length—at least twice as long as the usual *TV Guide* causerie. And even though the magazine ran a sidebar they called *Trail of Evidence* that gave pretty good proof Roddenberry lied continually about "City," they were reluctant to expend much more space on further "plaintiff's exhibits." But here we are at full length, and the Publisher wants you to see as much as we can reproduce.

Over the past thirty years, "The City on the Edge of Forever" has become not only the most famous *Trek* episode, it has also been a marketing and franchising bonanza for Paramount. From two hundred dollar acrylic light-boxes with three tiny celluloid frames of the show as illuminated insert, to two hundred dollar "crafted in fine pewter and Tesori® porcelain" desktop sculptures, to two hundred dollar posters sold on the shopping channels, "City" has become something of a cultural touchstone. Hell, it was even the punchline of a comic strip.

ace books, inc.

1120 AVENUE OF THE AMERICAS / NEW YORK, N.Y. 10036 / TN 7-5050

November 28, 1966

Dear Harlan,

    Thanks for your letter about the STAR TREK situation. From what I've seen of the show (I watched the first two or three and haven't felt a great urge since to turn it on) I'd say its demise would be no great blow to me, at least directly. However, you're right about it being important in opening up a larger sf market, so I'll cooperate with you on letter-writing, etc.

    I've made half a dozen Xeroxes of your letter and sent them to key fan newszines, which should alert the vast minions of fandom to the danger, too. If they have time between typing stencils for Apa L zines, I guess some of them will write letters. (I'm always dubious about the feasibility of getting fan support for anything practical, but sometimes fans surprise me.)

    Odd to hear STAR TREK's in trouble, by the way: the early ratings I saw in TV Guide and elsewhere showed it in the top ten nationally. TIME TUNNEL was in trouble for a while, but I hear they've now been given the go-ahead for the full season. It would be lousy if ST was canceled and TT went on.

Best,

Terry

Letter from the late Terry Carr, Senior Editor, Ace Books, in response to "The Committee" letter

And during those thirty years of fame and glory proceeding from the initial airing of the segment on 13 April 1967, Gene Roddenberry continued to represent me in interviews and from the lecture platform, as an undisciplined, talented-but-for-the-most-part-unhireable writer who had written the story of Edith Keeler all wrong. If you need any proof that I tell it just as it is, take a look at this page from *Cinefantastique* magazine, March 1987. Check out that large pullquote at the top.

making of a second pilot, "Where No Man Has Gone Before," and the bulk of the "The Cage" pilot was incorporated into a two-part episode entitled "The Menagerie."

Jeffrey Hunter played the part of Captain Christopher Pike in the "The Cage" pilot but "Jeffrey's wife did not want him doing science fiction," revealed Roddenberry. "So he turned down the series. William Shatner had become available and I kinda liked him ... "

For "The Menagerie" Parts 1 and 2, half of the two-parter was shot with Shatner in command of the Enterprise and with a less strident, better groomed Leonard Nimoy at his side. What audiences saw on the 11th and 12th weeks of the 1966 season was to be one of the classic STAR TREK adventures but it did not incorporate all the footage of "The Cage."

"The original print was never shown on television until it was cut up into the two-parter," said Roddenberry. "But then they discarded everything they didn't use." Roddenberry cleverly saved a copy of the full pilot, which is now on sale in video cassette.

"Part of it is in color and maybe 20% of it is in black and white because that's all there was left," he said. "They destroyed the color segues when they didn't use them in the two-arter. Originally there was only one color print. Desilu wasn't making a lot of money in those days and rather than spend the money to make a new negative they just took the print and chopped it up as the answer print. Everything that wasn't put into the two-parter 'Menagerie' was thrown away. I had a black and white print, run off as a record. By combining the black and white with the color we were able to complete 'The Cage.'"

Roddenberry was firm on the question of incorporating color and black and white segments for the episode's video release. "When they asked 'should we colorize these segments?' I said 'absolutely not! You have here a document of the way science fiction was in those days and the attitude of the studio toward it.'"

> **"Harlan Ellison is a genius. But he's not the most disciplined writer in the world. He had my Scotty dealing in interplanetary drugs!"**
>
> *- Series creator Gene Roddenberry -*

Sherry Jackson and Ted Cassidy as Ruk, androids from Robert Bloch's first season script "What Are Little Girls Made Of?" Below: Filming a split-screen shot of William Shatner as Kirk, who is subjected to duplication by a renegade scientist.

Although only an assistant art director on "The Cage," Matt Jeffries shares credit with Roddenberry for stamping the series with its unmistakable sense of authenticity. Roddenberry praised Jeffries. "Matt was, if I do say so myself, a brilliant choice. He had a good grounding in aero-nautical engineering which made our vessel look like it really worked." From flying B-17 missions over Africa during WWII to restoring a vintage 1935 biplane in his retirement, Jeffries' enthusiasm for aviation came to full flower in the design of the Enterprise, its bridge, engineering section, and other support levels.

Desilu supervising art director Rolland 'Bud' Brooks re-

called assigning Jeffries to STAR TREK. "Matt had worked for me as a set designer and Matt was an airplane nut—his interest in airplanes went beyond all bounds," chuckled Brooks. "I was sitting there thinking 'My god, we gotta come up with a lot of stuff here' and I thought of Matt. I couldn't think of anybody better to design the original flagship."

Since he was a member of the Aviation Writers Association, Jeffries had amassed a huge amount of design material from NASA and the defense industry which was used as an example of designs to avoid. "We pinned all that material up on the wall," recalled Jeffries, "and said, '*that* we will not do.' And also everything we could find on Buck Rogers and Flash Gordon and said; '*that* we will not do ... "

Through a process of elimination and selection they arrived at the ultimate design of the USS Enterprise NCC-1701. "I think the first time we had a review," said Jeffries, "I probably had a hundred different sketches. There were certain elements of some that we liked and certain elements of others that we liked and we kinda tossed the rest aside and began to assemble things with the elements that had some appeal to us."

Interestingly, one of the designs seriously considered for the Enterprise had the discus shaped primary hull replaced by one that was spherical. And the final Enterprise design, but for some last second switching, was to have flown upside down from its familiar configuration.

Initially a three-foot model was made and later a 14-foot model was constructed with what was unheard of attention to detail for TV modelmaking—even down to the nautically correct blinking red (port side) and green (starboard) running lights.

This attention to detail carried over to the design for what became one of television's most revered set pieces—the Enterprise Bridge. Replete with consoles, viewing screens, communication stations, and computer monitors, the Bridge was a masterpiece of intricate

Twenty years after being asked repeatedly *not* to spread these untruths, Roddenberry was *still* bumrapping me. Here is a salient excerpt from the 20th anniversary retrospective interview, as conducted by Ben Herndon:

> One of the persisting mysteries surrounding this episode concerns the expanded original version of the teleplay Harlan Ellison wrote as compared to the version that was filmed and broadcast with script changes penned by Roddenberry. •
>
> Roddenberry himself explained why certain alterations were made in the original script. "I think Harlan's a genius, but he's not exactly the most disciplined writer in the world," said Roddenberry.
>
> "He had my Scotty dealing in interplanetary drugs and things like that! Also, he wrote it so it would have cost $200,000 more than I had to spend. He just wrote huge crowd scenes and all sorts of things. I tried to get him to change it and he wouldn't, so I rewrote it."

Yeah, and now you *can* see the original. It's right here, just as I wrote it. And I defy you to find anyplace in the teleplay that remotely resembles Roddenberry's endless assertion, "He had my Scotty dealing in interplanetary drugs and things like that!"

•Hell, I'm tired of playing cutesy with you about who actually wrote the rewrite that aired. I've hinted at it, because *to me* it was a great revelation. But if you go to page 257 of the Afterwords section, you will find Dorothy C. Fontana's comments, wherein for the first time in our more than thirty years of mutual respect and friendship, she cops to having worked on the teleplay after Gene Coon's rewrite. Somehow, Dorothy didn't know about the *first* rewrite, the gawdawful version written by the man who briefly replaced John D.F. Black . . . Steve Carabatsos. Dorothy makes no reference to it, but I had a copy of that version and it was the existence of that inept attempt to rewrite me that convinced me I should drag my ass back to Desilu, for no remuneration and damned little approbation, to do the three or four rewrites that you will find reprinted in this book.

But what of Roddenberry's claim to have penned the aired version? Well if we are to believe Gene Coon—whose words come to us through the lips of Glen Larson and others—he wrote that version. But now we know that Dorothy Fontana whacked at it after *they* were done with it. I assert that Roddenberry may have fiddled, but that he did no substantive work. At least, nowhere in the UCLA *Star Trek* archive do we find even one page of a "City" script with Roddenberry's handwriting on it, or his typewriter's identifiable print, or anything that confirms either Dorothy's or his own contention that he rewrote on "City."

Peculiar, ain't it? I was supposed to have written only a first draft, according to Gene, but the UCLA archive contains at least three complete drafts and any number of rewrites, all neatly dated and catalogued; but nary a whisper of a script on "City" that can be directly laid at the altar of the man who twisted the truth so many times he came to believe his own fanciful mythology.

Gee, I wish everyone would buy into my untruths as they so happily did Roddenberry's, without ratiocination, without question. Hell, with that kind of blind adoration, even *I* could make the trains run on time.

Also, kindly find me huge crowd scenes.

Are we talking the line of extras in the soup kitchen? Are we talking the chump-change it would cost to populate a street in New York City during the Depression? How about those vast space armadas I'm supposed to have cobbled up? Where the hell are *they*?

Maybe now is the moment to suggest you leap ahead and actually *read* "The City on the Edge of Forever," as it was originally conceived. Perhaps you'll still like that abortive aired version, and perhaps you'll understand why I was so pissed at the way Roddenberry and his minions screwed over my script. And then, if you feel like it, you can go on past the first draft teleplay and read my revised second draft, in which I had even eliminated the Beckwith-LeBeque element, and gave Gene a *reasonable* way in which Dr. McCoy could have run amuck.

That was one of *five* rewrites, without pay, that I did to try and retain the integrity of the story. But no, Gene preferred having an accomplished ship's surgeon act in such a boneheaded manner that he injects *himself* with a deadly drug!

Yeah, sure, you were a sensational plotter and writer, Gene; and you can *schvitz* roses with Lysol to make 'em grow!

Such bullshit. Such never-ceasing, unapologetic, unabashed crapola. And this 1987 version of El Supremo's inability to tell the truth was hardly the first instance, nor was it the last.

"He had my Scotty selling drugs . . . "

Geezus bleeding Kee-rist on a crutch! *Scotty doesn't even appear in the goddam script!*

But it was a very different matter less than two months before the episode aired. According to Roddenberry in later years, I was *persona non grata*, a misfit who had cost the show a fortune. But on February 27th, 1967—a mere forty-five days before broadcast—the man who would lie about my ability and my creation for almost three decades sent me this telegram:

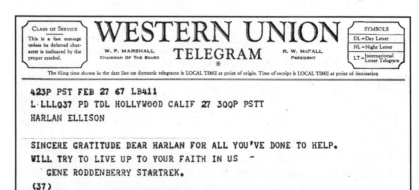

CLASS OF SERVICE   **WESTERN UNION**   SYMBOLS
This is a fast message   DL = Day Letter
unless its deferred char-   W. P. MARSHALL   NL = Night Letter
acter is indicated by the   CHAIRMAN OF THE BOARD **TELEGRAM**   R. W. McFALL   LT = International
proper symbol.   ®   PRESIDENT   Letter Telegram

The filing time shown in the date line on domestic telegrams is LOCAL TIME at point of origin. Time of receipt is LOCAL TIME at point of destination.

423P PST FEB 27 67 LB411
L·LLQ37 PD TDL HOLLYWOOD CALIF 27 3OQP PSTT
HARLAN ELLISON

SINCERE GRATITUDE DEAR HARLAN FOR ALL YOU'VE DONE TO HELP.
WILL TRY TO LIVE UP TO YOUR FAITH IN US ~
     GENE RODDENBERRY STARTREK.
(37)

But Gene spread his goo so eloquently, and the stone righteous *Trek* zombies slipped and slid in it with so much élan, that in later years it was like a Greek Chorus from anyone who needed to explain why I hadn't been writing anything for feature films or the series. Like, uh, here . . . a case in point. To be enjoyed after glomming the Paramount note attached to the cover sheet of the original story proposal for *Star Trek IV*, sent to me in December of 1984 by then Producer Harve Bennett, and Leonard Nimoy. (Please remember, as you read this anecdote, that you have seen me invited to talk about writing #IV, as the anecdote mentions #V)

LEONARD NIMOY

    Harlan:

    Enclosed, the concept as

    promised. Let's talk and

    arrange a meeting.

    Best,

                        STAR TREK IV:

                        A STORY PROPOSAL

                              By

                        Harve Bennett

                        Leonard Nimoy

                        August 10, 1984

Note from Leonard Nimoy regarding attached concept for Star Trek IV.

In the 4 June 1989 Arts & Leisure section of the *New York Times*, appeared an article written—but not headlined—by Robert F. Moss, itchily titled "To Sci-Fi Writers Hollywood is Mostly Alien." It is a longish piece purporting to explain the reasons "recognized" sf writers have not been more often hired to script sf/fantasy films.

In this *NY Times* article, Mr. Moss interviews all sorts of people, including me, and he quotes the producer of *Star Trek V: The Final Frontier* (Paramount). Said producer being one Harve Bennett, a guy I know. And Mr. Bennett said, among a number of things he said, as follows: "We brought in Ted Sturgeon to do a rewrite on *Star Trek II*, but he didn't make much of a contribution," and he described the late Grand Master as "too cerebral." Then the article reads like this:

> He [Bennett] claims to have had a disastrous experience with Harlan Ellison on a television series (a charge that Mr. Ellison denies) and characterizes him as an "extremely undisciplined writer," whose work is prolix, self-indulgent and often unshootable.
>
> But the evidence seems to exonerate Mr. Ellison. Though he wrote only one *Star Trek* segment, "The City on the Edge of Forever," it went on to become the most popular of the 79 episodes and appears to have served as the basis of *Star Trek IV*, the film series' biggest hit.

You will find the above-quoted sections on page 18 of the Arts & Leisure section of the *NY Times* for Sunday 4 June 1989, as I noted earlier.

It appears that Mr. Bennett, who solicited me—despite my lack of discipline, my prolixity, self-indulgence and generally disastrous character—to write *Star Trek II*, *Star Trek III* and *Star Trek IV* (and my agent, Martin Shapiro, phoned me a year or so ago asking me how I would respond to an invitation to write *Star Trek V*) long after our alleged "disastrous experience" on "a television series," told Mr. Robert F. Moss that he, Mr. Bennett, had this hideous imbroglio when he was shepherding *The Mod Squad*.

When Mr. Moss called to interview me for the *Times* article, he asked me about what Mr. Bennett had said. I replied as follows:

"Harve Bennett is a bastion of truth in an otherwise nasty world, and the idea that he might be telling an untruth is inconceivable. There is only one small flaw in his remarks. And it is this. I never worked on *The Mod Squad*. Dated Peggy Lipton a few times right around the time she appeared on the cover of *Life*, but I was never solicited to write for *The Mod Squad*, never submitted anything to *The Mod Squad*, never met with anyone from *The Mod Squad*. Perhaps the disastrous experience Mr. Bennett remembers was one of the brief chats we had at one of Marty's famous black tie New Year's Eve parties."•

The story of my "story conference" when Paramount and Roddenberry wanted me to write the first *Trek* feature has been told any number of times. Most recently in Shatner's second "memoir."

Gene completed his script in August 1975. As expected, Paramount president Barry Diller quickly and flatly passed, then asked him to take another crack. At the same time, unbeknownst to Gene, the studio began interviewing other respected science fiction writers, asking that they, too, submit outlines for the proposed *Star Trek* feature. Harlan Ellison was one of their first targets.

Ellison, as every decent Trekker knows, is the author of many of the finest pieces of science fiction ever written, as well as the man behind what's generally considered *Star Trek's* finest episode, "The City on the Edge of Forever." He's also a bit . . . eccentric. In fact, as legend has it, when he was asked by Paramount to write up his story outline in regard to a possible *Star Trek* movie, he balked, opting instead to commit his idea to memory. Once that was accomplished, he set up a meeting with a Paramount development executive, wherein he ran through a forty-five minute monologue and verbally unveiled a *Star Trek* adventure of truly epic proportions.

•Subsequent to the publication of the limited edition of this book last year, one of my faithful readers called me on this bit of historical recollection. And impaled me on my own words. In one of my two books of television criticism (which White Wolf will be reissuing in the *Edgeworks* series, probably in 1997), THE GLASS TEAT, I mention in one of my columns from that period (circa 1968-70) that Bennett and Rita Lakin had solicited me to come in and pitch a story idea for *The Mod Squad*. Nothing more is said of this liaison, and though I've combed my own extensive (and orderly) files, and searched through Leslie Kay Swigart's massive (but as yet unpublished) thousand-page-plus bibliography of all my writings, I find no *Mod Squad* treatment or teleplay or even story notes. So, to be precise, I was wrong when I asserted I had never been approached to work on that series. But as far as I can tell, my memory isn't playing me too many tricks, because there's no record of *The Mod Squad* request from Rita Lakin ever going any further.

Pacing about the office, speaking loudly and gesturing broadly for dramatic emphasis, Ellison conjured up a tale involving time travel back to prehistoric times, complete with battles against an evil race of reptiles and Captain Kirk's kidnapping of the entire *Enterprise* crew. Exhausted after his performance, Ellison supposedly turned to the executive and asked, "Well, whaddya think?" at which point he was told, "Hmmm, it's okay, I guess, but I was just reading this book right here called CHARIOTS OF THE GODS and in this thing, it says that the ancient Mayans were visited by creatures from outer space. Think you could squeeze some of those Mayans in there?"

Ellison, being Ellison, quickly, loudly, bluntly and politically suicidally pointed out the inherent stupidity of the man's idea, making clear the obvious fact that there were no Mayans in prehistory.

"Aw, so what," the executive supposedly replied, "nobody'll know the difference."

Ellison chimed, "I'll know the difference, you idiot." He then punctuated his remarks with a stream of profanity, a hasty exit and a strident door slam. Needless to say, his idea was quickly rejected.

As this second ghostwritten "memoir" by Shatner is about as reliable as the first one—and that *TV Guide* piece that appears earlier in this introduction should be compared side-by-side, page-by-page, with Shatner's self-serving fantasy about how *he* came up to my house to get me to finish the script—(Notice how everyfuckinbody in the world is responsible for the success of the "City" script . . . everybody and anybody . . . except me?) there are only a *few* hideous errors in the telling, apart from the anecdote being apparently lifted *in toto* from Edward Gross' book TREK: THE LOST YEARS (1989). Since we all know the Shatner TEKWAR novels were written by the fine sf/fantasy author Ron Goulart (who has a poison pill implant in his right lower bicuspid in case he is ever tempted to repeat that auctorial reality in public or private), so we know that one Chris Kreski wrote STAR TREK MOVIE MEMORIES for Shatner, and it's a shame proper credit wasn't given to Gross, but then, freewheeling use of other people's material seems to be only *de rigueur* for the *Trek* family and its associates.

(Oh, what's that? You think I'm kidding that Kreski and Shatner have pilfered Gross's material? Here take a look at what Gross wrote, and you tell me if you think this is "coincidental parallel development.")

In his excellent nonfiction assessment of horror and science fiction, DANSE MACABRE, Stephen King reported that rumor had Harlan Ellison going to Paramount with the idea of the *Enterprise* breaking through the end of the universe and confronting God himself. And that wasn't big enough, either.

Removing tongue from cheek, the author explained the real story to King, but before discussing that, it's important to note what writer James Van Hise wrote in his fanzine, *Enterprise Incidents*.

"The story Harlan came up with," Van Hise wrote in number eight of his magazine, "was never written down, but was presented verbally . . . the story did not begin with any of the *Enterprise* crew, but started on Earth where strange phenomena were inexplicably occurring. In India, a building where a family is having dinner, just vanishes into dust. In the United States, one of the Great Lakes suddenly vanishes, wreaking havoc. In a public square, a woman suddenly screams and falls to the pavement where she transforms into some sort of reptilian creature. The truth is suppressed, but the Federation realizes that someone or something is tampering with time and changing things on Earth in the far distant past. What is actually happening involves an alien race on the other end of the galaxy. Eons ago, Earth and this planet both developed races of humans and intelligent humanoid reptiles. On Earth, the humans destroyed the reptile men and flourished. In the time of the *Enterprise* when this race learns what happened on Earth in the remote past, they decide to change things in the past so that they will have a kindred planet. For whatever reason, the Federation decides that only the *Enterprise* and her crew are qualified for this mission, so a mysterious cloaked figure goes about kidnapping the old central crew. This figure is finally revealed to be Kirk. After they are reunited, they prepare for the mission into the past to save Earth. And that would have been just the first half hour of the film!"

Ellison gave Stephen King a little more information on his story meeting with Paramount.

"It involved going to the end of the known universe to slip back through time to the Pleistocene period when man first emerged," he said. "I postulated an alien intelligence from a far galaxy where the snakes had become the dominant life form, and a snake-creature who had come to Earth in the *Star Trek* feature, had seen its ancestors wiped out, and who had gone back into the far past of Earth to set up distortions in the time-flow so the reptiles could beat the humans. The *Enterprise* goes back to set time right, finds the snake-alien, and the human crew is confronted with the moral dilemma of whether it had the right to wipe out an entire life form just to insure its own territorial imperative in our present and future. The story, in short, spanned all of time and all of space, with a moral and ethical problem."

Paramount executive Barry Trabulus "listened to all this and sat silently for a few minutes," Ellison elaborated. "Then he said, 'You know, I was reading this book by a guy named Von Daniken and he proved that the Mayan calendar was exactly like ours, so it must have come from aliens. Could you put in some Mayans?'"

The writer pointed out that there were no Mayans at the dawn of time, but the executive brushed this off, pointing out that no one would know the difference.

"'*I'd* know the difference,'" Ellison exploded.

"'It's a dumb suggestion.' So Trabulus got very uptight and said he liked Mayans a lot and why didn't I do it if I wanted to write this picture," Ellison continued. "So I said 'I'm a writer. I don't know what the f-k you are!' And I got up and walked out. And that was the end of my association with the *Star Trek* movie."

Gross tells it even better. But they both omit one very important fact, and it is the omission of that fact in the Shatner-Kreski version that convinces me it was swiped from Gross: Roddenberry was *in the* room when I had this interchange with Trabulus. It was *Gene* who called me to come in for the meeting, in the very same office where we had done the series at Desilu, now Paramount.

Because neither Van Hise nor Gross ever mentioned it—he may not have known—Kreski-Shatner assumed this was a *sub rosa* meeting to do a back-door around Roddenberry's rotten first script. No way. Gene was sitting right there at the little round table in the corner near the windows, and he took part in the conversation.

That I didn't write it down before I told it, would only seem extraordinary to someone who didn't know diddlyshit about how business is done in Hollywood. The Writers Guild won't *allow* spec writing! You are not *allowed* to set down the plot before you have a deal. (There are, of course, hungry waifs who ignore this hard-won victory over Industry Greed by the excellent Writers Guild of America, who will write entire drafts of a screenplay on pure speculation. When they get it up the *tuchiss*, I have no pity for them.) So both Gross-Van Hise and Kreski-Shatner seeming to be startled that I "ran through a forty-five minute monologue and verbally . . . " is, in the case of the former, ignorance, but in the case of the latter, more than a revealing suspicion of monkey-see, monkey-do. (By the way, as a graciously offered writing note to Kreski-Shatner: the only way a *monologue* can be presented *is* "verbally"—that is, unless one is Hamlet delivering a soliloquy, or one is telepathic . . . out where I come from, pahdner, we call that "schoolgirl syntax.") But that is *precisely* how one makes a story pitch. You put together in your head the basic storyline, and you then sell it on your feet, like a stand-up comedian, to idiots in suits who have no more idea of how a plot should be constructed than a piece of ravioli has about Euclidian geometry.

As for my being "exhausted" after doing a mere 45 minutes . . . sheeeet, just ask anyone who's been to one of my 3-hour lectures!

And what end does this redundant exposure serve? If nothing else, it should show you, gentle reader, just how much malarkey you've accepted as True Word. Van Hise gets bits and snippets of half-remembered anecdotes, and publishes them without ever offering the finished copy to his sources for fact-checking. Then those mini-legends get circulated and distorted by fans who gossip and *never* get the specifics right (not to mention the inadvertent or purposeful warping of data on these idiot computer bulletin boards that run all night long disseminating half-baked bullshit no more valid than the *National Enquirer* edition of 12 November 1991 that blared the headline: STAR

TREK CREATOR'S SECRET—HE DIED HATING CAPT. KIRK.)
Then Edward Gross picks up the story and gets more specific, but *he*
wasn't there, *either*, so he makes the mistake of leaving Roddenberry
out of the scene. And then a Shatner-puppet filches the story, attempts
to rework the wording sufficiently so no one can shout, "Plagiarism!"
(they needn't have worried, neither Van Hise nor Gross has the money
to sue) and sets down the anecdote with several major errors now
concretized, drawing an utterly bogus conclusion that Paramount was
working behind Gene Roddenberry's back, thus reinforcing Gene's long-
since disproved claims that studio and network were out to scuttle him,
a song he sang from the git-go. And it makes Roddenberry look like El
Supremo, fighting off the hordes of duplicity, when in fact he was the
single largest blockage in the *Star Trek* flow.

But here is what I ask you to consider, and I realize now that I
grow weary writing this self-vindication, as weary as you must have
grown reading it: I ask you to perform two acts of simple logic.
No arcane thinking, no convoluted creation of conspiracies, no
long leaps between facts. Just *two* acts of cold, logical thinking.
And they are these:

• First, ask yourself if the depiction of the author of "City" as a
writer who couldn't handle the materials of his own story, as a mad
jackanapes without professionalism, as a talent to be admired but not
hired . . . rings true for a writer who was subsequently asked to write
Star Trek I, Star Trek II, Star Trek IV and *Star Trek V*? And asked to
write those larger, *more* expensive, *more* easily fucked-up productions
by *the same people who had been telling everyone Ellison was a bum!*

If I was so goddam notoriously impossible to work with, if I had
such a criminal disregard for budget, if I was a cannon on the loose . . .
why the hell did they come back to me again and again and again?

• And second, just read the damned script. Read all the treatments,
read the attempt I made to satisfy those subsequent demands for
revision, read the actual words I wrote! Then rent the damned video,
if you must, and compare. You may still go with what aired, but at least
you'll see that I wrote no Scotty selling drugs, I wrote no great crowd
scenes, I wrote no space armadas! I wrote a simple and poignant love
story, and I tried to say something about mortality and the importance
of courage when there is no hope and the nature of friendship and the
basic crapshoot that is history.

Read, and compare. The evidence is before you.

• • •

I don't have the space or the inclination to run all the letters from Roddenberry to me. Nor the space to place before you all of the times Roddenberry *in print* declared how much over-budget my show had gone . . . and each time it was thousands of dollars *more* than the last time, like the demagogue Senator Joseph McCarthy holding aloft a sheet of paper and declaring, "I hold in my hand the names of 136 card-carrying Communists in the State Department!" and the next time, "The names of 258 . . . " and the next time, "The names of 502 . . . ." But here's a sample.

Now, originally, I crowed like a madman at this ultimate admission by Roddenberry that, in fact, if I went over budget on "City" it was by a mere, piddling six thousand dollars! In the limited edition of this book, last year, I even went so far as to urge the reader to check out Roddenberry's own math in his letter to me. I said, "It don't parse, it don't add up, it's just simply *incorrect!*"

But on closer examination—and with a determination to be as truthful as the evidence at hand compels—it is clear that Roddenberry's budget letter presents a thorny ethical problem for me. As I pointed out, the Great Bird's figures don't add up. So I should caper and gibber and make hay out of this confession straight from his beak. But ethically, I'd be as bad as Roddenberry or the mooks who cobble up mythology about "City" and me. Because it's obvious, I think, that it was essentially a typographical error.

If you add another 6 to that 6000, you get $66,000. $191,000 + 66,000 = $257,000 . . . which is what Roddenberry says the show finally cost. So I didn't go over budget a stammeringly piddly *six* grand, but rather *sixty-six* grand. (And Solow & Justman's INSIDE STAT TREK roughly confirms that budget.) But the investigative journalist Joel Angel, whose book about Roddenberry I've cited previously, sent me a fax after reading the limited edition of this book, and he made reference to *his* investigations of archives dealing with *Star Trek*, and he advised me as follows:

> "Though Roddenberry says in his letter to you of 6/20/67 that 'City' came in at $257,000, there is no documentation in the archives to substantiate it. In the first year, according to the documents that *do* exist, no episode cost much more than $192,000. As you will see in Herb Solow's memo that follows, the approved budget was $185,000.
>
> "The only budget document I could find for the second year was Coon's 'Devil in the Dark,' which ran a month

before 'City.' Its projected cost, according to the documents, was $187,057; it came in at $192,863.

"Some examples of third year budgets: 'All Our Yesterdays,' projected cost: $182,282; final cost: $183,532. 'The Lights of Zetar,' projected cost: $168,000; final cost: $ 173 ,369. 'That Which Survives,' projected cost: $175,000 and that's exactly what it came in at.

"You may also like to know that in the third year, when budgets were cut, Roddenberry approved a raise for himself on at least one script, from the standard $4500 everyone else was getting, to $5500."

I think it's reasonable to assume that "City" ran $66,000 over budget . . . not $6000 as I trumpeted in the limited edition. But you wanna know something? Who gives a shit?! I was a freelance writer, like hundreds of others who worked *Star Trek* and every other television series, and it wasn't our job to board and budget the show! That was a job for Solow and Justman and Bernie Widin and the other staff members whose job it was to oversee such things. It was the responsibility of these "experts" to advise freelancers what the budget was, and ways in which it could be met if we went over the line. And, in truth, shows go over budget all the time, even scripts written by staff writers. It was, and is, a commonplace problem in the Industry, and not one that difficult to overcome case by case. If they wanted to.

And here's the capper to Roddenberry's bleats about the show going $66,000 over budget: it was the *aired version*, which The Great Bird of the Galaxy kept insisting was *his*, THAT WENT 66,000 FUCKING DOLLARS OVER BUDGET! Not my poor, miserable, inept, self-indulgent, extravagant first draft! If *he* couldn't come up with a script for "City" that came in on budget—after putting all those other "better writers" like Carabatsos, Coon, Fontana and himself to the chore—then how could poor, miserable, inept, etcetera etcetera Ellison be expected to do it!

I mentioned all this to Alan Brennert, the award-winning writer I've cited many times in this book (and to whom this volume is dedicated), and he told me:

"As a sometime-producer myself, I can assure you: no matter *who* wrote 'City,' it would have cost more than an average episode of *Star*

Desilu Productions Inc.

Inter-Department Communication

TO __GENE RODDENBERRY__   DATE __May 6, 1966__

FROM __Herb Solow__   SUBJECT __APPROVED BUDGET
FOR SERIES.__

At this morning's Desilu Board of Directors Meeting, the
members of the board, taking into account the series budget
as recently prepared, as well as the money being paid to us
by NBC, additional moneys to be carried by Desilu, etc.,
voted a resolution for the STAR TREK budget ceiling to be
$185,000.00 per hour. The board is aware that the cost of
the first group will come in at a higher figure, but the
authorization to me has been an average first year maximum
of $185,000.00.

I know all is being done to keep our costs down. I am hopeful that we continue to be optimistic on this point and that
the $185,000.00 budget ceiling will be a cost reality.

H.F.S.

hfs:ls

cc - Bob Justman
       John D. F. Black
       Bernie Widin

Weekly Cost Summaries?

	BUDGET est. as of 8/27/66	BUDGET EST. AS OF 2/4/67
CORBOMITE MANEUVER	204,584	188,274
MUDD'S WOMEN	215,629	197,100
ENEMY WITHIN	206,581	195,146
MAN TRAP	206,891	184,760
NAKED TIME	186,165	172,703
CHARLIE X	207,091	179,825
BALANCE OF TERROR	209,228	229,111
WHAT ARE LITTLE GIRLS MADE OF	226,528	208,033
DAGGER OF THE MIND	206,870	185,578
MIRI	220,828	212,852
CONSCIENCE OF THE KING		194,964
GALILEO SEVEN		217,037
COURT MARTIAL		187,067
MENAGERIE		212,765
SHORE LEAVE		200,912
SQUIRE OF GOTHOS		196,718
ARENA		187,757
ALTERNATE FACTOR		203,035
TOMORROW IS YESTERDAY		175,406
RETURN OF THE ARCONS		217,748
ARMAGEDDON		196,486
SPACE SEED		189,659
THIS SIDE OF PARADISE		186,634
DEVIL IN THE DARK		183,153
ERRAND OF MERCY		185,237
SERIES BUDGET / EPISODE	192,373	185,349

Trek, simply because of the period setting, New York City in the Great Depression. Sure, there was an old New York street on the Paramount lot, but you have to dress that street with vintage cars; you need to rent period clothes for your principals, your extras; to say nothing of the fact that you were making use of only *one* of the show's usual standing sets (the *Enterprise* bridge), and all the rest—the planet's surface, Edith's soup kitchen, the tenement basement, in fact *all* the Old Earth interiors—had to be constructed. Roddenberry *had* to've known this from the very first treatment, as did the people responsible for budgeting the segment, it didn't take them by surprise, and both they and NBC gave you the green light to go to teleplay first draft based on the treatment that contained everything I've mentioned. Hell, Roddenberry even boasted in his letter to you that he insisted on quality casting, sets, fx, and the like. Why would he commit to such inevitable budget overages if your script wasn't as good as it was? I find it the rankest sort of cowardice that he then, for the next thirty years, makes this big deal about *you* not being able to write the story to budget when even *he* couldn't! Or wouldn't.''

In his letter to me dated 20 June 1967, less than two months after the segment aired, Roddenberry wrote me:

> Dear Harlan: Despite the cuts in sets and cash the final budget figures on "City" were close to $257,000, or about $6,000 over our show budget of $191,000. We might have made it for around $20,000 less if I had not insisted on quality in casting, set constructions, special effects, and so on.

I'll tell you why I brought Alan Brennert into it at this point. In 1967—even allowing for what may or may not have been a typo—Roddenberry was saying I was $66,000 over budget. (In fact, what he was saying is that he was that much over budget because, don't forget, by that time they had "saved" my expensive script, they had "modified" my extravagance, so all they were left to shoot was their *own* over-budget version.)

By 1987, in an interview in *Video Review* (March 1987, page 46) that I cited earlier, but which bears refreshing in your mind, here's what the great model of perfectibility of humanity was saying:

> **VR**: I remember a time travel episode with Joan Collins.
> **RODDENBERRY**: I sent Joan a note the other day. I said, "What has happened to our Salvation Army virgin?"
> **VR**: That was a great episode.
> **RODDENBERRY**: It was a fun episode to do.
> **VR**: Who wrote that one?
> **RODDENBERRY**: Well, it was a strange thing. Harlan Ellison wrote the first draft of it, but then he wouldn't change it.
> **VR**: That's Harlan Ellison.
> **RODDENBERRY**: Yeah. He had Scotty dealing drugs and it would have cost $200,000 more than I had to spend for an episode.

And by 1990, he was telling the world I had been more than $350,000 over budget!

From $66,000 to $200,000 in just twenty years.

And by 1990, he was telling the world I had been more than $350,000 over budget! Yeah, and I also had Scotty dealing drugs.

A few loose ends, interesting digressions, a moment to catch our breath and depressurize so we don't get "the bends" from all this intense self-justification and naked animosity. Not to mention speaking considerable ill of the dead. (But then, I have also spoken some ill of the living. I'm an Equal Opportunity Opprobriumist.)

Not *everybody* ate from the poisoned mushroom of Roddenberry flack. The *New York Times Book Review* of 23 December 1993 carried a short review of Shatner's MEMORIES. And in that little notice, the reviewer, Rosemary L. Bray (whose name I never encountered prior to seeing it on that *Times* page, but whose name raises hosannahs from me every time I now hear it), wrote this:

" . . . bits of gossip and a record of happy accidents that led to some of the show's signature moments. For example, the episode snidely considered the best of any *Star Trek* season, 'The City on the Edge of Forever,' starring Joan Collins, was a watered-down version of a script by the science fiction writer Harlan Ellison, who so hated the entire experience and its result that he refused to associate with any of the staff again."

Well, almost right. I still associate with D.C. Fontana and occasionally talk to Johnny Black and even invited Herb Solow and Bobby Justman over to the house when they wanted information for their INSIDE STAR TREK. Leonard Nimoy and George Takei and De Kelley remain friends. We don't see each other much these days, though Leonard and I, and our wives, went out and had some excellent Indian cuisine about three months before my heart attack, and that's fairly recently. Walter Koenig and I see and talk to each other all the time.

But I don't talk to Roddenberry no more.

I've mentioned David Alexander elsewhere in this essay. He's a guy who was hired by Majel Roddenberry to write the "authorized"— that is, sanitized, prettified, heroificated—biography of Gene. It's been brought to my attention that I seem to manifest some rancor at Mr. Alexander. If I do, it is because I think Mr. Alexander plays with the facts and has done a hired-gun job that maintains myths and untruths that no self-respecting biographer should have allowed to stand. What I guess I'm saying, is that I don't think there is anything even remotely like evenhandedness in Mr. Alexander's snow-job about the Great Bird.

I won't even go into my feelings about Mr. Alexander actually trying, in a court of law, to be named "official biographer" so no one else—including Joel Engel, who wrote that *other*, warts-and-all Roddenberry biobook—would be able to contradict the Martinized version Majel had hired Alexander to write. (March 17, 1994; Case #SP 000 741; Superior Court of the State of California, in and for the County of Los Angeles.)

But what I *would* like to dwell on for a moment, because it is so goddam ludicrous and bogus that I can't even get pissed at it, all I can do is shake my head in dumbfounded disbelief at the bodacious *chutzpah* of Roddenberry and those who spent their time sucking up to him, is a little number Mr. Alexander and El Supremo ran in an interview in *The Humanist* (March/April 1991; Volume 51, Number 2).

Now remember, folks, before we tumble down *this* weird little rabbit hole into Roddenberryland, that nothing of the story or characters in "City" existed before I wildly dreamed up the plot and presented it to *Star Trek*. It was all outta my head, y' know what I'm saying here?

But in *The Humanist Interview* titled "Gene Roddenberry: Writer, Producer, Philosopher, Humanist" by David Alexander, we find the eye-opening exchange reproduced here.

Alexander suggests to Roddenberry that Sister Edith Keeler, a

CONTENTS

MARCH/APRIL 1991
VOLUME 51, NUMBER 2

mony of some special reason.

One time he went and wished he hadn't. It was 1933 when the great earthquake hit Long Beach. We had some relatives come into town, and Dad did the decent thing and took them to church. My dad was much like many humanists I've known: kind-hearted. He never called anyone on a religious question and never made a big thing about the fact that he was not religious. I remember when I was about three years old I had learned to recite a poem. I think it was "Away in a Manger." I had been called up onstage at church to perform it. I was a little ham—maybe I still am—but I remember the applause being so good. When my father came into the church a bit later, the preacher said, "You've got to see this," and he invited me up to the platform again and I repeated the poem.

My father suffered fools gladly. I would not cast those other people as fools, but my father suffered people's prejudices gladly, happily.

Mom had a hell of a time explaining why my dad never showed up in church. It was the things you might expect of a loving wife—"He works hard. He sees so much of this during his working life, he doesn't care to talk about it afterward," et cetera.

The Humanist: What was your father's background?

Roddenberry: He left school in the third grade. Later on, he taught himself to read and write. He was a very intelli-

gent man. He learned much like I learned. He met people and fastened on to what they were saying. My father was a very common man who got his high-school diploma while he was a police officer in Los Angeles. He was very pleased with that.

I received a letter which told me a great deal about him. Two elderly ladies wrote from Jacksonville, Florida, when the original series was on NBC. They had watched "Star Trek," saw my name, and wrote that they could have predicted that I would have done something like "Star Trek" because I had talked of such futuristic things when they had met me on my way to Europe *to fight in World War I.* They thought they had discovered my father and what he was doing long after he came back from the Great War. They thought I was my father. That told me quite a bit. They had remembered him all those years and said some very nice things about him.

The Humanist: That must have been exciting to have received that letter.

Roddenberry: Yes, it was. To have them say about my father that he held such thoughts when they knew him was exciting. There are many things about fathers and sons and you tend to think of the bad things. But in this case it was good stuff. It made me very proud that,

in spite of being not formally educated, he had dreamed such dreams.

The Humanist: This helps explain something about your favorite original series episode, "The City at the Edge of Forever," when Kirk and Spock travel back in time to Earth of the 1930s. This would have been contemporary with your father. Joan Collins played a character named Edith Keeler who ran a skid-row mission and talked about going to the stars. You drew on your father for parts of the Edith Keeler character.

Roddenberry: I'd like to say a few more things about him to set my mind straight. He was advanced far beyond his time. Once he took me out to the front yard of our Monte Vista Street house and said, "Gene, someday they'll rip out whole blocks of the city and put gigantic highways through here." He was talking about the freeways that I later saw being built. He said this to me in the 1930s.

During World War II, while I was still home, Dad had shown me a newspaper report on how the Germans had broken through the Russian lines. Dad was looking it over and said, "I've spent some time in open country, and I know something about the military. I figure they'll be stopped about here." He was pointing at Stalingrad.

He was a shrewd analyst of world events. I am reminded now that, being in my teens and very knowledgeable, I pooh-poohed his decisions and observations, but they were well ahead of our military men.

The Humanist: He was a basic Los Angeles street cop?

Roddenberry: Yes, he was a good beat cop. I think my father was very often embarrassed with what the police did in those days. He was an unusual man. I guess many of my beliefs about ordinary people and what they can do come out of respect for my father. He had a side to him that was diffident, quiet. He had an ugly side, too, but it was, I think, legitimate for him at that time, as I know how he grew up in the Florida-Georgia

character I created, and whom I based on the famous Aimee Semple McPherson, an historically-prominent evangelist of the 1920s and '30s, was actually Roddenberry's brainstorm, based on his father, whom he speaks of admiringly. (I won't reprise what other books about Roddenberry have said in relation to the Great Bird and his father, and how Bird felt about the old man, and what their relationship was. I am sworn not to get into Roddenberry's personal life here, for which pledge I am infinitely grateful.)

Above: Flamboyant Pentecostal preacher "Sister" Aimee Semple McPherson (1890–1944) was the first evangelist to recognize the potential of radio to reach a vast "congregation" (Library of Congress).

Now, doesn't that absolutely fry the fish, folks! Don't it just warm that illegitimate corner of all our hearts in which lies the most corrosive, mendacious beast of self-aggrandizement we can imagine?

Not only was the miserable, lying sonofabitch shameless in trying to grab credit for having *written* the script, he was not above tacitly acquiescing to the suggestion that it was all his own invention, right from the git-go.

Was I infuriated when one of my readers sent me *that* steaming Alexandrian turd? No, of course not. I am a sensible, rational person, ready to accept the fallaciousness of the existence of Santa Claus, the Tooth Fairy, and the ability of my poor, stunted brain to create a character so fully-formed and coherent that even now when she goes out on the book-signing circuit, Joan Collins is asked repeatedly about Sister Edith Keeler.

Which brings me to a beauty.

And I don't mean Collins.

If you've read the script, you will remember that Edith Keeler is an humanitarian whose philosophy is one of kindness and compassion. It is stated in the script that she develops, over the next few years, a coherent identifiable philosophy that many people in that post-World War I, semi-Isolationist society found appealing. It is set forth in the teleplay that her philosophy catches on—something like Scientology without the phony scams—and it is sufficiently appealing that it produces a tone in the body politic that briefly keeps America out of the war against Hitler. A brief period that permits the development of the first atomic bomb not by America, but by The Third Reich, and that leads to Germany winning World War II.

It is a "what if?" plot, and standard extrapolative play in the genre of speculative fiction. It is not a coarse, solve-the-problem-in-53 minutes oversimplification. But apart from the idiot bullshit dialogue that Roddenberry shoved into Sister Edith Keeler's mouth—the kind of fuzzy-headed social thinking that could give you diabetes—she was a strong, decent woman. That's why she remains appealing.

And how does the Bimbo Queen, Joan Collins, remember this glorious role, in this landmark show that still draws raves for her limited abilities? Well, read for yourself, from page 113 of Ms. Collins's INSIDE JOAN COLLINS.

cious appetite and devoured material—and actors and actresses to make the material come alive. She would get small roles in the big series of the time: "The Bing Crosby Special," "Mission Impossible." She even played opposite her old classmate David McCallum from RADA in a "Man from U.N.C.L.E." episode.

And she did a "Star Trek." The segment, titled "City on the Edge of Forever," later became a cult classic. Every Trekkie knows it and remembers it. The story gimmick is strictly a sci-fi time-warp wrinkle, with the *Enterprise's* Dr. McCoy—"Bones"—swept up into another time and another world, and Captain Kirk and Spock tracking him down. McCoy has wound up, sick and incapacitated, in a mission for poor souls during the Great Depression in New York. Joan is a female mission worker fascinated with the charms and the utter charisma of none other than Adolph Hitler! She's quite probably a Nazi plant. Kirk falls in love with her and seems to be swallowing her Nazi philosophy. Spock warns Kirk that Hitler nearly ruined the world in the years following. When an out-of-control truck threatens to kill Collins, Shatner at first leaps to the rescue, but, recalling Spock's warning, lets fate take its course and allows her to be killed, keeping the world from being destroyed by the monster of Berlin—through her proselytizing, presumably.

Meanwhile, Newley was deeply enmeshed in *Dolittle*, at this point working in New York, and Joan was all alone at the house. She was startled one night to get a phone call from none other than her laid-back Californian discotheque associate Ryan O'Neal. It was Joan's birthday, and although Newley had promised to be there with her, he had been unable to break away from his work.

O'NEAL: Happy birthday! Where's your husband taking you tonight?

JOAN: He's stuck in the Big Apple.

O'NEAL: Well, uh, we wouldn't want you to be alone on your birthday, would we?

JOAN: No. We wouldn't.

And if *that* journey "inside" Joan Collins doesn't remind you of a visit to a forlorn, empty venue where the wind whistles forever across a sterile terrain, try *this* one from her own classic autobiography PAST IMPERFECT, page 248:

"So I worked . . . . and 'Star Trek'—'The City on the Edge of Forever' became one of the most popular episodes. As Edith Cleaver [sic], a young mission worker for down-and-out men in New York in the Depression, I try to prove to the world that Hitler was a nice guy. Bill Shatner as Captain Kirk falls in love with Edith, and Dr. Spock [sic]—he of the ears—allows her to get run over by a truck lest her teachings lead the world to total destruction."

I don't know which one of them is the greater pinhead—Jay David who wrote the former book for Carroll & Graf in 1988, or the nameless editor at Simon & Schuster who apparently never fact-checked, much less read for sanity, the semiliterate blather of this latter—but there really ought to be a hell on Earth for literary dodgem-cars like that. The less said about Ms. Collins's ratiocinative powers, the better off we'll be but, amazingly, Collins seems to have taken the INSIDE JOAN COLLINS dementia version of my plot as gospel. She was interviewed last year on a British chat show, and she claimed that in "City" she was "in love with Adolph Hitler."

I thought having Shatner getting it all mixed up was bad.

I didn't know when I was well off.

Which brings me to the last, most recent item. During the last few years, Herb Solow and Bobby Justman—whose positions as executives of Desilu and *Star Trek* back in the days "City" was being done—called on me to be interviewed for their recently-published tome, the Gigantic INSIDE STAR TREK: *The Real Story*. Though I was reluctant to spill most of what you've read in *this* book, I felt (and continue to feel) warmly toward both of them. We go a long way back, and they have always treated me decently, and we've had a bemusing sort of relationship in which they perceive me as some sort of barely housebroken creature. So I spoke to them. They both came over one day, and we sat and I talked and told them vast amounts of stuff, and they taped it, as I recall.

Then, as the year or so passed, Herb would call me once in a while to check on something . . . and I'd answer his Queries as best I could. I knew they would treat me square in the hook. They are decent guys.

But then, a few months ago—as I write this—the book came out, and though they reported the "City" matter at length in a chapter all its own, and they gave credit where it was due, even to buttressing my main contention in *this* book that Roddenberry was an unregenerate credit-thief (see page 185 of IINSIDE STAR TREK), they ended the section with this anecdote:

---

writer-director Frank Pierson sitting several tables away. Some months earlier, Howard had decided to hate Frank Pierson (an Academy Award-winning writer and former President of the Writers Guild) because Frank rewrote Howard's friend Carol Sobieski's screenplay, "Neon Ceiling," a drama that Howard felt needed no changes whatsoever. Obviously agitated by Harlan's remarks, Howard, a powerfully built man, announced he was going to tackle Frank and shove him through the huge plateglass window to plunge eight floors to the street below. We managed to restrain him. It was that kind of evening!

The Writers Guild rule for award consideration was that the writer, not the producing company, submitted the script and could submit whatever version he or she chose, be it the writer's first draft or the final shooting script, which usually had undergone many revisions and rewrites by others. Two different panels of judges then made the individual award decisions.

Some years after receiving the Writers Guild award, Ellison was in a bar when he ran into writer Don Ingalls. "Fandango," a script Ingalls wrote for *Gunsmoke*, was one of the four other contenders that lost out to Ellison's script. Ingalls had also written for *Star Trek*, and they discussed not only the series but Ellison's award-winning script. After a few drinks Harlan boasted that, before submitting his own final draft for consideration, he had "polished it up a little bit to make it even better." To this day, Ingalls remains amused by his friend Ellison's award-winning stratagem.

HERB: So when I finally realized that Harlan was a sorcerer's reincarnation, it answered that burning question: "Why did he do what he did at the Awards dinner?" Easy. The Wizard made him do it.

On the Edge of Forever: Waiting for Harlan   289

I couldn't believe what I saw there. I couldn't believe that at no time in the preceding few years, of all the times we spoke, neither Herb nor Bobby thought to ask me about the validity of what Don Ingalls had told them. Not once.

Now, anyone who knows me at all . . . anyone who has read my books and followed my essays . . . anyone who is in my company for more than an hour . . . knows what's wrong with that Ingalls anecdote.

What's wrong is that I *don't drink*.

I have *never* drunk.

Can't stand the taste of alcohol, it makes me sick. As a consequence, I have no tolerance for alcohol of any kind. I do not drink beer, wine, hard liquor. I also don't use drugs, but that's another matter.

I've even written at length about this. Look up a piece I wrote about working in a carnival when I was thirteen years old. It's in one of my books. It's titled "Gopher in the Gilly."

What I'm saying here, is that anyone who knows anything at *all* about me knows that I don't drink.

Consequently, I don't go into bars.

I don't think I've been in a dozen bars in my whole life, even accompanying friends or buddies throughout my young adulthood.

And I sure as hell have never been drunk.

I barely knew Don Ingalls. He wrote some segments of *Voyage to the Bottom of the Sea* when I was working at 20th Century Fox on the same series, and I guess I've run into him a few times over the years; but we are not close friends, just casual acquaintances; and I sure as hell never went drinking with him in a bar somewhere.

Additionally, I have in my files the *exact* copy of "City" that was submitted to the Writers Guild for consideration in judging that year's awards, and it is exactly like the script in this book. There are no changes (with the exception of a few infelicities of grammar introduced into this edition) from the original version. It is a copy of my best draft of "City." I never ever in any way "altered" or "polished up" my teleplay before submitting it. As I say, I have the very one that was entered, with the WGAw cover sheet still on it.

So why does Don Ingalls say this, a story that is patently bullshit, untrue, made up? Well, it's been thirty years, and they just cannot let me have the credit for my own work. Even good guys like Bobby and Herb had to accept this unsubstantiated story from Ingalls—who was a very close buddy of Roddenberry's, I've been told they were both cops together, but I don't know Ingalls well enough to call him and ask him, and frankly, I ain't gonna bother, he probably believes that crap by this time, he's been dining out on it for three decades.

Don't ask me why Ingalls has to make himself look as if I stole an award from him, this many years after the fact of his losing and my winning, but maybe Ingalls wasn't happy that I copped the award (my second in as many years), and maybe he has altered memory to suit his saving face. I don't know.

What I *do* know is that this anecdote never happened.

Not any part of it.

Not a bar, not me being drunk, not hoisting a few with a guy I barely knew, not doctoring up my teleplay so I could enrich my chances to win. It's all bilge and rat-puke.

Ask *anyone* who knows anything about me.

So I called Herb, and I got very testy with him, particularly when I asked him why he verified so many other things in the book, but never sought to solicit any response from me, though he'd certainly had the opportunity in all the times we'd talked. And Herb got defensive and said well, we just heard it from Don, and we believed it, and blah blah blah.

So I *told* Herb that I don't drink. That I *never* drank, not from the time I was born. I even told him that the one time someone had forced some alcohol on me had been maybe twenty years ago, at some dumb party somewhere, and some clown made a big thing about what a "party pooper" I was because I wasn't bagged like everyone else, and he gave me maybe an inch of beer in a glass, and to shut him up I swigged it, and got instantly, totally falling-down sick to my stomach.

I told this to Herb, and I also told him that I had the very copy of "City" that the judges had looked at, way back in 1967, that it was in my files and I'd drive it over to him right then and there along with a copy of the limited edition of this book, containing the same damned script, so he could compare them if he had a mind to do so, but he got cranky with me, he didn't like being told his book wasn't as properly vetted and researched as he wanted to believe; and he told me that he would put in a footnote in later editions, and in the paperback, to the effect that "Harlan says he doesn't drink and Ingalls' story isn't so."

Big fucking deal.

Let's end the section in this book, the section that once again posits my inability to write, and let's try to be a good pair of guys with Harlan, and treat him not as quite the mountebank we could if we were meanspirited. But let's end the section with a bogus anecdote that says, in pretty plain language, "Ellison wasn't really good enough to win that

Writers Guild award with his original version, my pal Gene's version was *much* better, and Ellison had to cheat at the last minute even to get the judges fooled."

So Herb will add a footnote that says, "Harlan says it ain't so." Yeah. Great. And the next day, I got the following fax from Herb:

SOLOW TWO ENTERTAINMENT

FAX MEMO
[one (1) page]

May 20, 1996

TO: **Harlan Ellison**

In thinking about our conversation yesterday, may I address one of the points you made about the Ingalls' story.

I understand your insistence that you haven't had a drink in 20 years and that you haven't been in a bar in 20 years.   If you will re-read Ingalls' story and locate it in time, you will see that he was referring to a meeting that took place approximately 27 to 28 years ago.

You know that both Bob and I respect you and your talent.   Please respect our concern for accuracy and our three years of effort in writing a fair and objective book.

Best.

Herb.

29060 CLIFFSIDE DRIVE • MALIBU • CALIFORNIA 90265 • TEL (310) 457-2215 • FAX (310) 457-5955

TOTAL P.01

See what he did. He wants me to respect his "concern for accuracy" but he couldn't even understand what I was saying about that one inch of beer twenty years ago. *He* heard it as my saying that I drank up till twenty years ago, but stopped, and so Ingalls had to be telling the truth because his anecdote took place earlier than twenty years ago. No, dummy, I *never* drank, have never ever drunk, not now, not twenty years ago, not sixty-two years ago.

I do not drink, period, no mitigation.

But there it is, thirty years, and still going strong. The Curse of Roddenberry.

The supreme, overwhelming egocentricity of Gene Roddenberry, that could not permit him to admit anyone else in his mad-god universe was capable of grandeur, of expertise, of rectitude. And his hordes of Trekkie believers, and his pig-snout associates who knew whence that river of gold flowed . . . they protected and buttressed him. For thirty years.

If you read all of this book, I have the faint and joyless hope that at last, after all this time, you will understand why I could not love that aired version, why I treasure the Writers Guild award for the original version as that year's best episodic-dramatic teleplay, why I despise the mendacious fuckers who have twisted the story and retold it to the glory of someone who didn't deserve it, at the expense of a writer who worked his ass off to create something original, and why it was necessary—after thirty years—to expend almost 30,000 words in self-serving justification of being the only person on the face of the Earth who won't let Gene Roddenberry rest in peace.

1 August 1995
Revised and expanded June 1996

TREATMENTS

21 March 1966
13 May 1966

March 21, 1966

STAR TREK
"The City on the Edge of Forever"
written by Cordwainer Bird

TEASER:

FADE IN aboard the *USS Enterprise* somewhere out near the Rim. CLOSE ON a small isometrically-shaped metal container, as it is opened by a hand. CAMERA HOLDS CLOSE as the lid opens with tambour doors, so that the interior rises, and a strange dull light floods the frame. As the container opens, the black velvet interior slides up to reveal possibly half a dozen strange and wondrous glowing jewels. Yet they are not jewels. They are the infamous and illegal Jillkan dream-narcotics, the Jewels of Sound. They are faceted solids, but not stone, more like a hardened jelly that burns pulsingly with an inner light: gold, blue, crimson, orange.

We HEAR a VOICE O.S., a voice that shakes slightly, trying to maintain a tenuous control. "Beckwith, give me one. Stop it, Beckwith!" and as the CAMERA PULLS BACK we see one of the *Enterprise*'s officers LT/JG LeBEQUE, a French-Canadian with a strong face; but a face that is now beaded with sweat. And holding the Jewels of Sound is RICHARD BECKWITH, another officer, a man whose face shows intelligence and . . . something else. Cunning, perhaps, or even subdued cruelty. Cruelty kept rigidly in check, channeled to specific uses. Beckwith smiles as he stares with fascination at the Jewels of Sound.

"How long have you been my man, Lieutenant?" Beckwith asks, softly. He isn't taunting, merely interested. "How long have you been hooked on the Jewels?"

The Lieutenant's face tightens. He isn't a toady, neither is he a weak man. But the Jewels of Sound have been listed illegal throughout the Galaxy because only one exposure is needed to make a man a confirmed addict. Swallow one Jewel, experience the Circe call of the strange music and lights the Jewels offer, and you are lost forever. And so LeBeque will swallow his pride, and answer the man who holds the delight he needs so desperately, "You gave me my first taste on Karkow, that was a year ago. I need one, Beckwith, stop playing with me."

Beckwith extends one, a golden Jewel. But as the Lieutenant reaches for it, he closes his fist over it, closing off the light, and LeBeque winces, as though the loss of it physically hurts him. "I want to know our next putdown planet, and what the security log says about valuable commodities. I'll want a landfall pass and I'll want you to cover for me while I trade with the natives."

"After the slaughter on Harper Five, you'll do it again? If Kirk finds out—"

"He *won't* find out, will he, LeBeque? He won't find out, or you'll never hear these Jewels inside you again. Remember that. I'm coming back from this a rich man, and I'll never have to go to space again. Nobody's going to get in the way of that, LeBeque. I want to live a quiet life, but that takes resources."

LeBeque gropes for words, "So you cheat aliens, get them hooked on illegal dream-narcotics, and steal what they could trade for cultural advances."

"Hooked like you, LeBeque. Hooked like you."

"Yes, like me. And I'm already paying."

"But you'll pay a little more. Do I get what I need?"

LeBeque nods slowly. Beckwith gives him the Jewel and the *Enterprise* Lieutenant swallows it. CAMERA HOLDS past Beckwith smiling knowingly at LeBeque, and as a look of almost orgasmic pleasure crosses the Lieutenant's face we REVERSE ANGLE from LeBeque's POV and we see THRU HIS EYES as Beckwith's face begins to shimmer with weird lights, like a Van deGraaf generator. Then we HEAR the incredible music of the Jewels—sounds from another time, another space, sounds that reach into LeBeque's head and strum the synapses of his brain, as the lights collide and merge and swivel and twirl and dance in patterns of no-pattern, and Beckwith's face fades away with that damnable knowing smile, and for SEVERAL BEATS we SEE THRU the drug-drunken eyes of a man in the grip of an alien narcotic. Then, as we COME BACK INTO FOCUS we HEAR the VOICE of MR. SPOCK as he yells, "LeBeque! Damp that starboard unit, you're running into the red! You'll blow the entire drive! LeBeque!" and we COME BACK INTO FOCUS finding ourselves in the control central with LeBeque being dragged back away from the damping controls by Spock and several other crewmen.

He reels back and the HIGH PIERCING WHINE of machinery stressing to implosion level subsides as Spock damps the units. The extraterrestrial spins on LeBeque and coldly informs him, "You've been walking around this control country like a man under water for the past two hours. If you're feeling unwell Mr. LeBeque, relieve yourself and leave the bridge."

"T–two hours . . . ?" LeBeque murmurs, shaking his head as though to clear it. He excuses himself from the bridge and WE GO WITH HIM as he passes down cross-corridors in the ship, pausing to fight with himself, emotions playing across his face that tell us the man despises himself for what he has allowed himself to become. Then, making a decision, he heads for Beckwith's cubicle and as we come to them in 2-SHOT, we hear LeBeque say, "I've had it. Whatever Kirk wants to do with me, I'll deserve it; but I'm turning you in, Beckwith."

He turns to go, and has taken only two steps into the corridor when Beckwith, wild with panic, emerges from behind him and we ZOOM IN on Beckwith as he raises a massive block of green jade and swings it heavily again and again at LeBeque, out of the frame. Another ZOOM IN on a trio of crewmembers, two men and a woman as they round the junction of corridors and see the murder and then we HARD CUT TO

The Assembly Salon of the *Enterprise* where a court martial is concluding. Kirk is presiding, with Spock and the SCOTTISH ENGINEERING OFFICER and THE MEDIC in charge. Much of the ship's complement is on hand to hear CAPTAIN JAMES KIRK summarize:

"The responsibility of those of us who come out from Earth is to come in peace, to spread the best of mankind among the other races of the stars. Those who seek to pervert this responsibility, to profiteer from the contact between races, to fill their own pockets at the expense of understanding and brotherhood, serve a devil that has no name. Richard Beckwith, by the evidence of this court-martial you have been proved guilty of fomenting insurrection on a less-advanced planet, of luring unsophisticated aliens into the vilest sort of narcotics addiction, of smuggling contraband and of murder in cold blood. The sentence of this court, by the articles of any justice applicable to these crimes, is that you be carried to the nearest uninhabited planet—for we would not sully the soil of a settled world by the imposition of your body—and there be put to death in the manner proscribed by the articles of punishment under which this ship goes to space. Do you have anything to say to this court?"

Beckwith smiles. "I've always wanted to end this jaunt with a quiet, elegant life. What could be more elegant than an entire planet for my graveyard."

And as we HOLD ON Beckwith, we FADE OUT.

ACT ONE:

FADE IN the bulk of the *Enterprise* hanging above the silver-gray ball of a lost planet far out in the heart of The Coalsack. Kirk speaking: "Ship's Log, star-date 3134.8. At last we have found a desolate mote in the emptiest reaches of nowhere between galaxies. Astrogators call it The Coalsack for stars are few and far between. We have found one such star, without a name, labeled merely with a number. And circling that dying sun is but a single planet. My men have seen it and turned their faces away. Most of the viewports have been made opaque; they don't want to even think about a world so lost, so lonely, that it is only serviceable as an execution chamber for a creature not even worth calling a man. I am taking Spock and two other officers, and a firing squad of twelve men down."

They transport down to the surface of the dead world. It is a featureless ball of silver-gray mists and cold. They wear insulation suits and breatherpaks. But when they are down, and about to commence the execution, one of the techs in the group announces there is radiation from over the horizon. Kirk is troubled: the protocols of the ship's articles postulate a courtesy of not executing criminals aspace, on an inhabited world. They must check it out before they can dispose of Beckwith.

They strike out toward the source of radiation and in the far distance see a series of great mountain peaks, rising up like shards of glass from an ocean of silver. They get a distant impression of a great city on the furthest of those peaks, a series of spires that tower into the cadaverous gray sky without warmth or welcome.

But they go toward the spires and soon they find themselves on a mountain top near the city. As they top a rise, they are astounded to see a group of men ... but such men as the explorers from Earth have never known:

Old they are. Old as the chill and dying sun that casts only shadows on this empty planet. Old as thought, old as time, old as the cinder on which they live. Nine feet tall, and shapeless beneath the long white robes that reach to the mist-laden ground. Even taller if one allows their mitered headpieces. Taller still by the lengths of their snow-beards, the only part of them other than their lined and weary faces that shows from their clothing.

Kirk and Spock register astonishment at finding these ancient creatures, but the old men finally speak, after long beats in which their motionlessness makes us suspect they may be stone. And this is what they say:

We are the Guardians of Forever. We have been here since before your sun burned hot in space, before your race came into being. We have been here when this area of space was so filled with young suns that it was always high noon from their light.

"But why do you stay here when this world is cold and empty?" Mr. Spock demands.

Only on this planet do the myriad pulse-flows of time and space merge. Only here do the flux lines of Forever meet. Only here on this empty corpse of a world is there a gateway to the past, where the time machine created by the Ancients can work. Only here. And we were set to watch the time machine, so many hundreds of centuries ago that even we do not have clear memories of it.

The Guardians explain that they are almost immortal, that they have been guarding "the time machine" for so many eons that Kirk and his party are the first visitors they have had since two hundred thousand years before dinosaurs walked the Earth. Kirk expresses astonishment at the concept of a "time machine," that he had always thought it was the fable of lab technicians when they had had too much pure grain to drink. The Guardians nod their heads in the direction of a shimmering pillar of light, set between the gray-silver rocks. The time machine. Built on lines of creation that mortal Man will not discover for a hundred hundred times the span of years he has been in existence. Created out of pure matter, and harnessed to this world where the passage of time and space meet just so. The pillar of light rises up and disappears. Into that fire of forever lies the passage to the past.

Kirk advises one of his techs to bind Beckwith in a straitjacket of force-fields, till they have spoken more with these ancients, and made some decision as to whether the sentence can be carried out here, or they must go to space again, to find a truly uninhabited world.

Beckwith is taken away and Kirk asks the Guardians if they would consider it an imposition to tell them more about the time machine. They smile a little wearily, and say they would be pleasured to do so. "We want to know," Kirk says gently, and they answer: *We have nothing to do but desire to show you.* Uncounted millennia they have stood here, silent, and to exercise their craft is their delight.

They explain how the time machine works, and then they offer to show Kirk the past. He asks if they can show him the past of any world, and they say yes. Kirk asks to see the past of Old Earth. They show him the time of the mastodons, the time of the clipper ships, the time of the Depression, 1930. And the men of Earth marvel.

Is it possible to go back, they ask.

Yes, it is possible to go back, but not wise. Man and non-Man must live in their present or in their future. But never in their past, save to learn lessons from it. If passage back is effected, the voyager may add a new factor to the past, and thus change everything from that point to the present all through the universe. It is dangerous.

The time machine has been left set at the year 1930, Old Earth. As Kirk and Spock talk with the Guardians, the ancient men tell them that time moves at its normal pace all through the universe, but not here, not within the sphere of influence of the machine, for it is akin to standing on the king's cross, a zone of no-time. Spock then says to Kirk, "You see how old they are, centuries older than any human or alien we have ever encountered? Yet they say that time moves barely at all here. Can you imagine how old they must be to have aged so much."

The thought is staggering to Kirk, but he has barely a moment to think about it, for Beckwith manages to cleverly escape his guards, grabs a weapon and kills one of the guards as he makes a long run toward the time machine. Roused from their ruminations by the sounds of gunfire, Kirk and Spock plunge forward to stop Beckwith. He slams Spock across the jaw with the butt of the phaser rifle and keeps going, a broken-field dash that Kirk suddenly realizes is toward the time machine, Kirk takes a flying dive toward Beckwith, and manages to throw him off-balance. But Beckwith does a little dance-step of maneuvering and though he loses the phaser rifle, he hurls himself forward and in a *whooooshing* of space rushing to fill the vacuum where he has been Beckwith vanishes into the pillar of light, even as Kirk grabs up the phaser and fires a blast of coruscating energy at the pillar of light—now once again empty.

Beckwith has gone back. Back to the past.

Kirk dashes back to Spock. The extraterrestrial gets lumpily to his feet. He is all right. The Guardians of Forever are in a panic. They say the fact of adding Beckwith to the past has changed everything. Kirk says everything looks the same. *Yes, here, on this world, everything is the same,* they explain, *but from here outwards everything is different. It is another universe out there.*

"How? How is it changed?" Kirk demands.

They do not know. Only that the fabric of time has been warped, the river that is the time-flow has been diverted, and everything in the present has been altered. At that moment the Guardians' city, high on one of the crags far behind them, begins to shimmer, and send out waves of light. The Guardians say they are being summoned by others, that the great ancient machines that govern the time pillar of light are registering traumas in time, and they must return to their city.

And they vanish.

Kirk realizes he and Spock and the men must get back up to the *Enterprise* as quickly as possible, to see what has changed there. He sends the men up first, in translation shifts that leave only himself and Spock and the two officers for the final shift.

For a moment they contemplate what alterations in time Beckwith's jump-back could have caused, but as Spock points out, "Speculation at this point is senseless."

Not so senseless, however, when they translate up to the ship, materialize in the translation chamber and find that the control room they left as a USS exploratory vessel has altered drastically. As they stare about the room, the neatly-uniformed men are gone, and in their place Kirk and Spock find themselves staring at a motley horde of evil-looking, evil-smelling space pirates. A crew of deadly cutthroats with phasers leveled at them. The pirates are a strange and anachronistic blending of modern science and traditional Jolly Roger garb. The eleven men already sent up, eleven *Enterprise*-garbed men, are prisoners. And as one of the pirates steps forward to speak, a terrifying latter-day descendant of Edward Teach, Blackbeard, Kirk finds himself about to be gunned down mercilessly.

"Welcome to the *Condor*," the pirate Captain smirks, as we HOLD on Kirk's expression of disbelief, and we FADE OUT!

ACT TWO:

Kirk and Spock realize what has happened: some strange turn in time has altered their ship into a buccaneer vessel. They leap out of the translation chamber and Kirk grapples with the Pirate Captain. It is the signal for the captive *Enterprise* men to overcome their captors. There is a bloody pitched battle in pilot country and finally the *Enterprise* men manage to empty the control room. But now there are not 530 men of the *Enterprise* on the other side of that triple-strength door. There are 530 killer vandals and their women, who are even at this moment readying weapons to blast through into the control room. Kirk and Spock know they must go back to the nameless planet and follow Beckwith into the pillar of light. They must bring him back from the past, to straighten out time.

They enter the translation chamber, and leaving their twelve remaining living fellow crewmen to hold the ship, they begin to dissolve. The Scotch Engineering officer, watching them, urges, "Hurry back, Cap'n, or we might not be 'ere when y'ret —"

But they are gone.

The Guardians have returned. Kirk and Spock say they will go back. They ask the Guardians to send them to the same time Beckwith arrived in. The Guardians say there is a problem. Because of the internal stresses put upon the time-flow by the passage of Beckwith, they cannot send the two spacemen back to the precise time. Either earlier or later. Kirk says earlier, and they will wait for Beckwith, and grab him when he comes through.

The Guardians warn Kirk and Spock of two things: first, Beckwith's go-back has caused only a *temporary* temporal alteration. If they can bring him back, everything will go back the way it was, like a river following its natural course.

But in each time-period there is a focal point, the Guardians warn them. *Something or someone that is indispensable to the normal flow of time. Something that may be completely innocent or unimportant otherwise, but acts as a catalyst, and if tampered with, will change time permanently.*

They say that Beckwith will try to reach this focal point, and in some way alter it, so that time stays forever altered. Kirk wants to know how Beckwith knows what the focal point is. The Guardians assure him Beckwith doesn't know, but that because of the stresses and fluxes of the time-flow, Beckwith will be inexorably drawn to this focal point, and will alter it, even without knowing he is doing so.

"Then how can we stop him?" Kirk asks.

The Guardians tell him the machines in their city, machines which probe and delve into the time-flow continuously, have isolated the focus point in the era Beckwith has invaded. They tell Kirk and Spock it is a girl, EDITH KOESTLER, who is scheduled to be run down and killed by a moving van at a specific time. Beckwith's subliminal drive will take him to the path of this occurrence, and he will somehow prevent its happening thus fixing time permanently into the altered shape it has now assumed.

They must capture Beckwith, and bring him back into the present, the now, before he can meet Edith Koestler, and alter her fate.

They go into the pillar of light a week earlier than Beckwith, and when they appear in the past, they find themselves in Chicago of 1930, on Old Earth.

It is, literally, the city on the edge of Forever ...

Linked to a tall-spire city on a frozen mountain peak across the stars and hundreds of years in the future, another city on the opposite edge of Forever, by the tenuous thread of life called Kirk and Spock and Beckwith.

But now that they are here, in the past, they must learn to make their way, at least until Beckwith comes through the time machine. Yet imagine the circumstances—they are men out of time, out of joint with the world around them. They have trouble understanding the language (after all, even English alters to indistinguishability in three hundred years), they have no skills that can be put to use in this "regressive" age. Their clothes are peculiar. They have no place to live, no money (and don't even understand the medium of exchange or have a way of earning money) and most obvious of all—

Spock is an obvious extraterrestrial.

This is brought forcibly home to them as they appear on a crowded Chicago street, directly in front of an old man selling apples and hot chestnuts from a Depression-style pushcart. The old man sees them !pop! into existence, and at the sight of Spock, he clutches at his heart and falls over. People in the crowd, seeing the old man writhing on the ground, and seeing Spock, immediately draw the conclusion Spock has harmed him. They start yelling for the cops. A policeman emerges from a shop down the street, at the noise, and fires at Spock and Kirk.

They take off, down the street, around the corner, into an alley, over a fence, into a backyard and down another street till they come to ground in a basement of an apartment building.

There they make the necessary adjustments to change their Translations into language-interpreting devices. "I can almost make out what they're saying," Kirk tells Spock. "But it's odd, all run together, filled with words I know, many of them key sentence words. It's English, all right, but as difficult for me as, say, the English of Shakespeare's time would be for them. We'll use the Translations till we've picked up the style of the language, and then perhaps we can make it without them."

They know they must find Edith Koestler. But to do that, they must be able to move freely in the city. Kirk cautions Spock to stay there, back in the end of that dirty basement, till he can find them lodgings, and clothes of the period. Spock agrees and Kirk goes off.

But this is the year of the Depression. Work is scarce, money is almost impossible, even clothes are a problem. And Kirk, so much worse off than men familiar with the times, with ties to the period, with knowledge of how to do it and where and how much it costs, finds himself at a loss. He manages to steal some clothes off a clothesline and returns to the apartment house.

He and Spock change, and they are about to leave, when the custodian of the building discovers them. He assumes they are bindlestiffs, just bums, sleeping in the basement, and though they think he is going to make a fight with them, he seems to be a good man; he asks them if they need work, and they say yes. He tells them they can sleep down in the basement till they find something better. "At least it's warm near the furnace." In exchange they will carry out the cinders and shovel the coal to keep the furnace stoked, and promise not to steal from any of the tenants.

They thank him, and he says it's only for a short time, till something happens for them.

A short time ...

As the waters of Forever RIPPLE and WE FIND OURSELVES back on the changed *Enterprise*, in the control room with the doomed men, as the Pirate Captain readies a bank of destructive heat-beams, and trains them on the control room doors. As the doors glow red from the bombardment, and one of the younger officers in the besieged control country asks the Scotsman, "Where are they ... what are they doing ... are they coming to help us ...?"

And as We CLOSE TIGHT on the metal, turning to slag, we contemplate Kirk and Spock, back there ... and we FADE OUT.

ACT THREE:

Kirk has a menial job. Spock has passed himself off as an oriental, he's washing dishes in a beanery. They are existing in the grimy underside of Chicago life, while seeking the girl who is the focal point for this time-phase.

Spock locates her and Kirk takes a room in the same building. Time is growing short. Beckwith will come through from the future in three days. Kirk meets Edith Koestler, and strangely, wonderfully, they communicate. Kirk, who has all his life been alone on ships in space, who has known casual liaisons with women in port cities and on pleasure planets, finds himself drawn to this girl, who seems to embody a simplicity, and a warmth, that he had only read about secretly in cheap novels.

For three days they grow to know each other. Kirk is pleasured. Spock grows worried. He cautions Kirk against "going native."

But the time for worrying is past as the day of Beckwith's appearance arrives. They wait at the appointed time in the pop-out place, and when Beckwith materializes, in the center of a crowd, they try to grab him but he once again manages, through dint of desperation, to escape them. They track him through the city, but he loses himself.

And now, forewarned that they are trying to get him, Beckwith realizes that he cannot be safe, anywhere in time, unless he kills Kirk and Spock.

So the hunted turns hunter. He stalks Spock first, and almost manages to assassinate him, but at the last moment Spock saves himself. And Beckwith vanishes again.

They realize they must do something different to find him before he gets to the girl. Kirk stays with her, while Spock goes searching through the underworld, and finds a man who will hire himself out to locate Beckwith. But when Spock goes to get the man's report, he finds him dead.

Beckwith has developed cunning. Time is running out.

ACT FOUR:

Kirk and Spock take shifts staying with Edith Koestler. Spock takes his turns in hiding, for the girl knows nothing of him. But for Kirk, the hours spent with the young girl are the happiest of his life. And we see, we sense the growing dilemma for him. Kirk has fallen in love. He has come into the past to do a job, a simple job, but because he has found himself inextricably involved with his emotions, the situation has become perilous.

Spock and Kirk discuss this. They enter into a heated argument. At least, on Kirk's part. Spock is cool and analytical about the problem. Kirk has his choice: on one side, this girl and her life; this girl and her love. On the other, the men of the *Enterprise* who may even have already given their lives; and this universe.

Kirk flees from Spock's logic.

We PLAY SCENES of Kirk's deepening involvement with the girl, so that when Beckwith finally arrives on the scene, still unaware that he is moving inexorably toward this focus-point, this unknown girl who means nothing to him, yet means everything to him—we feel a total empathy for Kirk. The truck that is destined to run her down is lumbering through the street. Kirk sees Edith starting to cross. He sees Beckwith notice the girl and the truck, and start to move to save her. We CLOSE on EACH OF THE PRINCIPALS in SLOW MOTION SHOTS that prolong the agony of the moment. Edith moving into the streets. Beckwith starting toward her to save her. Kirk starting toward Beckwith to prevent his act. *And Kirk not being able to do it!*

He cannot sacrifice her, even for the safety of the universe. But at that moment Spock, who has been out of sight, but nearby, fearing just such an eventuality, steps forward and freezes Beckwith in mid-step. Edith keeps going and we QUICK CUT to Kirk as we HEAR the SOUND of a TRUCK SCREECHING TO A HALT. As Kirk's face crumbles, we know what has happened. Destiny has resumed its normal course, the past has been set straight. RIPPLE-DISSOLVE to *Enterprise* in INTERCUT then back.

Spock helps Kirk back to the location for return to the future. They materialize on the planet and receive the parting words of the Guardians, who tell them the past has been repaired. They ask one favor: leave Beckwith with them for punishment. Spock agrees, for Kirk is in no condition to make any decisions.

They translate back up to the *Enterprise,* but for a moment we stay with Beckwith and the Guardians. "What are you going to do with me?" he asks fearfully.

We are going to give you Forever as you wished, they tell him, and motion toward the pillar of light that waits. Beckwith smiles a smile of triumph. Somehow, he knows not how, he has won. He dashes to the pillar of light, and plunges into it . . .

. . . and finds himself materializing *in the heart of a sun.* An execution that goes on forever and ever, for the Guardians have altered their machines so that Beckwith is caught in a time-Möbius. An interlocked time-phase that puts him into the heart of a blazing inferno just long enough to die, then snaps him out to a moment before he died, then puts him back then takes him out, over and over and over and over . . .

Later, on the *Enterprise,* alone in his stateroom, Kirk receives a visit from Spock, and between them we see a depth of friendship that explains now how a man of deep feeling could be so close to an alien of cold logic. Kirk is felled by sadness, and Spock seems to understand. For the Captain, there is something irretrievably lost, but Spock makes sense when he says, "No woman was ever loved as much, Jim. Because no woman was ever offered the universe for love."

And Kirk understands. FADE OUT on the stars once more. The stars, like Kirk's love, eternal.

May 13, 1966

STAR TREK
"The City on the Edge of Forever"
written by Harlan Ellison

PROLOGUE:

FADE IN establishing shot *USS Enterprise,* somewhere out near the Rim, hanging suspended above a strange, silvery planet. OVER this shot and subsequent pantomime shots, we HEAR the VOICE of KIRK:

KIRK'S VOICE OVER

Ship's Log: star-date 3134.6. Our chronometers still run backward. When it started, we followed the radiations, all the way to the Rim of the Galaxy. We have found the planet-source of the radiation, but something else is happening . . .

(beat)

When we left Earth, each of the 450 crewmembers of the *Enterprise* was checked out stable. But locked in this ship for two years, they have experienced the stresses of time and space. We have continuous psych-probes, but we know some have been altered. There may even be those who have gone sour. We can never know till the flaw shows up. And by then, it's too late . . .

Our OPENING SHOT has MOVED IN on the *Enterprise* THROUGH A DISSOLVE to a shot CLOSE on a small, isometrically-shaped metal container, as it is opened by hand. Kirk's speech over is heard (after beat) as we HOLD CLOSE on the lid of the box, opening with tambour doors, so that the interior rises, and a strange dull light floods the frame. As the container opens, the black velvet interior slides up to reveal possibly half a dozen strange and wondrous glowing Jewels. Yet they are not jewels. They are the infamous and illegal Jillkan dream-narcotics, the Jewels of Sound. They are faceted solids, but not stone, more like a hardened jelly that burns pulsating with an inner light: gold, blue, crimson, orange.

We HEAR a VOICE O.S., a voice that shakes slightly, trying to maintain a tenuous control. "Beckwith, give me one. Stop it, Beckwith" and as the CAMERA PULLS BACK we see one of the *Enterprise's* officers LT/JG LeBEQUE, a French-Canadian with a strong face; but a face that is now beaded with sweat. And holding the Jewels of Sound is RICHARD BECKWITH, another officer, a man whose face shows intelligence and—something else. Cunning, perhaps, or even subdued cruelty. Cruelty kept rigidly in check, channeled to specific uses. Beckwith smiles as he stares with fascination at the Jewels of Sound.

"How long have you been my man, Lieutenant?" Beckwith asks, softly. He isn't taunting, merely interested. "How long have you been hooked on the Jewels?"

The Lieutenant's face tightens. He isn't a toady, neither is he a weak man. But the Jewels of Sound have been listed illegal throughout the Galaxy because only one exposure is needed to make a man a confirmed addict. Swallow one Jewel, experience the Circe call of the strange music and lights the Jewels offer, and you are lost forever. And so LeBeque will swallow his pride, and answer the man who holds the delight he needs so desperately. "You gave me my first taste on Karkow, that was a year ago. I need one, Beckwith, stop playing with me."

Beckwith extends one, a golden Jewel. But as the lieutenant reaches for it, he closes his fist over it, closing off the light, and LeBeque winces, as though the loss of light physically hurts him. "I want to know about that planet out there—and what the security log says about valuable commodities. I'll want a landfall pass and I'll want you to cover for me while I trade with the natives."

"After the slaughter on Harper Five, you'll do it again? If Kirk finds out—"

"He *won't* find out, will he LeBeque? He won't find out, or you'll never hear these Jewels sing inside you again. Remember that. I'm coming back from this a rich man, and I'll never have to go to space again. Nobody's going to get in the way of that, LeBeque. I want to live an elegant life, but that takes resources."

LeBeque gropes for words. "So you cheat aliens, get them hooked on illegal dream-narcotics, and steal what they could trade for cultural advances."

"Hooked like you, LeBeque. Hooked like you."

"Yes, like me. And I'm already paying."

"But you'll pay a little more. Do I get what I need?"

LeBeque nods slowly. Beckwith gives him the Jewel and the *Enterprise* Lieutenant swallows it. CAMERA HOLDS past Beckwith smiling knowingly at LeBeque, and as a look of almost orgasmic pleasure crosses the lieutenant's face, we REVERSE ANGLE from LeBeque's POV and we see THRU HIS EYES as Beckwith's face begins to shimmer with weird lights, like a Van deGraaf generator. Then we HEAR the incredible music of the Jewels—sounds from another time, another space, sounds that reach into LeBeque's head and strum the synapses of his brain as the lights collide and merge and swivel and twirl and dance in patterns of no-pattern, and Beckwith's face fades away with that damnable knowing smile, and for SEVERAL BEATS we SEE THRU the drug-drunken eyes of a man in the grip of an alien narcotic. Then, as we COME BACK INTO FOCUS we HEAR the VOICE of MR. SPOCK as he yells, "LeBeque! Damp that starboard unit, you're running into the red! You'll blow the entire drive! LeBeque!"

And we COME BACK INTO FOCUS finding ourselves in the control central with LeBeque being dragged back away from the damping controls by Spock and several other crewmen.

He reels back and the HIGH PIERCING WHINE of machinery stressing to implosion level subsides as Spock damps the units. The extraterrestrial spins on LeBeque, and coldly informs him,

"You've been walking around this control country like a man under water for the past two hours. If you're feeling unwell, Mr. LeBeque, relieve yourself, and leave the bridge."

"T—two hours . . . ?" LeBeque murmurs, shaking his head as

though to clear it. He excuses himself from the bridge and WE GO WITH HIM as he passes down cross-corridors in the ship, pausing to fight with himself, emotions playing across his face that tell us the man despises himself for what he has allowed himself to become. Then, making a decision, he heads for Beckwith's cubicle, and as we come to them in 2-SHOT we hear LeBeque say, "I've had it. Whatever Kirk wants to do with me, I'll deserve it; but I'm turning you in, Beckwith."

He turns to go, and has taken only two steps into the corridor when Beckwith, wild with panic, emerges from behind him and we ZOOM IN on Beckwith as he raises a massive block of green jade and swings it heavily, again and again at LeBeque, out of the frame. Another ZOOM IN on a trio of crewmembers, two men and a woman, as they round the junction of corridors and see the murder and then we HARD CUT TO:

CORRIDOR OF *ENTERPRISE* framing a LONG SHOT IN PERSPECTIVE as Beckwith races toward the transporter chamber. There is a guard on the door, but Beckwith rushes INTO FRAME at such a breakneck pace that he is on the guard, and smashes him to the deck before the other can raise his weapon to challenge. Beckwith plunges through the hatch into the chamber, and the hatch sighs shut behind him, even as a throng of *Enterprise* crewmen— led by CAPTAIN JAMES KIRK, Spock, YEOMAN JANICE RAND and DR. McCOY—fill the frame and dash away from us, down the corridor toward the chamber.

McCoy drops, to aid the guard who lies twisted at an odd angle, possibly dead. Kirk and Spock find the hatch sealed from the other side. Yeoman Rand breaks out a phaser and begins to puddle the sealtite as they HEAR the SOUND of the SHIP'S TRANSPORTER. As they burst through the hatch, into the transporter room, they find the transporter still glowing, the TRANSPORTER CHIEF half-conscious, struggling to sit up and pointing at the still-active machine. "B-Beckwith . . . " he mumbles.

"He's loose on that planet down there," Kirk says tightly. "Let's go get him . . . "

CAMERA HOLDS on Kirk as the crew rush everywhichway to get a patrol ready to transport down after the killer. CAMERA HOLDS as Kirk turns to stare at the still-glowing transporter and on that eerie humming as we FADE OUT.

ACT ONE:

FADE IN the surface of the dead world. CLOSE ON booted tracks as CAMERA ANGLE WIDENS to show us the terrain. A featureless ball of silver-gray mists and dust-like powder that covers the ground. As though some cosmic god had flicked an ash and it had grown into a world. As CAMERA PULLS BACK we see the tell-tale shimmering and coalescing that mean crewmen from the *Enterprise* are materializing from the transporter. As Kirk, Spock, Yeoman Rand and FIVE ENLISTED CREWMEN appear, we HEAR the VOICE of KIRK OVER:

> KIRK'S VOICE OVER
> Ship's Log: star-date 3134.8. This cinder, this empty death of a planet. This desolate mote in the emptiest reaches between galaxies. Its loneliness has the men of my patrol on edge. I know what they feel. This is the source of the peculiar radiation that had our clocks running backward. And now, Beckwith is down here—somewhere. Oh, we'll find him, we have to. But there is something more important that has them frightened. A dead world such as this should be frigid, it should have no atmosphere.
> (beat)
> But we aren't cold—and we can breathe.

While we HEAR VOICE OVER we see Spock indicating the tracks to Kirk, and the Captain deploying his men in a search-pattern as they move forward. VOICE OVER CONTINUES as we LAP DISSOLVE TWICE THRU scenes of the patrol moving across the wilderness, being directed by one or another of the patrol members who stay with the tracks. When we first saw them materialize, they were wearing insulation suits and breatherpaks (transparent plastic envelopes over their heads) but now that Kirk has informed us there is air, the plastic envelopes have been thrown back like hoods.

They carry phasers, and one of the crewmen has a small radiation console strapped to his chest. The DISSOLVES are different only in ANGLE and CLOSEUP for the scenery is seemingly changeless.

As we DISSOLVE THRU TO the last of these tracking shots, the crewman with the console advises Kirk that the strange radiation that affected the ship's clocks is becoming stronger, coming from the direction in which the tracks lead, over the horizon.

They strike out toward the source of radiation and in the far distance see a series of great mountain peaks, rising up like shards of glass from an ocean of silver. They get a distant impression of a great city on the furthest of those peaks, a series of spires that tower into the cadaverous gray sky without warmth or welcome.

They follow the tracks that head straight for the mountains, and the radiation grows more potent. Soon they find themselves on a mountain top near the city. As they top a rise—and the tracks vanish on the harder surface—they are astonished to see a group of men ... but such men as the explorers from Earth have never known:

Old they are. Old as the chill and dying sun that casts only shadows on this empty planet. Old as thought, old as time, old as the cinder on which they live. Nine feet tall, and shapeless beneath the long white robes that reach to the mist-laden ground. Even taller if one allows their mitered headpieces. Taller still by the lengths of their snow-beards, the only part of them other than their lined and weary faces that shows from their clothing.

Kirk and Spock register astonishment at finding these ancient creatures, but the old men finally speak, after long beats in which their motionlessness makes us suspect they may be of stone. And this is what they say:

We are the Guardians of Forever. We have been here since before your sun burned hot in space, before your race came into being. We have been here when this area of space was so filled with young suns that it was always high noon from their light.

"But why do you stay here when this world is cold and empty?" Mr. Spock demands.

Only on this planet do the myriad pulse-flows of time and space merge. Only here do the flux lines of Forever meet. Only here on this empty corpse of a world is there a gateway to the past, where the time vortex created by the Ancients can work. Only here. And we were set to watch the time vortex, so many hundreds of centuries ago that even we do not have clear memories of it.

The Guardians explain that they are almost immortal, that they have been guarding "the time vortex" for so many eons, that Kirk and his party are the first visitors they have had since two hundred thousand years before dinosaurs walked the Earth.

Spock inquires if they have seen another Earthman, and the Guardians say no. Yet as we INTERCUT to a rocky niche nearby, we see the hunted Beckwith, listening to every word being said. He looks around him, trying to find a way to escape, but it is a cul-de-sac. The only way out is past Kirk and the *Enterprise* patrol—and the Guardians. The look of desperation grows on his face, but it is mixed with a viciousness that tells us Beckwith is far from finished.

Kirk expresses astonishment at the concept of a "time vortex," that he had always thought it was the fable of lab technicians when they had had too much pure grain to drink. The Guardians nod their heads in the direction of a shimmering pillar of light, set between the gray-silver rocks. The time vortex. Built on lines of creation that mortal Man will not discover for a hundred hundred times the span of years he has been in existence. Created out of pure matter, and harnessed to this world where the passage of time and space meet just so. The pillar of light rises up and disappears. Into that fire of forever lies the passage to the past.

Kirk asks the Guardians if they would consider it an imposition to tell him more about the time vortex. They smile a little wearily, and say they would be pleasured to do so. "We want to know," Kirk says gently, and they answer: *We have nothing to do but desire to show you.* Uncounted millennia they have stood here, silent, and to exercise their craft is their delight.

They explain how the time vortex works, and then they offer to show Kirk the past. He asks if they can show him the past of any world, and they say yes.

Kirk asks to see the past of Old Earth.

They tell him to watch the pillar of light. At first there is no change, but in a moment the light itself begins to roil and thicken—like quicksilver mixing with smoke—and then a scene takes form *in* the light. It is a view of dense primordial jungle, blazing under a young sun. Then there is a crashing through the jungle, and the Earthmen reel back in astonishment as the behemoth bulk of a giant wooly mammoth bursts out of the foliage.

They show him the time of the Mastodons; the time of the

Clipper Ships; the time of the Depression, 1930. And the men of Earth marvel.

As we HOLD PAST BECKWITH in F.G. to the Earthmen watching the pillar of light, we HEAR Kirk ask if it is possible to go back in time, back to, say, Old Earth. The Guardians indicate it is possible.

But it is not wise. Man and non-Man must live in their present or their future. But never in their past, save to learn lessons from it. Time can be dangerous. If passage back is effected, the voyager may add a new factor to the past, and thus alter everything from that point to the present, all through the universe. Time is elastic. It has a tendency to revert to its original shape when the changes are minor. But when the change is life or death ... when the sum of intelligence has been altered then the change can be permanent ... and cataclysmic. So we do not go back. For one hundred thousand years no one has gone back.

The time vortex has been left set at the year 1930, Old Earth. As Kirk and Spock talk with the Guardians, the ancient men tell them that time moves at its normal pace all through the universe, but not here, not within the sphere of influence of the machine, for it is akin to standing on the king's cross, a zone of no-time. And that explains why there is atmosphere and warmth on this dead world. If they can control time, how much simpler it is to control their environment. It also explains the radiations received by the *Enterprise,* the radiations that caused their chronometers to go berserk. Spock then says to Kirk, "You see how old they are, centuries older than any human or alien we have ever encountered? Yet they say that time moves barely at all here. Can you imagine how old they must be to have aged so much."

The thought is staggering to Kirk, but he has barely a moment to think about it, for at that moment Beckwith leaps from his hiding place and makes a long run toward the time vortex. Kirk and Spock plunge forward to stop Beckwith. He slams Spock across the jaw and keeps going, a broken-field dash that Kirk suddenly realizes is toward the pillar of light. Kirk takes a flying dive toward Beckwith, and manages to throw him off-balance. But Beckwith does a little dance-step of maneuvering and hurls himself forward and in a whooooshing of space rushing to fill the vacuum where he has been, Beckwith vanishes into the pillar of light, even as Kirk grabs up a phaser and fires a blast of coruscating energy at the pillar of light— now once again empty.

Beckwith has gone back. Back to the past.

Kirk dashes back to Spock. The extraterrestrial gets lumpily to his feet. He is all right. The Guardians of Forever are in a panic. They say the fact of adding Beckwith to the past has changed everything. Kirk says everything looks the same. *Yes, here on this world, everything is the same,* they explain, *but from here outward, everything is different. It is another universe out there.*

"How? How is it changed?" Kirk demands.

They do not know. Only that the fabric of time has been warped, the river that is the time-flow has been diverted, and everything in the present has been altered. At that moment the Guardians' city, high on one of the crags far behind them, begins to shimmer and send out waves of light. The Guardians say they are being summoned by others, that the great ancient machines that govern the pillar of light are registering traumas in time, and they must return to their city.

And they vanish.

Kirk realizes he and Spock and the men must get back up to the *Enterprise* as quickly as possible, to see what has changed there. He sends the men up first, in transporter shifts that leave only himself and Spock for the final shift.

For a moment they contemplate what alterations in time Beckwith's jump-back could have caused, but as Spock points out, "Speculation at this point is senseless."

Not so senseless, however, when they transport up to the ship, materialize in the chamber and find that the room they left as a USS exploratory vessel has altered drastically. As they stare about the room, the neatly-uniformed men are gone, and in their place Kirk and Spock find themselves staring at a motley horde of evil-looking renegades. A crew of deadly cutthroats with phasers leveled at them. The renegades are a strange and anachronistic blending of modern science and mismatched garb. The six crewmembers already sent up, five *Enterprise* men and Yeoman Rand, are prisoners. And as one of the pirates steps forward to speak, Kirk finds himself about to be gunned down mercilessly.

"Welcome to the *Condor*!" The pirate CAPTAIN smirks, as we HOLD on Kirk's expression of disbelief and we FADE OUT!

ACT TWO:

Kirk and Spock realize what has happened: some strange turn in time has altered their ship into a buccaneer vessel. They leap out of the transporter chamber and Kirk grapples with the Pirate Captain. It is the signal for the captive *Enterprise* men to overcome their captors. There is a bloody pitched battle in the transporter room and finally the *Enterprise* men manage to empty the chamber. But now there are not 530 men of the *Enterprise* on the other side of that triple-strength door. There are 530 killer vandals and their women, who are even at this moment readying weapons to blast through into the chamber. Kirk and Spock know they must go back to the nameless planet and follow Beckwith into the pillar of light. They must bring him back from the past, to straighten out time.

They enter the transporter chamber, and leaving their six remaining living fellow crewmen to hold the ship, they begin to dissolve. Yeoman Rand, her uniform ripped from the battle, exposing a handsome expanse of leg, urges them tightly, "Hurry back, Captain. Or we might not be here when you ret—"

But they are gone.

The Guardians have returned. Kirk and Spock say they will go back. They ask the Guardians to send them to the same time Beckwith arrived in. The Guardians say there is a problem. Because of the internal stresses put upon the time-flow by the passage of Beckwith, they cannot be sent back to the exact, same, precise moment. Either earlier or later. Kirk says earlier, and they will wait for Beckwith and grab him when he comes through.

The Guardians warn Kirk and Spock of two things: first, Beckwith's go-back has caused only a *temporary* temporal alteration. If they can bring him back, everything will go back the way it was, like a river following its natural course.

But in each time-period there is a focal point, the Guardians warn them. *Something or someone that is indispensable to the normal flow of time. Something that may be completely innocent or unimportant otherwise, but acts as a catalyst, and if tampered with, will change time permanently.*

They say that Beckwith will try to reach this focal point, and in some way alter it, so that time stays forever altered. Kirk wants to know how Beckwith knows what the focal point is. The Guardians assure him Beckwith *doesn't* know, but that because of the stresses and fluxes of the time-flow, Beckwith will be inexorably *drawn* to this focal point, and will alter it, even without knowing he is doing so.

"Then how can we stop him?" Kirk asks.

The Guardians have been speaking in generalities, in parables (though for purposes of this outline they have stated their points concisely), and now they try to tell Kirk what he needs to know, but once again their ethereal natures turn the clues into riddles:

You must stop him by bringing him out of the past. He will seek that which must die, and give it life. Stop him.

Kirk is confused. "I don't understand. Can't you tell me more?"

Blue it will be. Blue as the sky of Old Earth and clear as truth. And the sun will burn on it, and there is the key.

Even Spock, analytical and logical, does not understand. But though they ask again and again, the Guardians can tell them nothing more. So they turn to the pillar of light, still tuned to Old Earth, 1930. They walk toward it, and the flames leap up about them as they step through.

They go into the pillar of light, a week earlier than Beckwith, and when they appear in the past, they find themselves in New York of 1930, on Old Earth.

It is, literally, the city on the edge of Forever . . .

Linked to a tall-spire city on a frozen mountain peak across the stars and hundreds of years in the future, another city on the opposite edge of Forever, by the tenuous thread of life called Kirk and Spock and Beckwith.

But now that they are here, in the past, they must learn to make their way, at least until Beckwith comes through the time machine. Yet imagine the circumstances—they are men out of time, out of joint with the world around them. They have no skills that can be put to use in this "regressive" age. Their clothes are peculiar. They have no place to live, no money (and don't even understand the medium of exchange or have a way of earning money) and most obvious of all—

Spock is an obvious extraterrestrial.

This is brought forcibly home to them as they materialize on a crowded New York street. In the midst of a bread-line demonstration. On a soap-box, a man is inciting the crowd to riot, charging that all the foreigners are clogging the soup kitchens, stealing jobs good Americans should have, sending the country further and further into the Depression. Kirk and Spock are momentarily disoriented, having come from a bleak landscape a million light-years away, and hundreds of years in the future, and they find themselves looking about with confusion. Their movement draws the attention of the haranguer, and when he sees Spock, his eyes open wider.

"There's one of 'em! There's one of the foreigners trying to take the bread out of our mouths! Let's show him how we feel about things!"

The crowd turns in blind fury, propelled by empty bellies, and begins attacking Spock. Kirk leaps to his aid, and in a moment there is a street corner imbroglio that both realize they cannot win. In a moment that is clear of attackers, Kirk levels the phaser he has brought through with him and trains it on a lamppost. It vanishes at a blast of light, and the crowd falls back in terror.

Kirk and Spock take this moment as a means of escape. They bolt, with the crowd regrouping behind them.

They take off, down the street, around the corner, into an alley, over a fence, into a backyard and down another street, till they come to ground in a basement of an apartment building.

They know they must find the focal point the Guardians spoke about. But to do that, they must be able to move freely in the city. Kirk cautions Spock to stay there, back in the end of that dirty basement, till he can find them lodgings, and clothes of the period. Spock agrees and Kirk goes off, leaving the alien with the phaser.

But this is the year of the Depression. Work is scarce, money is almost impossible, even clothes are a problem. And Kirk, so much worse off than men familiar with the times, with ties to the period, with knowledge of how to do it and where and how much it costs, finds himself at a loss. He manages to steal some clothes off a clothesline and returns to the apartment house.

He and Spock change, and they are about to leave, when the custodian of the building discovers them. He assumes they are bindlestiffs, just bums, sleeping in the basement, and though they think he is going to make a fight with them, he seems to be a good man; he asks them if they need work, and they say yes. He tells them they can sleep down in the basement till they find something better. "At least it's warm near the furnace."

In exchange they will carry out the cinders and shovel the coal to keep the furnace stoked, and promise not to steal from any of the tenants.

They thank him, and he says it's only for a short time till something happens for them.

A short time ...

As the waters of Forever RIPPLE and WE FIND OURSELVES back on the changed *Enterprise,* in the chamber with the doomed men, as the Pirate Captain readies a bank of destructive heatbeams, and trains them on the control room doors. As the doors glow red from the bombardment, and one of the younger officers in the besieged transporter chamber asks Yeoman Rand, "Where are they . . . what are they doing . . . are they coming to help us?"

And as we CLOSE TIGHT on the metal, turning to slag, we contemplate Kirk and Spock, back there . . . and we FADE OUT.

ACT THREE:

Kirk has a menial job. Spock has passed himself off as an Oriental, he's washing dishes in a beanery. They are existing in the grimy underside of New York life, while seeking the focal point for this time-phase.

Then, by chance (or as Spock later murmurs, "There are no coincidences in Time.") the alien locates the "focal point." On his way home one night from the hash-house where he washes dishes, he passes a street corner revival. He hears the lyrical sound of a woman's voice, as clear and as vibrant "as truth." He stops, pauses to listen as SISTER EDITH KEELER speaks to a crowd of disgruntled derelicts, poor men—as all men in these days of pennilessness are poor—about the brotherhood of man. About the need to trust, the need to love . . . not in the manner of the fanatic, to love merely because it keeps the belly from growling; but to love because it is the only salvation for mankind, the only way to find the path to the stars.

Spock listens to the beautiful girl say things that the space travelers of his own age have learned. Thoughts that are thousands of years ahead of their time. And then he realizes: she is wearing a blue cape, a cape as blue as the sky of Old Earth. A cape that is fastened across her throat by a huge golden brooch in the shape of a sunburst. And her name is Keeler . . .

Blue it will be. Blue as the sky of Old Earth and clear as truth. And the sun will burn on it, and there is the key.

Spock rushes back to tell Kirk. They follow the girl after her revival meeting, and see the tenement in which she lives. Kirk takes a room in the same building.

Time is growing short. Beckwith will come through from the future in three days. Kirk meets Edith Keeler, and strangely, wonderfully, they communicate. Kirk, who has all his life been alone on ships in space, who has known casual liaisons with women in port cities and on pleasure planets, finds himself drawn to this girl, who seems to embody a simplicity, and a warmth, that he had only read about secretly in cheap novels.

For three days they grow to know each other. Kirk is pleasured. Spock grows worried. He cautions Kirk against "going native."

But the time for worrying is past as the day of Beckwith's appearance arrives. They wait at the appointed time in the pop-out place, and when Beckwith materializes, in the center of a crowd, they try to grab him but he once again manages, through dint of desperation, to escape them. They track him through the city, but he loses himself.

And now, forewarned that they are trying to get him, Beckwith realizes that he cannot be safe, anywhere in time, unless he kills Kirk and Spock.

So the hunted turns hunter. He stalks Spock first, and almost manages to assassinate him, but at the last moment Spock saves himself. And Beckwith vanishes again. Time is running out.

ACT FOUR:

Kirk and Spock take shifts staying with Edith Keeler. Spock takes his turns in hiding, for the girl knows nothing of him. But for Kirk, the hours spent with the young girl are the happiest of his life. And we see, we sense the growing dilemma for him. Kirk has fallen in love. He has come into the past to do a job, a simple job, but because he has found himself inextricably involved with his emotions, the situation has become perilous.

On one occasion, as they pass down a New York street, Edith hears a jaunty tune of the time, a raggy version of "Please":

Please, lend your little ear to my pleas;
Lend a ray of cheer to my pleas;
Tell me that you love me, too.
Please, let me hold you tight in my arms.
I could find delight in your charms;
Ev'ry night my whole life through. •

It comes from a down-below-the-street music shop, and as she tells Kirk how much she loves music, she pulls him toward the downstairs entrance. She slips, and as she starts to fall, arms flailing, Kirk moves to catch her. We HEAR in ECHO CHAMBER the VOICE of the Guardian OVER: *He will seek that which must die, and give it life. Stop him. Stop ... stop ... stop ...*

And Kirk pulls his hand back. Edith falls. But she only sprains her ankle. She looks up at Kirk with confusion, as he rushes down to help her—now that he knows this is not the moment of death the Guardian hinted at. She cannot understand why he did not try to stop her fall, but she says nothing. We see it all through their expressions.

But Kirk is tormented, twisted by the fate that says he must not interfere with the course of Time.

Spock and Kirk discuss this. They enter into a heated argument. At least, on Kirk's part. Spock is cool and analytical about the problem. Kirk has his choice: on one side, this girl and her life; this girl and her love. On the other, the men of the *Enterprise* who may even have already given their lives; and the universe.

Kirk flees from Spock's logic.

We PLAY SCENES of Kirk's deepening involvement with the girl, so that when Beckwith finally arrives on the scene, still unaware that he is moving inexorably toward this focus-point, this unknown girl who means nothing to him, yet means everything to him—we feel a total empathy for Kirk. The truck that is destined to run her down is lumbering through the street. Kirk sees Edith starting to cross. He sees Beckwith notice the girl and the truck, and start to move to save her. We CLOSE on EACH OF THE PRINCIPALS in SLOW

MOTION SHOTS that prolong the agony of the moment. Edith moving into the street. Beckwith starting toward her to save her. Kirk starting toward Beckwith to prevent his act. *And Kirk not being able to do it!*

He cannot sacrifice her, even for the safety of the universe. But at that moment Spock, who has been out of sight, but nearby, fearing just such an eventuality, steps forward and freezes Beckwith in mid-step. Edith keeps going and we QUICK CUT to Kirk as we HEAR the SOUND of a TRUCK SCREECHING TO A HALT. As Kirk's face crumbles, we know what has happened. Destiny has resumed its normal course, the past has been set straight. RIPPLE-DISSOLVE to *Enterprise* in INTERCUT then back.

Spock helps Kirk back to the location for return to the future. They materialize on the planet and receive the parting words of the Guardians, who tell them the past has been repaired.

Kirk is almost in a state of shock from the death of Edith Keeler, and as Spock speaks to the Guardians, Beckwith lunges away from him, throws himself once more into the pillar of light. Spock starts toward it, but the Guardians stop him.

"He went back again!"

Spock is coldly furious.

No. The vortex cannot be set for the same time twice. You were told that.

"But he's escaped."

Not this time. He wanted Forever. The vortex has given him Forever. Like the Möbius strip that has no end, he is locked in Time, he can never escape. His Forever will be in the heart of an exploding sun. He named his own doom.

HARD CUT to special effect shot of Beckwith materializing out of the pillar of light . . .

. . . and finding himself materializing in the heart of a sun. An execution that goes on forever and ever, for the vortex has warped time so that Beckwith is caught in a time-Möbius. An inter-locked time-phase that puts him into the heart of a blazing inferno just long enough to die, then snaps him out to a moment before he died, then puts him back, then takes him out, over and over and over and over . . .

Later, on the *Enterprise,* alone in his stateroom, Kirk receives a visit from Spock, and between them we see a depth of friendship that explains *now* how a man of deep feeling could be so close to an alien of cold logic. Kirk is felled by sadness, and Spock seems to understand. For the Captain, there is something irretrievably lost, but Spock makes sense when he says, "No woman was ever loved as much, Jim. Because no woman was ever offered the universe for love."

And Kirk understands. FADE OUT on the stars once more. The stars, like Kirk's love, eternal.

THE END

PROLOGUE

FADE IN:

1   *ESTABLISHING SHOT— ANGLE IN SPACE*

The *USS ENTERPRISE* hanging in mid-foreground over a strange, silvery planet under a wan and dying red sun. CAMERA MOVES IN on ship and OVER this (and subsequent pantomime shots), we HEAR the VOICE of KIRK:

> KIRK'S VOICE (OVER)
> Ship's Log: star-date 3134.6. Our chronometers still run backward. We have followed the radiation to its planet-source here at the Rim of the Galaxy, but something else is happening . . .
> *(beat)*
> When we left Earth, each of the 450 crewmembers of the *Enterprise* was checked out stable. But it's been two years—so much stress on them. We have continuous psych-probes, but we know some have been altered. Even some who may have gone sour: we can't know till the flaw shows up. And by then, it's too late . . . much too late . . .

While VOICE OVER carries, CAMERA MOVES IN on *Enterprise* smoothly till we

RAPID LAP-DISSOLVE TO:

2   *INT. ENTERPRISE—BECKWITH'S CABIN— XTREME CLOSEUP*

on a small, isometrically-shaped metal container as it is opened by a hand. VOICE OVER is heard (after beat) as we HOLD CLOSE on the lid of the box, opening with tambour doors, so the interior of the box rises

(MORE)

(CONTINUED)

and a strange DULL LIGHT FLOODS the FRAME. As the container opens, the black velvet interior slides up to reveal possibly half a dozen glowing jewels. They are faceted solids, but not stone; more like a hardened jelly that burns pulsing with an inner light: gold, blue, crimson. As KIRK'S VOICE OVER ends we hear:

> LeBeque's Voice O.S.
> *(trembling)*
> Beckwith, stop it! Give me one!

CAMERA PULLS BACK to MED. 2-SHOT showing LT/JG LeBEQUE, a French-Canadian with a strong face—a face now beaded with sweat, a face in torment—and another officer, RICHARD BECKWITH, a man whose face shows intelligence and . . . something else. Cunning, perhaps, or even subdued cruelty. Beckwith holds the pulsing Jewels in their container. He smiles unpleasantly as LeBeque stares transfixed by the Jewels. Beckwith, without moving, taunts him with them.

> Beckwith
> *(conversationally)*
> Jewels of Sound. So expensive, so illegal. You want me to give you a dream-narcotic they've banned all through the Galaxy? Tsk-tsk, Lieutenant, how far you've fallen.

> LeBeque
> I won't beg, Beckwith.

> Beckwith
> No? How long have you been my man, Lieutenant? How long have you been hooked on the Jewels?

(CONTINUED)

2   *CONTINUED:—2*

LeBeque's face tightens, his fists clench at his sides. He isn't a weak man, nor a toady. But Beckwith holds his life.

> LEBEQUE
> You gave me my first taste on Karkow,
> that was a year ago. One taste and I was
> addicted. I need one . . . stop playing
> with me.

Beckwith extends one, a golden Jewel. But as LeBeque reaches for it, Beckwith closes his fist, and the light is shut off. LeBeque gasps, winces, as though physically hurt. Then with his hand still extended, Beckwith gets down to business.

> BECKWITH
> *(directorially)*
> I want to know about that planet out
> there. What the log says about valuable
> commodities. I'll want a landfall pass,
> and I'll want you to cover for me when
> I trade with the natives.

> LEBEQUE
> *(amazed horror)*
> After the slaughter you caused on
> Harper Five, you'll do it again? If Kirk
> finds out —

> BECKWITH
> *(chilled steel)*
> He won't find out, will he, Lieutenant?
> If he does, you'll never hear these
> Jewels sing inside you again. I'm your
> only source, remember that.
> *(beat)*
> I'm coming back from this a rich man,
> (MORE)

(CONTINUED)

and I'll never have to go to space again.
Nobody's getting in my way, LeBeque: I
want to live an elegant life, but that
takes resources.

                    LeBeque
                  (it takes guts)
So you cheat aliens, get them hooked
on illegal narcotics, and steal what they
could trade for cultural advances?

                    Beckwith
Hooked like you, LeBeque. Hooked like
you.

                    LeBeque
                   (bitterly)
Yeah, like me. And I'm already paying.

                    Beckwith
                 (with finality)
But you'll pay a little more. Do I get
what I want?

LeBeque nods painfully, reluctantly. Beckwith slowly
opens his hand and the golden light shines. LeBeque
grabs it quickly and swallows it. CAMERA HOLDS past
Beckwith smiling knowingly at the Lt/Jg as a look of
almost orgasmic pleasure crosses LeBeque's face.

3   REVERSE ANGLE— *LeBEQUE'S POV— WHAT HE SEES*

as shot THRU HIS EYES as Beckwith's face begins
to shimmer with weird lights, like a Van deGraaf
generator, like heat lightning off a rain-slick
pavement. We HEAR the incredible MUSIC OF THE
                    (MORE)

3   *CONTINUED:*

JEWELS as they reach through LeBeque's head: part electronics, part orchestral and something like a scream from a creature dying horribly. Everything goes OUT OF FOCUS as the LIGHTS collide and merge and swirl and dance in patterns of no-pattern, and for SEVERAL BEATS we SEE THRU the drug-drunken eyes of a man in the grip of an alien narcotic. The MUSIC RISES and the SCREAM BUILDS as Beckwith's face fades away with that damnable smile and everything blurs as we

COME BACK INTO FOCUS TO:

4   *INT. BRIDGE—MEDIUM CLOSE ON LeBEQUE*

as everything leaves its fuzziness and we HEAR the VOICE of MR. SPOCK O.S. and we see LeBeque at a huge bank of ship's controls, knife-switches depressed, and a control bar in his hand, gauges oscillating wildly and all of them in the DANGER RED country. There is a frightening HIGH PIERCING WHINE of machinery stressing to implosion level that is the tail end of the SCREAM we have heard through the drug-vision. The FOCUS COMES SHARPER thru VOICE O.S.

Spock's Voice O.S.
(urgent but Spock-ish)
Mr. LeBeque! Damp that starboard unit,
you're running in the red. You'll blow
the entire drive! LeBeque!

And as CAMERA PULLS BACK we see LeBeque being dragged away from the controls by TWO CREWMEN as Spock steps in quickly but calmly to damp the power controls. The WHINE SUBSIDES RAPIDLY.

Spock turns to LeBeque. He is as coldly furious as
(MORE)
(CONTINUED)

4   *CONTINUED:*

an alien without emotion can get. Menace in his
voice.

>   SPOCK
> You've been walking around this bridge
> like a man under water for two hours. If
> you're unwell, Mr. LeBeque, have yourself
> placed on relief, and leave the bridge.

>   LEBEQUE
>   *(horrified)*
> T-two hours ... oh god ...

He shakes his head as though to clear it, and then stumbles
away, up the risers to the hatch which sighs open at his
approach. He pauses for a beat at the portal, hand on the wall
to steady himself as we HOLD PAST Spock who watches him
with concern. He goes through the portal.

5   *INT. CORRIDOR—CAMERA WITH LeBEQUE—HAND-HELD*

as he passes down the passage, pausing for a moment to
fight with himself, and the Arriflex camera SQUIBS ABOUT
his FACE showing us the self-loathing, the torment. Then he
makes a decision that is visible in his expression and goes
away from us as we

                                            QUICK CUT TO:

6   *INT. BECKWITH'S CABIN—ANOTHER ANGLE THAN
    SCENE 2*

as LeBeque careens in through the portal. Beckwith looks up
from some paperwork he's doing at a desk on which dozens
of disc-books in jewel-cases are held in place by bookends
that are TWO HUGE FACETED BLOCKS OF BRILLIANT
GREEN JADE, prominent in the ANGLE of the SHOT.

                                            (CONTINUED)

6 *CONTINUED:*

> LeBeque
> *(shaking)*
> I'm done. I almost disabled the ship.
> Whatever Kirk wants to do with me, I'll
> deserve it; but I'm turning you in,
> Beckwith.

He whirls to leave as Beckwith leaps up from the desk, reaching for one of the blocks of jade.

7 *INT. CORRIDOR—HAND-HELD*

CLOSE on LeBeque as he COMES TO CAMERA, hurrying. Beckwith seen over his shoulder, plunging after him, raising the block of jade as LeBeque passes out of FRAME and CAMERA HOLDS on Beckwith swinging the heavy weight. PAST HIM we see a PAIR OF CREWMEMBERS (man and woman) coming around the corner as the SOUND of a heavy weight hitting something soft is HEARD O.S. and CAMERA ZOOMS IN on the FACE of the FEMALE CREWMEMBER as she SCREAMS and we

> HARD CUT TO:

8 *LONG ANGLE DOWN ANOTHER CORRIDOR—OPEN ON BLACK FRAME*

as the BLACK FRAME becomes Beckwith dashing away from CAMERA IN PERSPECTIVE toward the Transporter Chamber. There is a GUARD on the portal, but Beckwith rushes INTO FRAME at such a breakneck pace—full out, dammit!—that he is on the Guard, grabs his phaser rifle and smashes the man to the deck with the butt of it, before the man can raise a hand to stop him. CAMERA WITH him as he plunges through the hatch and it closes behind him as CAMERA WHIP-PANS back down the corridor in the direction from which Beckwith came.

> (MORE)

> (CONTINUED)

8   CONTINUED:

Around the bend in the corridor boils a throng of *Enterprise* personnel—led by CAPTAIN JAMES KIRK, Spock, YEOMAN JANICE RAND and DR. McCOY—all ad-libbing "He came this way . . . " "Down there, the guard . . ." "The Transporter chamber . . . " "It's Beckwith . . . " *etcetera.*

They dash TOWARD CAMERA and FRAME BLACK as HAND-HELD CAMERA GOES WITH and FRAME OUT OF BLACK as they dash away from us. McCoy drops to one knee, to aid the Guard, who lies twisted at an odd angle, possibly dead. Kirk and Spock try the hatch. Sealed from the other side. Yeoman Rand moves in between them with a phaser and begins to puddle the sealtite as we HEAR the SOUND of the SHIP'S TRANSPORTER.

9   INT. TRANSPORTER CHAMBER—FULL SHOT

as they burst through the hatch. The Transporter is still glowing. On the floor the TRANSPORTER CHIEF, half-conscious, struggles to sit up. He points to the machine.

> TRANSPORTER CHIEF
> *(mumbling)*
> B-Beckwith . . . he went down . . .

> KIRK
> *(tight, to Spock)*
> Fit out a patrol! Jump!

CAMERA HOLDS on Kirk as the crew rushes everywhichway to equip a patrol to transport down after the killer. Kirk turns to stare at the still-glowing Transporter with its EERIE HUMMING and we see his concern as we

FADE TO BLACK
and
FADE OUT.

END PROLOGUE

ACT ONE

FADE IN:

10 *EXT. PLANET—ESTABLISHING—DAY*

CLOSE on booted tracks as CAMERA ANGLE WIDENS to
show us the desolate face of the barren world. Silver-
gray sands that take a good impression of the Beckwith
tracks receding toward the horizon. Nothing else. No
rise, no hill, no foliage, no break or relief from the sheer
flat desolation of the terrain. As though some cosmic
god had flicked an ash and it had grown into a world.
A burnt-out ember of a sun hanging dolorously in the
cadaverous sky. As we HOLD a beat on the empty
panorama, we HEAR the VOICE of KIRK OVER:

KIRK'S VOICE (OVER)
Ship's Log: star-date 3134.8. This
cinder, this empty death of a world.

As these lines are SPOKEN OVER we see the
tell-tale shimmering and coalescing that means
crewmembers from the *Enterprise* are materializing
from the Transporter. As Kirk, Spock, Yeoman Rand
and THREE ENLISTED CREW appear, VOICE OVER
CONTINUES:

KIRK'S VOICE (OVER)
This is the source of the strange radiation
that had our clocks running backward.
How odd that Beckwith should choose
this ghost of a world for his escape. I am
transporting two shifts for patrol—Rand,
Spock, myself, and six enlisted crew. We'll
find him.

As these lines are SPOKEN OVER we see Spock indicating
the tracks to Kirk, and pointing in the direction
(MORE)

(CONTINUED)

10 CONTINUED:

they vanish; we see Kirk deploying his crew-patrol in a search-pattern as they move forward. VOICE OVER CONTINUES as we

LAP-DISSOLVE THRU:

11 *LONG SHOT—THE SCENE*

The patrol (now comprising nine people: we have not seen the last three materialize, but Kirk has told us about it), moving across the wide empty face of the planet as VOICE OVER CONTINUES:

KIRK'S VOICE (OVER)
But something more important has us nervous. A world with a dying sun such as this ... it should be frigid, without atmosphere ...
(beat)

CONTINUOUS
LAP-DISSOLVE THRU:

12 *MED. SHOT—THE TERRAIN—ON THE PATROL*

CAMERA MOVES IN SLOWLY as VOICE OVER CONTINUES and: (NOTE: we should see 3 scenes overlapping.)

KIRK'S VOICE (OVER)
(after beat)
But we aren't cold ... and we can breathe.

CONTINUOUS
SLOW LAP-DISSOLVE TO:

13 *EXT. PLANET—ANOTHER ANGLE—MED CLOSE SHOT*

PAST Yeoman Janice Rand IN F.G. as she turns her head sharply to look just PAST CAMERA. A console is strapped on her, just below the bosom, and dials dot the face of the machine. A HUM grows stronger from machine.

(CONTINUED)

13 *CONTINUED*

RAND
(into camera)
Captain, there's the source of the
radiation.

CAMERA PULLS BACK RAPIDLY to show Kirk,
Spock and the rest just behind her, and as CAMERA
FILLS we see the full landscape. Mountains on the
horizon. Mountains that rise up into the sky, till
they become vague and wispy. Rising straight out of
the flat terrain like pilasters.

SPOCK
The tracks . . . straight for the mountains.

CAMERA DOLLIES BACK IN and PANS LEFT to
come in CLOSER on Kirk and, past him—as if they
were miniatures right over his shoulder—the
mountains, with a strange glittering on one far,
distant peak.

KIRK
(almost dreamily)
Mr. Spock: do you see the city up there?
Do you see it, too?

SPOCK'S VOICE O.S.
It is there, Captain. It is illogical, but it
is apparently real.

KIRK
(in awe)
Like a city on the edge of forever.

CAMERA HOLDS as Kirk moves away toward the
horizon and the others move with him. CAMERA HOLDS
on the far distant view of that gleaming city, seen in
almost opaque dimness as we

DISSOLVE TO:

14 PLATEAU OF THE GUARDIANS—LATER DAY—CLOSE SHOT

ON KIRK as he climbs up the last of what is obviously a rocky defile. The stones are a peculiar silvery material, with buried shimmers of light in them. As Kirk climbs up onto the plateau, CAMERA GOES WITH HIM as the ANGLE OPENS to show us bracing rock walls and niches all around us.

15 THE PLATEAU—ESTABLISHING SHOT—KIRK'S POV

PANNING SHOT from Kirk's immediate right, around the bowl of the plateau. Gray sky past the rock prominences, light and eerie mist that gives the entire area an ethereal look, niches up in the rock walls, boulders of the same bright substance here and there, on a higher peak—but still quite far-off—the city, glittering like a hyper-sensitive's dream. And as the CAMERA PANS AROUND we see, for the first time, THE GUARDIANS OF FOREVER. The shot continues a beat and then CAMERA ZOOMS IN on them who, for that beat, had looked almost like part of the stone walls. But as CAMERA CLOSES in the ZOOM, we see they are men. But such men as have never before been seen:

The instant impression is age. Old, terribly old, as old as time itself, as old as the dying sun overhead. Nine feet tall, gray-silver in tone, shapeless beneath the long white robes that reach to the mist-laden ground. They seem incredibly tall, not merely because they are a *motionless* nine feet in height, but because of their hair which rises up like mitered headpieces, because of the beards that hang down from their silent and ancient faces. Though only their heads show, they seem almost religious in tone; there is a vast dignity, an immense holiness about them. They do not move *ever,* and for a beat we suspect they may be stone.

16 CLOSING SHOT—WITH KIRK

as he moves toward them. They wait and watch, silently. Spock moves in behind, then the others, fanning out. One of the crewmen hefts his phaser, but without seemingly seeing him, Kirk makes a gentle motion with his hand, to lower the weapon. They move closer. Finally, after many beats:

>   KIRK
>   *(with wonder)*
>   Who are you?

>   1ST GUARDIAN
>   *(a voice of power)*
>   We are the Guardians of Forever.

>   KIRK
>   You live in that city?

>   1ST GUARDIAN
>   Since before your sun burned hot in
>   space. Before your race was born.

>   SPOCK
>   This place is dead, empty. Why do
>   you stay?

>   1ST GUARDIAN
>   Only on this world do the million
>   pulse-flows of time and space merge.
>   Only here do the flux lines of Forever
>   meet.
>   *(beat)*
>   Only here can exist the gateway to the
>   past, where the Time Vortex of the
>   Ancients can work. Only here.
>   *(beat)*
>   And we were set to watch the Time
>   Vortex, so many hundreds of centuries
>   ago that even *we* do not have clear
>   memories of it.

                                    (CONTINUED)

16 CONTINUED:

> KIRK
>
> The gateway to the past? A time
> machine?

> 1ST GUARDIAN
>
> Not a machine. A creation, a Vortex.

Kirk is about to ask what they mean, but Spock—
logical—cuts in.

17 ON SPOCK

> SPOCK
>
> Have you seen another man, dressed as
> we are?

> 1ST GUARDIAN
>
> What we see has already been, or is yet
> to be. No. No other like you.

18 ROCKY NICHE—CLOSE PAST BECKWITH

past him hidden in a shadowy crevice, the phaser
aimed at Kirk, listening. He looks around himself,
trying to find a way out, but we see it is a cul-de-
sac. The only escape route is past the *Enterprise*
crewmen. He looks desperate but vicious, far from
finished. KIRK'S VOICE CARRIES.

> KIRK
>
> There are legends in space. About you.

> 1ST GUARDIAN
>
> You are the first visitors we have had
> for twice two hundred thousand years.

19 ANGLE PAST KIRK IN F.G.

to the Guardians, the mist rising, the light changing. Kirk approaches another step. We can see something in him we have never seen before: wonder, absolute all-consuming wonder. He has found a key to the secrets of the universe that compel him. He is being filled to the top with amazement, and he leans forward almost like a child.

> KIRK
>
> I always thought stories about time
> machines were the drunk-stuff of lab
> technicians when they'd had too much
> pure grain to drink.

> 1ST GUARDIAN
>
> That which is . . . *is.*

And he turns his head only infinitesimally. Kirk looks in the direction the Guardian has indicated, and his eyes open wide, delight and amazement and confusion and belief there.

20 THE TIME VORTEX—ESTABLISHING

Set in a tall, narrow rocky defile, it rises up, different to each who see it. A pillar of flame, a shaft of light, a roiling brightness of smoke, whatever wonder you care to make of it, the obvious aspects are light, height and insubstantiality. Construct it as you choose.

> 1ST GUARDIAN O.S.
>
> Pure matter. Built by a science man will
> not understand for a hundred thousand
> times the span of years he has already
> existed.

and the others near him, wondering, listening.

> KIRK
> *(awed)*
> And it's possible to go back ... and
> forward ... in time ...?

> 1ST GUARDIAN
> All time, all space. They meet in this
> brightness, the Vortex.

> SPOCK
> *(very scientific)*
> Can you give us a demonstration? Is
> that possible?

The Guardian's answer is oddly tinged with weariness
and pleasure.

> 1ST GUARDIAN
> Time is weary for the craftsman who
> cannot demonstrate his craft. We have
> nothing to do but desire to show you.
> The past.

> KIRK
> Can you show us the past of any world?

There is the faintest possible nod of: Yes, we can.

> KIRK
> *(softly)*
> The past of Old Earth ... please ...

The Guardians look toward the pillar of light and
as Kirk does so, the CAMERA SHOOTS PAST HIM. At
first there is no change, but in a moment there is
movement in the light ... a thickening ... a roiling

> (MORE)

(CONTINUED)

21 *CONTINUED:*

like oil . . . like quicksilver mixed with smoke . . . and a scene begins to take FORM IN THE VORTEX. (NOTE: this, and other scenes in Vortex will be MATTE INSERTS.)

22 *CLOSE ON VORTEX—FEATURING MATTE INSERTS (STOCK)*

A *scene* of primordial times; great saurians; a woolly mammoth; steaming prehistoric jungle; reality!

It FADES OUT to be replaced by:

A *scene* in the days of the Clipper ships; something typical of the period; reality!

It FADES OUT to be replaced by:

A *scene* of New York City in the time of the Depression, 1930-32.

(NOTE: At Director's discretion, INTERCUTS of the Earthmen marveling at this demonstration may be inserted.)

23 *PAST BECKWITH TO VORTEX*

as he watches with as much rapt attention as Kirk and his patrol. But the cunning is there, the arched brow and the faintly smiling mouth. The animal has sensed an avenue of escape, as we HEAR KIRK SAY:

KIRK
Could we go back, any of us . . . say, to
this time, 1930 of Old Earth?

Beckwith strains for the answer.

24 UP-ANGLE ON GUARDIANS

SHOT FROM TILT they look immense, rising up, almost Messianic in tone, something reverential as they speak about their religion—time.

> 1ST GUARDIAN
> Yes, but it is not wise. Man and non-Man must live in their present or their future. But never in their past, save to learn lessons from it. Time can be dangerous. If passage back is effected, the voyager may add a new factor to the past, and thus change time, alter everything that happened from that point to the present ... all through the universe.

25 SPOCK AND GUARDIANS PAST HIM

fascinated by the concepts, not the magic of it all.

> SPOCK
> Then time is not a constant. It is not rigid?

> 1ST GUARDIAN
> Time is elastic. It will revert to its original shape when changes are minor. But when the change is life or death—when the sum of intelligence alters the balance—then the change can become permanent ... and terrible.

> SPOCK
> Like changing the flow of a river.

> 1ST GUARDIAN
> A river, a wind, a flow, elastic. It makes
> (MORE)

(CONTINUED)

25 *CONTINUED:*

> no difference how you imagine it to
> yourself.

> KIRK
>
> How long has it been since anyone
> went—

> 1ST GUARDIAN
>
> We do not go back. We guard. For one
> hundred thousand years no one has
> gone back.

> SPOCK
> *(to Kirk)*
>
> Captain, I understand now why we
> can breathe here, and why our
> chronometers turned backwards.

The Time Vortex has been left set at 1930. While
CAMERA DOES NOT dwell on it, whatever shot we enter,
we should see the scene of the Depression back there,
to remind us it's on.

> KIRK
>
> They've created a zone of no-time here.

> SPOCK
>
> Within the sphere of influence of the
> Vortex, time does not move. All
> through the rest of the universe it
> flows at its normal rate, but here—

> KIRK
> *(softly)*
>
> If they can control time, how much
> simpler it must be for them to control
> the atmosphere.

(CONTINUED)

1ST GUARDIAN

There is wisdom that lesser species
have not grasped. Perhaps you who call
yourselves "men" will be next to guard
all of time.

SPOCK

But if this is true ... how old you are ...
if time does not move at its normal rate
here ... how long have you been here
to get as old as you are ...

26 FULL SHOT—THE SCENE—HAND-HELD

But they have no time to ponder an answer, for at
that moment Beckwith breaks from cover and
makes a long run toward the Time Vortex. He is
halfway there before they realize what is happening.
Kirk and Spock plunge forward to stop him. Spock
gets to him first, and knocks the phaser out of
Beckwith's hands, but Beckwith slams Spock across
the jaw and keeps going. He grabs Yeoman Janice
Rand as a shield and roughhouses her in front of
him, ever closer to the Vortex. She half-turns and
elbows him; he leaves her and Kirk reaches him just
as he closes on the Vortex. Kirk sees he is going for
the Vortex (from which the 1930s scene is gone, but
which still flickers and glows so we know it is in
operation) and makes a flying dive for him. But
Beckwith does a little dance-step of broken-field
maneuvering and flings himself forward. CAMERA
WITH HIM as he dives headfirst into the Vortex.
There is the SOUND of a LOUD WHOOOOSH! as
space rushes to fill the vacuum where he has been,
even as Kirk grabs up the phaser lying near him on
the ground and fires at the Vortex. A blast of
coruscating energy hits the light pillar, but does
nothing. The Vortex is empty. Beckwith is gone.

27 *WITH KIRK*

as he crawls back to Spock, who is just rising. Yeoman Rand joins them, and the rest of the crew patrol.

> KIRK
> *(to Spock)*
> Are you—

> SPOCK
> I am undamaged, Captain.

Kirk looks at Janice Rand. She nods tightly that she's fine also. Then Kirk turns quickly, speaks to the Guardians.

> KIRK
> He went back?

> 1ST GUARDIAN
> *(panic)*
> Yes. The Vortex was active. Your world, Old Earth.

> KIRK
> But you said—

> 1ST GUARDIAN
> All past history has been changed.

> KIRK
> But how can that be . . . it all looks the same here?

> 1ST GUARDIAN
> Yes, here. But from here outward, everything has been changed. It is another universe in which we stand.

(CONTINUED)

27 *CONTINUED:*

> SPOCK
> How has it been changed?

28 ANGLE ON GUARDIANS—CITY IN B.G.

high on that farther crag, the CITY BEGINS TO PULSE & GLOW. We SEE IT over the Guardians' shoulders. One of the other two who has been bone-silent all through this action, suddenly begins to show animation. His body quivers ever so faintly under the robes, and his face makes a slight movement.

> 1ST GUARDIAN
> The time-flow has been diverted. We
> are being summoned. The machines of
> the Ancients are registering traumas in
> time. We must return.

And THEY VANISH! The Vortex dies out. Kirk, *et al* alone.

29 TWO-SHOT—KIRK & SPOCK

with the crew patrol behind them. Yeoman Rand prominent.

> KIRK
> We have to get back to the ship.

> SPOCK
> *(to Rand)*
> Yeoman. Signal *Enterprise* for Transporter
> pickup; give these coordinates.

> RAND
> Yes, sir.

She fiddles with the console, BLEEPS a signal.

(CONTINUED)

29 CONTINUED:

KIRK

If they were right—If it's changed ...

SPOCK

Conjecture has no merit.

KIRK

Yeoman, stay with us for the second
shift. Send the lower ranks up first.

RAND

Yes, sir. Pickup commencing.

CAMERA ANGLE EXPANDS as the six enlisted personnel
group together. They begin to shimmer as we have seen
previously, then vanish.

RAND

Captain?

Kirk looks at her.

RAND (CONT'D.)

What's happened up there, sir?

KIRK

(distant)

Beckwith may have killed again ...

DISSOLVE TO:

30 INT. TRANSPORTER CHAMBER—CLOSE ON KIRK
& SPOCK

in the last stages of materialization. Rand behind them.
As they appear corporeally, suddenly we see Kirk's face
assume a BROAD EXPRESSION of disbelief and
consternation. Rand's eyes widen in total confusion.

(MORE)

(CONTINUED)

30 CONTINUED:

Even Spock is momentarily set back. Rand gives a small YELP of anxiety.

31 REVERSE ANGLE—PAST KIRK IN EXT. F.G.

(NOTE: this *must* be shot past the three people in the transporter to show the entire chamber before them.)

WHAT THEY SEE: the six enlisted personnel herded into a corner, being held at bay by men and women with weapons totally unlike those used by the *Enterprise* crew. The captors are RENEGADES. Their dress is not regulation uniforms, but motley garb, each one wearing what he or she feels like. They are unkempt, and as vicious-looking as a crowd of free-booters can look. There are as many in the group as needed to hold the *Enterprise* crew at bay.

In the forefront of the group stands the RENEGADE CAPTAIN whose evil nature is so evident on his face that no one could doubt for a moment that this man is the vilest scum of a million worlds. He has a weapon of extreme ugliness pointed at Kirk and Spock and Rand. His smile is the smile of an animal.

RENEGADE
(with chill warmth)
Welcome to the *Condor*.

HARD CUT TO:

32 CLOSE ON KIRK

his expression of—yes, possibly—fear and bewilderment and then dawning realization that he has, indeed, wandered helplessly into a world he never made. HOLD ON THAT thought as we

FADE OUT.

END ACT ONE

ACT TWO

FADE IN:

33 *INT. TRANSPORTER CHAMBER—ESTABLISHING*

the renegades holding the *Enterprise* patrol at bay.
Kirk and Spock make a slight move, but guns come
up, and they settle back. The Renegade Captain seems
perplexed, but still a threat.

> RENEGADE
> Whoever you are, you shouldn't have
> come aboard.

34 *CLOSE 2-SHOT—KIRK & SPOCK (RAND IN B.G.)*

Kirk's bewilderment has passed. He speaks in an
undertone to Spock.

> KIRK
> He was right. Time's been altered.

> SPOCK
> Renegades.

> KIRK
> This isn't the *Enterprise* anymore.

35 *PAST RENEGADE CAPTAIN TO THEM*

on the Transporter stage. Beside the Renegade is a
TECHNICIAN who is operating the complex
Transporter console.

> RENEGADE
> Now step down off that stage slowly.

36 SAME AS 34

Kirk frantically seeks an escape route. We see it in his face.

> KIRK
> *(to Rand, softly)*
> Yeoman ... give that console full
> feedback!

37 CLOSE ON JANICE RAND

as she hesitates a fractional beat to understand his order. Then CAMERA TILTS DOWN SLIGHTLY to show us the console still strapped on her, and her hands moving to two big calibrated knobs. She suddenly twists them as far as they will go. There is an ABRUPT PIERCING WHINE.

38 SAME AS 33—HAND-HELD

as the Transporter console erupts in a shower of sparks and a WHAMMMM! and the Technician is thrown half across the room. The Renegade Captain and his men naturally turn with a start, and in that instant, Kirk leaps off the Transporter stage.

> KIRK
> *(yells)*
> Go!

And Spock joins him in a flying leap that carries him off the stage and onto the nearest renegade. The *Enterprise* crewmen begin punching, grabbing weapons. There is a pitched battle in the cramped confines of the Transporter chamber and the tactic resolves itself into forcing the remaining members of the *Condor's* crew out the hatch, and sealing it behind them. The final tally has one *Enterprise* crewman dead on the floor, and three *Condor* renegades in similar condition.

39 MEDIUM SHOT—KIRK PROMINENT

as several of the patrol with phasers stand guard at the port, waiting for a counter-attack. The remainder gather around Kirk. Janice Rand is trying to pull her torn uniform around her. Spock has a cut on his cheek. He is bleeding yellow.

RAND

Captain, where's the *Enterprise* crew?

KIRK

Not here. Maybe nowhere.

SPOCK

Logically, with time altered, they were
possibly never born, or they have
become *those.*

He jerks his head in the direction of the hatch and the renegades.

KIRK

There are 450 enemies out there.

CUT TO:

40 CORRIDOR OUTSIDE TRANSPORTER CHAMBER

as the Renegade Captain regroups.

RENEGADE

Nimblek, Owstian, blast through that
hatch!

Two renegades with weird hand-weapons move on the hatch, start to blast at it. The door gets smoky, smudgy.

41 INT. TRANSPORTER CHAMBER—ANOTHER ANGLE

CLOSE ON CREWMAN nearest hatch. He turns head sharply into CAMERA and speaks as FRAME OPENS to SHOW FULL SCENE.

(CONTINUED)

CREWMAN

Cap'n. I feel heat. They're blasting.

SPOCK
(to Kirk)

There are too many variables to this problem.

KIRK

We have to change things back.

SPOCK

Then all the possibilities come back to a single course of action.

KIRK
(nods understanding)

Yeoman Rand . . . can you hold this chamber?

RAND
(unsure)

How long, sir?

KIRK

Indefinitely.

There is a beat of silence. Everyone knows what he means. She nods. Kirk looks at Spock.

KIRK

Let's get back.

They hasten to the Transporter stage, get on. Rand moves to the main control panel that her feedback exploded.

(CONTINUED)

41 CONTINUED:— 2

> RAND
>
> I'll have to cut in alternate circuits,
> Captain. My feedback burned out the
> central sources.

> KIRK
>
> Do your best, Yeoman.

As she works, rehooking circuits, moving hurriedly,
Spock moves off his Transporter plate to Kirk's side.

42 EXTREME CLOSE TWO-SHOT—KIRK & SPOCK

as Spock leans in to speak so the crew won't hear him.

> SPOCK
>
> They may not allow us to go back after
> Beckwith.

> KIRK
>
> They've got to.

> SPOCK
>
> Time is something sacred to them.
> They may not think as we do—that it
> should be changed back.

> KIRK
> *(more insistent)*
>
> They've *got* to!

> RAND'S VOICE O.S.
>
> Ready, Captain. It's jerry-rigged, but it
> ought to hold.

> KIRK
> *Energize!*

43 *ANGLE ON KIRK, SPOCK IN CHAMBER*

The dematerialization EFFECT—they become transparent . . .

> RAND
> Hurry back, we might not be here
> when you—

. . . they dissolve. A few faint sparkles fade. Empty
chamber.

44 *EXT. PLANET—PLATEAU OF THE GUARDIANS OF TIME*

as we left it. The REMATERIALIZATION EFFECT
occurs: first the sparkling, then the transparent
outlines of bodies, then the solid appearance of Kirk
and Mr. Spock. They look around and then the
Guardians POP INTO EXISTENCE where they had
stood before.

> 1ST GUARDIAN
> The universe you knew . . . never
> existed. The ship you came in . . . never
> existed. The men and women you
> knew . . . never existed.

> KIRK
> *(fiercely)*
> Let us follow Beckwith. We'll change
> Time back.

> 1ST GUARDIAN
> The rope of the time stream knots, and
> knots again. It is far more dangerous
> attempting to unsnarl the past than it is
> to let Time flow on. Let it go.

(CONTINUED)

44 CONTINUED:

> KIRK
> *(anguished)*
> Not that *easy* for us! Everything we
> knew, everyone we care about . . .
> they're gone . . . or changed . . .

> 1ST GUARDIAN
> You are children, believing you can put
> smoke back in its bottle.

> SPOCK
> Is Time immutable? Or can it be set
> back as it was before Beckwith's
> intercession caused the knotting?

> 1ST GUARDIAN
> The man Beckwith . . . he is a serious
> impediment in the Time-flow. He is
> scar-tissue. A clot in the chronal
> bloodstream. Do you know the
> concept "evil"?

> KIRK
> *(tense)*
> We do. Send us back. We'll retrieve him.

> 1ST GUARDIAN
> There is a problem, of course. There is
> *always* a problem. Time cannot be
> doubled.

> SPOCK
> *(grasps immediately)*
> Basic physics. Two objects cannot
> occupy the same space at the same
> time. You cannot send us back to the
> precise time of Beckwith's appearance,
> can you?

(CONTINUED)

1ST GUARDIAN
Before. Or after. But not the same.

Spock looks at Kirk. They communicate silently, analyzing the options, the two intelligent problem-solvers considering all the possibilities. Finally: they nod to each other.

KIRK
Before he gets there. He won't know we're already settled in.
> *(beat)*

How close can you set us down in the past?

1ST GUARDIAN
Soon. Close, perhaps. But we have no way of calculating such things.

SPOCK
Captain, the tricorder. I can set it now to resonate in phase with the Vortex. That will establish a baseline for dating, and once in the Past, we can get our chronological bearings.

KIRK
We'll grab him when he comes through. We'll be waiting.
> *(beat)*

I just hope we won't have been waiting for *years.*

SPOCK
If we bring him back, then the river resumes its natural course, everything goes back the way it was?

(CONTINUED)

44 CONTINUED:—3

1ST GUARDIAN
(nods)
But in each time-period there is a focal
point. An object, a person, something
that is indispensable to the normal
flow of time. Unimportant otherwise,
but as a catalyst ...

KIRK
And if Beckwith tampers with it—time
is changed permanently.

SPOCK
Will Beckwith know what this focal
point is?

1ST GUARDIAN
No, but the stresses of the time-flow
will *draw him to it.* If he influences
it, nothing can restore the shape of
the past.

KIRK
(intense)
Then how can we stop him?

1ST GUARDIAN
(mystically)
Bring him back. He will seek that which
must die, and give it life. Stop him.

KIRK
I don't understand. Can't you tell us
more?

1ST GUARDIAN
Blue it will be. Blue as the sky of Old
Earth and clear as truth. And the sun
will burn on it, and *there* is the key.

(CONTINUED)

44 CONTINUED:—4

Kirk and Spock look at each other. The Guardians
have obviously said all they can say. They nod with
resignation at each other, and turn to the Time Vortex,
just as it flickers to life. They move toward it. Flames
and light burgeon, and the SOUND of the Vortex is
HEARD. Rapidly changing colors wash across Kirk
and Spock.

45 ANGLE ON TIME VORTEX

as they step up to it, hesitate a beat, then step in.
Flames leap up about them (or whatever SPECIAL
EFFECT is employed) and they vanish. CAMERA PANS
SMOOTHLY BACK to Guardians.

1ST GUARDIAN
As night falls, they run like hunters, and
for all our wisdom, we are helpless.

RIPPLE-DISSOLVE TO:

46 LIMBO SHOT

against the blackness, in SOLARIZED IMAGE, Kirk and
Mr. Spock, REVERSE-IMAGE as though they were
negatives, hurtling toward CAMERA out of the dark,
a sense of intense motion. They hurtle STRAIGHT
FOR CAMERA and

FRAME TO BLACK.

47 EXT. NEW YORK STREET—1930—LATE DAY—
ESTABLISHING

a seamy, down-at-the-heels street; murky glass
storefronts; automobiles of the period, but very few;
prominent in the scene is a store with a large sign
proclaiming:

CCC CAMPS—SIGN UP HERE

(CONTINUED)

47 *CONTINUED:*

and beside it another store with a sign that says *FREE SOUP* and a smaller sign with an arrow that says *FORM A LINE*. In front of these two shops there is a small group of men. They are in a line, and though we can only see six or seven shabby men in caps and shapeless coats outside on the sidewalk, the way they are queued up, with the line disappearing into the soup kitchen, we know there are many more in the crowd. On a soapbox between the two stores, a tall, wild-eyed man with a typical moustache of the time, dressed in the same shabby garb, wearing a frayed "newsboy's cap," holding an American flag on a pole, is haranguing the crowd. The penniless men listen to the ORATOR, who is slowly inciting them to riot, as we SEE the sudden materialization of Kirk and Spock at the rear of the crowd. Kirk faces the Orator, but Spock is turned the other way, as though they had come through time turned-about.

48 *CLOSE ON KIRK & SPOCK*

as they look around, startled and disoriented. They find each other, and there is wonder in their eyes. Not till this moment have they believed what the act of time-travel was really like. Now they turn to the Orator as he howls.

> ORATOR
> What kind of a country *is* this, where
> men have to stand in bread lines just to
> fill their bellies? I'll *tell* you what kind!
> A country run by the foreigners! All the
> scum we let in to take the food from
> our mouths, all the alien filth that
> pollutes our fine country. Here we are,
> skilled workers, and they want us to
> sign up for CCC camps. Civilian
> *(MORE)*

(CONTINUED)

48 CONTINUED:

> Conservation Corps, men—is *that* what
> we're gonna do? Work like coolies inna
> fields while these swine who can't even
> speak our language take the—

He CONTINUES UNDER as we CLOSE on Kirk and Spock. Spock looks at Kirk with disbelief.

SPOCK
Is this the heritage Earthmen brag
about? This sickness?

KIRK
(disgusted)
This is what it's taken us five hundred
years to crawl up from.

49 REVERSE ANGLE—ORATOR'S POV

as he sees Spock in the rear of the crowd. The fanaticism of his harangue is suddenly halted. He rises on tip-toe and suddenly points a finger.

ORATOR
There! There's one! There's one of
them foreign trouble-makers. Whyn't
we *show* him how we like his kind!

The crowd turns almost in a body, and there is a definite MURMUR THRU THE CROWD as they see Spock—an obvious alien though they have no idea *how* alien—who looks around uneasily. Kirk edges away with his phaser leveled, and we wonder for a beat if Kirk is possibly deserting his companion.

ORATOR
(hysterically)
They're the ones sending this country
(MORE)

(CONTINUED)

49 *CONTINUED:*

deeper into the Depression! *They're* the ones that want your babies to die with swollen bellies, *they're* the ones!

But he doesn't need to finish. The crowd suddenly HOWLS and goes for Spock. Spock lays about with vigor, sending men sprawling. Kirk backs away. And then, he levels the phaser at a lamppost, and with a SIZZLE the weapon goes off, disintegrating the lamppost. The crowd falls back in horror. Spock and Kirk run like hell out of FRAME.

50 *EXT. NEW YORK STREETS—LATE DAY MONTAGE*
thru
56 as they run. An attempt should be made in this sequence by use of CAMERA TILT and SMASH-CUT and LAP-DISSOLVE and ARRIFLEX to give a tone of plunging disorientation. They are in another time, strictly speaking an alien world, and they are being pursued by a mob, though we need not show the mob. But by use of ERRATIC ANGLES (up from street-level; flashing past camera; down on them as they race by) with MUSIC OVER we can obtain a sense of phantasmagoria in seven shots:

DOWN A LONG EMPTY STREET OF ECHOING BUILDINGS

AROUND A CORNER AND AWAY FROM US INTO AND DOWN THE LENGTH OF AN ALLEY KNOCKING OVER GARBAGE CANS IN THEIR WILD FLIGHT

STRAIGHT FOR US AS THEY JUMP TO CATCH THE TOP OF A FENCE AND TENNESSEE-ROLL OVER IT

THROUGH A BACKYARD HUNG WITH WASH

KIRK GRABS SPOCK AND PULLS HIM DOWN
(MORE)

(CONTINUED)

50 CONTINUED:
thru SOME STEPS INTO A SHADOWY BASEMENT
56 ENTRANCE.

57 *INT. BASEMENT—WITH SPOCK & KIRK*

as they plunge through the darkness, their momentum carrying them all the way to the rear near a coal bin from which coal spills onto the basement floor itself. A furnace of the old stoke type. They slip behind it and slide down to sit with their backs against the wall as CAMERA CLOSES ON THEM.

SPOCK
Barbarian world!

KIRK
They were hungry, and afraid.

SPOCK
As violent as any aborigine world we ever landed on.

KIRK
All right, we're safe now.

SPOCK
I would call this anything but "safe." Barbarians!

KIRK
You're an accomplished ethnologist, Spock; you know all races go through a violent phase.

SPOCK
My race never languished in such ignorant behavior for thousands of years. We went to space in peace.
(MORE)

(CONTINUED)

57 *CONTINUED:*

Earthmen came with all of *this* behind them.

> KIRK
> *(aroused)*
> And that's why you hit space two
> hundred years after us!

> SPOCK
> Try to tell me Earthmen uplifted my
> race. Tell me that, and use Beckwith as
> an example of nobility.

> KIRK
> I should have left you for the mob!

Spock is about to say something that borders on pique.
He starts, stops, resumes his mask of imperturbable
alien calm.

> SPOCK
> I spoke out of turn ... Captain.

Kirk simmers down. He chuckles.

> KIRK
> Mr. Spock. You're picking up dirty
> habits hanging around with Earthmen.
> Emotionalism.

> SPOCK
> *(piqued, but not about to show it)*
> We have some immediate problems ...
> Captain.

> KIRK
> *(bemused)*
> You draw a certain amount of
> attention, Mr. Spock. We'll have to
> disguise you.

(CONTINUED)

Spock says nothing, but there is a look of disgust on his face. He half turns away. Kirk rises.

> KIRK
> There's a line of clothes back there. I'll see if I can, uh, liberate some period costumes for us.

> SPOCK
> See if you can locate a ring to go through my nose.

Kirk smiles with amusement, and slips out of the basement as Spock settles back uneasily, looking around, and we

DISSOLVE TO:

58 *INT. BASEMENT—ANOTHER ANGLE*

ON SPOCK & KIRK now dressed in ill-fitting (NOTE: please please *please* let these clothes not be tailor-made for them, it always looks phony!) 1930s-style garb. They are buttoning the last buttons as we COME TO THEM.

> KIRK
> We'd better get out of here.

> JANITOR'S VOICE O.S.
> What's your hurry, fellahs?

They turn sharply and in the dim light from the stairwell leading upstairs we see a man in overalls, a JANITOR, who is watching them.

> KIRK
> We were just going. It's cold out there.

(CONTINUED)

58 CONTINUED:

The Janitor comes down toward them. He has a shovel in his hands, but though he holds it ready, there is nothing menacing about the pose. He is an older man, early fifties, with a friendly, open face. He approaches. Spock fades back a bit, letting shadows obscure him.

> JANITOR
> Oh, don't fret it none. I get a lot of bindlestiffs down here. You can hang around awhile if you like, get the chill off.

> KIRK
> *(uneasily)*
> No, we'd better be going.

They start past him and he turns to watch them.

> JANITOR
> Hey . . . Bo.

Kirk and Spock stop, turn around.

> JANITOR
> I need a couple of men to clean up the alley, sweep out the airshaft—you know, tenants always dumping stuff down there.
> *(beat)*
> I'd be willing to let you bunk out down here in exchange. Give you some bedding.

Kirk and Spock look at each other.

> KIRK
> Well, that's kind of you, but . . .

(CONTINUED)

JANITOR

Long as you don't swipe nothing, it'll
work out fine. You need a place, I need
some help.

CAMERA MOVES IN PAST Janitor to CLOSE 2-SHOT of
Kirk and Spock as Kirk looks at Spock and murmurs
sotto voce:

KIRK
(smiling)
Worse than any barbarians?

HARD CUT TO:

59 *INT. STAIRWELL—TENEMENT BLDG.—DAY—SPOCK &
KIRK*

They are sweeping up. Kirk lays down his broom and
starts to wrestle a huge garbage can loaded with
refuse toward a small dolly. Spock wears a stocking-
cap, pulled down over his pointed ears. He shovels
refuse into another can. He pauses, and wipes his
perspiring forehead with his sleeve. He has been
made up to faintly resemble a Chinese.

SPOCK

It seems dubious we will find the focal
point of this period, hidden away in a
garbage dump.

Kirk leans on the dolly. He wipes his face, leaving a
black smudge.

KIRK

I was thinking about that. If Beckwith
will be drawn to it, won't the same
apply to us?

(CONTINUED)

59 CONTINUED:

> SPOCK
>
> Perhaps. But what if he gets to it before
> we do?

> KIRK
>
> Where's the tricorder?

Spock disappears into the darkness of the basement, and there is the SOUND of METAL GRATING. In a moment he returns. He hands the tricorder to Kirk.

60 CLOSER SHOT—ON TRICORDER

as Kirk activates it. He speaks into the machine.

> KIRK
>
> Memory Banks.

> VOICE OF TRICORDER
> *(filter)*
> Activated.

CAMERA ANGLE WIDENS to include Kirk holding the device; almost a 2-SHOT:

> KIRK
>
> Integrate all data on Old Earth, year
> 1930 old style. Compute for variables
> resulting in major alterations of
> historical flow.
> *(beat)*
> When these variables have been
> postulated, integrate for the crisis
> points.

> VOICE OF TRICORDER
> *(filter)*
> Integration procedure involves seventh
> (MORE)

(CONTINUED)

level extrapolation and attendant
internal function overloads and failure.

> KIRK
> Give estimated time for completion of
> procedure.

> VOICE OF TRICORDER
> *(filter)*
> Procedure initiated.
> *(click)*
> Three hours, Earth time.

> KIRK
> Proceed.

He turns off the tricorder and hands it back to Spock
who vanishes once again into the darkness, as Kirk
speaks to his unseen presence.

> KIRK (CONT'D.)
> Think we can keep busy shoveling
> garbage for three hours?

> SPOCK'S VOICE O.S.
> *(voice from dark)*
> That is not what troubles me, Captain.
> *(beat)*
> That much integrating, at that level, for
> that intensive a period, may well burn
> out the circuits. The tricorder is a self-
> contained unit, with no dependence
> on the *Enterprise's* power. And as the
> *Enterprise* no longer exists, that is
> fortunate.

> KIRK
> I hear an unspoken "but."

(CONTINUED)

60 *CONTINUED:—2*

SPOCK'S VOICE O.S.

But ... it is a unit of finite power.
Setting it this excessive a task may
burn out the circuits. Its value to us in
this barbaric past is inestimable.

KIRK

As long as we get our answer, it won't
matter.

SPOCK'S VOICE O.S.

If we get the answer.

Spock has returned out of the darkness and is at work
once more. Kirk stares at him with amusement.

KIRK

You don't make a half-bad Chinese
laborer. They barely looked at you in
that "movie theater" last night. Twenty-
three skidoo, kiddo.

SPOCK

(not amused)

"Movie theater." You have an amazing
facility for picking up the local
language patterns, Captain—"twenty-
three skidoo" indeed—but we do not
seem much closer to locating that
monster, Beckwith.

KIRK

Time is relative. He hasn't even come
through yet. We have a lot of time ...

SPOCK.

A lot . . . and none at all.

(CONTINUED)

SPOCK CLOSE as the preceding line is spoken. He has no humor about the situation. And there is a tone of caution that cannot be ignored.

DISSOLVE TO:

61 INT. BASEMENT—ANOTHER ANGLE

CLOSE ON TRICORDER as Spock holds it in his hands. CAMERA PULLS BACK to MED. 2-SHOT as they talk to machine.

> VOICE OF TRICORDER
> *(filter)*
> Integration completed.

> SPOCK
> List all focal points.

> VOICE OF TRICORDER
> *(filter)*
> Preliminary listing involves six hundred and sixteen thousand five hundred and ninety focal points.

> SPOCK
> Eliminate all but those within a ten-kilometer radius of our present coordinates.

> VOICE OF TRICORDER
> *(filter)*
> Unable to comply.

> KIRK
> Explain.

> VOICE OF TRICORDER
> *(filter)*
> Circuits damaged in seventh level intensity. Only partial data available. You were warned.

(CONTINUED)

61 *CONTINUED:*

> KIRK
> *(resignedly)*
> Proceed.

There is tortured clicking and whirring from the machine. Then, amidst static, it speaks.

> VOICE OF TRICORDER
> *(filter)*
> Blue. The burning sun. The key.

It clicks and hums and then quits entirely. Spock hands the dead unit to Kirk. Kirk hefts it with frustration.

> KIRK
> That takes care of *that.* Wasn't the blue,
> the sun, wasn't it what the Guardian
> said, something like that? Did you make
> any sense out of it?

> SPOCK
> A description, perhaps. It was no help
> *before* we came through the Vortex,
> and it is not much help now.

Kirk holds out the tricorder.

> KIRK
> Can you repair it?

> SPOCK
> Dubious, Captain. The transistor has
> not been invented yet; nor the printed
> circuit; nor the mnemonic
> (pronounced nee-mon-ic) memory
> cube; nor—

> KIRK
> You made your point, Mr. Spock.

(CONTINUED)

> SPOCK
> But, as always, sir, I can try.

Kirk chuckles and hands it to Spock.

> KIRK
> I'm going out to get a job today.

> SPOCK
> Perhaps I should do the same.

> KIRK
> Forget it. I need you working on that
> tricorder, so we can get a fix on how
> long it'll be before Beckwith arrives.
> *(beat)*
> Besides, it's too risky.

The Janitor emerges from the entrance to the basement.

> JANITOR
> What's too risky...?

> KIRK
> Uh, nothing . . . his going out for a
> job . . .

> JANITOR
> Listen, these days, *everybody's* on the
> dodge. Least thing'll get a man pinched.
> Saw some Bo just last week got thrown
> in the pokey for tryin' to steal bread an'
> macaroni for his kids.
> *(beat)*
> What'd the Chinee do?

> KIRK
> Some, uh, friends of his are in trouble.

As he says this we

CUT TO:

62 *INSERT SHOT—TRANSPORTER ROOM ON* ENTERPRISE

NOTE: this is intended as a shock-value shot, only a few frames in duration, almost subliminal in nature. It should be there, hold a scant beat, and be gone. Longer will be confusing. It is intended to link the Old Earth action with the imperativeness, the sense of *moment,* of action in the future. A jab in the eye, not a punch in the mouth.

The beleaguered *Enterprise* patrol as one of the crewmen wrenches open the door and Yeoman Rand fires a phaser through the instant-open hatch, at the Renegades, and the hatch—with its tell-tale burned spots—is thrust closed immediately by hand. The action takes place in only three or four beats and we

CUT BACK TO:

63 *SAME AS 61* PRECISELY

as though we haven't lost a beat in the conversation, as though we have seen through the eyes of thought of Kirk or Spock, to the urgency of what they must do.

> KIRK
> Uh ... he can work around here ... he
> needn't go *out* to work ...

But the Janitor is hearing the objection.

> JANITOR
> Leave it t'me. I got a job down the
> street he can fill ...

CUT TO:

64 *INT. RESTAURANT KITCHEN—ANGLE ON SPOCK*

FRAME OBSCURED by a large cloud of steam. As CAMERA PULLS BACK we see Mr. Spock, still wearing

(MORE)

(CONTINUED)

the stocking-cap pulled down over his ears, in an old-style button-down undershirt with the sleeves rolled up, industriously working over a zinc double-sink filled with filthy dishes. Horsehair scrub brush, cake of brown lye soap. As he works, we HEAR the VOICE of the COOK O.S.

> COOK'S VOICE O.S.
> Okay, Chinee No-Talk, time to quit!

Mr. Spock straightens up, with difficulty. His face is drenched with sweat, the front of his wool undershirt stained with a thousand kinds of refuse. He turns and CAMERA PANS WITH him as the Cook comes INTO FRAME.

> COOK
> Night shift comin' in, you can knock off.

Mr. Spock starts to leave, slowly, painfully, the way it feels after a day of boring, nauseating drudgery. He takes his seedy jacket from a peg near the sinks, and starts away as the Cook stops him.

> COOK (CONT'D.)
> Hey, Yellow Peril! Payday today. You
> been onna job a week, doncha even
> know when you collect?

Spock stops. There is an expression of infinite weariness there, and resignation. The Cook takes some money from his pocket.

> COOK (CONT'D.)
> Lessee now ... fifteen cents an hour for
> ten hours a day ... that's, uh, nine
> dollars fifty for the week ...

(CONTINUED)

64 CONTINUED: — 2

He starts to count it out. He hands it over to Spock and starts to put the rest of the money back in his pocket. Spock's hand snakes out quickly, and he grabs the Cook's wrist in a grip that is obviously painful. The Cook's face screws up in anguish and he bends a little to the angle of Spock's pressure. Then, in a very calm voice, Spock addresses him.

> SPOCK
> *(matter-of-factly)*
> *Ten* dollars and fifty cents for the week.
> Seventy hours at fifteen cents an hour.

> COOK
> *(in pain)*
> Hey! Leggo, you're gonna bust it.

> SPOCK
> *(calmly)*
> *Ten* dollars and fifty cents ...

> COOK
> *(real anguish)*
> Okay, okay, *ten, ten,* anything you
> say ... yeah, I figgered it wrong ...

Spock releases him. The Cook rubs the wrist furiously.

> COOK (CONT'D.)
> Jeez, you don't haveta ruin a stiff jus'
> cuz he misfigured somethin', do ya?
> Here's your lousy buck ...

He hands Spock the extra dollar. Spock moves toward door.

(CONTINUED)

COOK (CONT'D.)
(shouts after)
You sure learned to figger money
pretty quick . . . an' you dint speak so
good last week like that . . . you was
just *playin'* dumb . . .

But Spock has slammed the door to the alley exit as
we HOLD on the Cook and he says his last line.

DISSOLVE TO:

65 *EXT. NEW YORK STREET—EVENING (DAY FOR NIGHT)*

as Spock moves down the block out of the alley.
CAMERA WITH HIM as he PASSES THRU FRAME. It
is a typically-dressed 1930 scene, with enough
people on the street to give an impression of a
populated evening. Cars in the street, vendors with
pushcarts, street lamps illuminating a stickball game.
And on the corner, as Spock nears it, we see a crowd
gathered. Not a large crowd, but enough bodies to
indicate a sizeable small gathering. There is a woman
on a tiny dais, there on the corner, and around her
are several Salvation Army types (though *not* in
Army uniforms) with bass drum, cornet, triangle and
clarinet. She is speaking to the crowd as Spock
draws abreast of them. We HEAR HER VOICE as he
comes toward the group. The VOICE of SISTER
EDITH KEELER, the voice of truth.

NOTE: an actress with a VOICE that is warm, mature
and truthfully effective is absolutely necessary in
this role.

EDITH
(to crowd)
Shadow and reality, my friends. That's
the secret of getting through these bad
(MORE)

(CONTINUED)

65 *CONTINUED:*

> times. Know what is, and what only
> seems to be. Hunger is real, and so is
> cold. But sadness is not.

Sister Edith Keeler is a young woman, possibly middle twenties, but with a voice that is instantly arresting. (It was said of the old-time radio announcer, Graham MacNamee, that anyone passing a room in which there was a radio playing his voice was compelled to stop. Sister Edith's voice has that wonderful quality.) She is quite lovely. Not beautiful, but fresh and vibrant, truly alive. With no adolescence in her loveliness, but a kindness, a radiance. She wears a simple dress, but over it she wears a blue cape fastened at her throat by a scatter pin in the shape of a sunburst. The color of the cape is an attractive, though not gaudy, blue. And the sunburst is not overly obvious at first.

EDITH

> And it is the sadness that will kill you,
> that will ruin you. We all go to bed a
> little hungry every night, but it is
> possible to find peace in sleep
> knowing you have lived another day,
> and hurt no one doing it.

Spock is passing them now, and he turns with a nod of agreement in f.g. as she says these words of profound simplicity.

66 *XTREME CLOSE ON SPOCK*

as his eyes widen and he sees something.

67 *REVERSE ANGLE—SPOCK'S POV—WHAT HE SEES*

CAMERA ZOOMS IN on Edith's cape as we HEAR

(MORE)

(CONTINUED)

67 CONTINUED

in ECHO OVER or FILTER OVER the words of the Guardian.

> VOICE OF GUARDIAN
> *(echo filter)*
> Blue it will be. Blue as the sky of Old
> Earth . . .

Edith's VOICE UNDER runs concurrently with this phantom sound.

> EDITH
> Love is only the absence of hate.

CAMERA MOVES UP to her FACE as she says the preceding line while VOICE of GUARDIAN OVER continues.

> VOICE OF GUARDIAN
> *(echo filter)*
> . . . and clear as truth. And the sun will
> burn on it . . .

as CAMERA MOVES DOWN OVER CAPE to the sunburst scatter pin.

68 CLOSE ON SPOCK

as his eyes widen with recognition of the focus point in this time era. And as we HOLD on Spock, he MOVES TOWARD HER in FRAME and we see revealed a placard that was obscured before, while the VOICE of the GUARDIAN ends its phantom reminder.

> VOICE OF GUARDIAN
> *(echo filter)*
> . . . and there is the key.

(CONTINUED)

68 CONTINUED:

And we HOLD on the edge of the crowd with SPOCK prominent and the placard whose message is simply:

Hear SISTER EDITH KEELER Speak.

SLOW FADE TO

SOFT-FOCUS IRIS ON WORD "KEELER"
and
FADE OUT.

END ACT TWO

ACT THREE

FADE IN:

69 *EXT. NEW YORK STREET—DAY*

MED. SHOT on Sister Edith Keeler, selecting a few meager fruits and vegetables from a pushcart at the curb on the busy street we saw in Scene 65, but shot from a DIFFERENT ANGLE. CAMERA ANGLE WIDENS to INCLUDE Spock and Kirk PROMINENT IN F.G., watching her from the security of an apartment entrance.

> KIRK
> You're certain?

> SPOCK
> The cloak was blue as the sky of Old
> Earth, fastened by a sunburst pin, and
> they said "there was the *key.*" Her
> name is *Kee*-ler.

> KIRK
> An amazing coincidence.

> SPOCK
> There are no coincidences in time. The
> Guardian said Beckwith would be
> drawn to the focal point. As were we.
> It was inevitable.

Edith moves away, waving gaily to the push-cart vendor who calls something bright and friendly after her. She moves down the sidewalk as CAMERA MOVES WITH HER even though HOLDING the *Enterprise* men in f.g. as their heads move to follow her passage. She stops to talk to two women, who seem bent under a burden of sorrow.

> (MORE)

(CONTINUED)

They straighten and smile as she leaves them. She pauses to talk to a child sitting on the curb, playing with a cat. The child laughs. The CONVERSATION BETWEEN Kirk and Spock goes on OVER this.

> KIRK
>
> She seems such a pleasant woman.

> SPOCK
>
> She is a catalyst. Things will happen to time because of her.

> KIRK
>
> I wonder what things . . . ?

> SPOCK
>
> Or what things will *not* happen. *That* is not our concern. We have to stay with her. Beckwith will find her, and so, logically, *we* will find Beckwith.

70 *EXT. TENEMENT—ANOTHER STREET—DAY*

as Edith ENTERS FRAME and climbs the worn and sooty stoop and enters the building. CAMERA PULLS BACK to show Kirk and Spock standing beside a closed-up store with GONE OUT OF BUSINESS soap-written on the front window.

> SPOCK
>
> This is where she came last night. She is in cubicle number eighteen.

> KIRK
> Apartment.

> SPOCK
> *(shrugs)*
> Nomenclature.

(CONTINUED)

70 CONTINUED:

> KIRK
>
> I'd probably better get an apartment here, if I can, if there's a vacancy.

> SPOCK
>
> Will I be able to live here? These people seem to have all sorts of irrational categories for who can live where. Ghettos? Is that right?

> KIRK
>
> Sometimes.
> *(1/2 beat)*
> Yes, you can live here, too, but you'd better keep out of sight as much as possible. Find some place where you can keep an eye on her apartment without being seen, and you can work on the tricorder.

> SPOCK
> *(without amusement)*
> I am amused at your perception of what I must do to return the tricorder to a functional condition, Captain. "Work" is not the word I would have chosen.
> *(beat)*
> Perhaps "reinvent" might suffice.

> KIRK
> *(musing)*
> We've been here—what is it—eight, nine days?

> SPOCK
> Nine of these 24-hour Earth days.

(CONTINUED)

KIRK

How far ahead of Beckwith's arrival do
you think the Vortex set us down?

SPOCK

I could only conjecture.

KIRK

A couple of weeks? A month? Not a
year! You don't think it could be a year,
do you?

SPOCK

I could only conjecture.

KIRK
(exasperated)
Yes, Spock, I *understand.* You can only
conjecture. I urge you to *do so*.

SPOCK

He could have already come through.

KIRK

Are you serious? Then why haven't we
seen him, or felt him, or —

SPOCK

We won't know, if I extrapolate
correctly, until he is drawn to the
Keeler woman.

KIRK

Will it take him as long to reach her as
it took us?

SPOCK
(shrugs)
There is no way of knowing.

(CONTINUED)

70 CONTINUED:—3

> KIRK
>
> It's incredible to think of Beckwith
> coming through hundreds of years, in a
> straight line to her, today, tomorrow,
> the day after tomorrow ...

> SPOCK
>
> We traveled the same line ...

We SEE the special look Spock is giving his Captain, whose eyes are still on that building; a look that seems perplexed and a shade concerned, as he adds:

> SPOCK
>
> *(murmurs)*
>
> ...straight to her.

HOLD on SPOCK and KIRK each locked with secret thoughts as we

> DISSOLVE TO:

71 EXT. ROOFTOP—NIGHT—HIGH ANGLE—DESCENDING BOOM SHOT

TO Kirk and Spock, flat-out on their stomachs on the tenement roof, staring across an airshaft to a lit window, apartment eighteen. From time to time, Edith can be seen, moving back and forth. She SINGS a popular song of the period which can be HEARD UNDER. Kirk has just crawled in.

> KIRK
>
> Okay, go get some sleep. I'll spell you.

> SPOCK
>
> Is there anything to eat?

> (CONTINUED)

                              KIRK
          I bought nine pounds of cabbage and
          asparagus. The grocer is beginning to
          look at me.

                              SPOCK
          It is the only Earth food I can keep
          down. No hydroponics, no synthetics,
          my system needs *youbash* and *keva* ...

                              KIRK
          I can imagine how inconspicuous
          you'd be with purple *keva* juice
          running down your Chinese face. Stick
          with the asparagus.

                              SPOCK
          She is keeping a regular schedule.

                              KIRK
                            (musing)
          Mmmm. She's quite lovely, isn't she, Mr.
          Spock?

There's that EXPRESSION of concern again. SPOCK
in b.g. of FRAME with KIRK in f.g. watching that lit
window.

                              SPOCK
          This is not an easy pursuit to begin
          with, Captain. Complications could
          make it impossible.

                              KIRK
                       *(as if hearing him
                        for the first time)*
                            What?

                                              (CONTINUED)

71 *CONTINUED:—2*

> SPOCK
>
> I have a theory, Captain, that the easiest
> world for a spaceman to "go native"
> on—is his own world.

> KIRK
>
> Don't be ridiculous. The stakes are too
> high here.

> SPOCK
> *(with meaning)*
> That was precisely my point.

He crawls away in the dark as Kirk looks after him for SEVERAL MEANINGFUL BEATS and then slowly looks back toward the brightness of the window, and Edith silhouetted, with her SONG on the ascendant. HOLD on Kirk, ambivalent.

> DISSOLVE TO:

72 *INT. TENEMENT—SHOT UP STAIRWELL—DAY*

as Edith comes down TOWARD CAMERA brightly. There is joy in her movement, enthusiasm and spring in her step. A man could delight in this female, so very womanly and yet so self-possessed in her maturity. A VOICE O.S. halts her.

> KIRK'S VOICE O.S.
> Hello.

She is CLOSE TO CAMERA now and as she pauses with her hand on the banister, she looks back up the way she came and we see Kirk leaning over the railing on the floor above. HOLD Edith CLOSE IN F.G. to Kirk in b.g. above her.

> EDITH
> Hello.

> (CONTINUED)

KIRK
(nervous beat)
I wanted to say hello.

EDITH
(amused)
And you do it very well. Would you like
to try it again? Hello.

KIRK
(grins widely)
I guess it was a pretty lame way to get
to meet you.

EDITH
On the contrary. It worked marvelously
well. I'm Edith Keeler.

Kirk comes around the newel post, down the stairs
to her as CAMERA FOLLOWS holding her in f.g.

KIRK
I'm Jim Kirk. I just moved in. I saw you
a couple of times.

EDITH
You have a very pleasant accent. Iowa?

KIRK
Uh, Iowa. Yes, that's very good, most
people don't catch it.

EDITH
I have a good ear. From singing in
church choir. You get to know pitch.

Now they stand beside each other.

(CONTINUED)

72 CONTINUED:—2

> KIRK
> *(at a loss now)*
> Well . . .

> EDITH
> You're quite handsome.

> KIRK
> *(nonplussed)*
> Why, uh, thank you. And you're quite
> lovely.

> EDITH
> Now that all that is out of the way,
> would you like to take a walk with me?
> I'm going to pick up some stolen
> merchandise.

Kirk is astonished. His expression tells us so. She notes his consternation.

73 2-SHOT—KIRK & EDITH

> EDITH (CONT'D.)
> *(laughs)*
> Don't be bothered. I'm not a thief.
> Some young boys I know, well, they
> made a mistake. I talked to Lt. Gleeson
> at the precinct, and he said if the goods
> were returned—

> KIRK
> *(pleasured)*
> You do quite a lot of that sort of good
> work, don't you?

> EDITH
> I try to keep busy.

> (CONTINUED)

73 CONTINUED:

KIRK

There seems to be enough misery to
keep a *platoon* busy.
(beat)
You seem sturdy, but it must wear you
down.

EDITH
(confides)
There *is* a Depression on; the secret is
not getting "depressed."
(brightly)
Shall we walk now?

KIRK
Love to.

74 REVERSE ANGLE

ON THEM as they move together toward the vestibule
door that will open onto the street. They carry the
FOREGOING DIALOGUE with them as they leave the
tenement. As they go out the door, CAMERA PANS
SWIFTLY RIGHT to a mirror hanging on the wall,
which gives us an ANGLED VIEW UP the stairwell.
Spock is there, watching, troubled.

CUT TO:

75 LIMBO SHOT—EDITH & KIRK

against darkness, walking, apparently talking to one
another, Edith laughing lightly at one point, as
LIGHTS FLICKER BEHIND THEM then vanish, as
STROBE LINES shoot past, giving us a sense of space
and time elapsing. And slowly they reach toward one
another without looking, and hold hands, still
walking as we

DISSOLVE THRU TO:

76 *INT. EDITH'S APARTMENT—KIRK & EDITH—NIGHT*

a plain little room. The INTERIOR of WHAT WE SAW EXT. IN Scene 71 across the airshaft. (if feasible, suggest use apartment in Sc. 71, redecorated and shot in reverse to save cost of another set-up.) Feminine touches, but nothing very elegant. She lives in the same simplicity of decency which she preaches. A little square table covered with oilcloth (*not* a tablecloth) is in the center of the room and Edith comes from kitchen to the table set for two, carrying a hot dish of something. We HEAR a KNOCK on the outside door.

> EDITH
> It's open, Jim.

Kirk comes in, a little wearily, and assays the room. He is dressed in work clothes. He slumps into a chair, pulls off a shoe.

> EDITH
> What's the matter?

> KIRK
> *(rubs foot)*
> Ah, I bought a cheap pair of shoes.
> They're too tight.

She goes into the kitchen and putters there as we HEAR the SOUNDS of her activity. She speaks to him from there, O.S.

> EDITH'S VOICE O.S.
> How is it going on the job?

> KIRK
> Drearily. But at least I'm learning how
> to operate a steam shovel.
> (MORE)

(CONTINUED)

76 *CONTINUED:*

> *(ironic)*
> Should be of immense help in my
> chosen profession.

She pops her head out, a dish towel in her hand.

> EDITH
> There are times when you say things
> that don't mean what you said, know
> what I mean?

Kirk knows. We can see in his face his amazement and possibly his concern. She is watching him. He motions her toward him. She comes, carrying the dish towel, and he pulls her down into his lap as CAMERA CLOSES ON THEM.

> KIRK
> Why do you say that?

> EDITH
> Sometimes you seem, well, disoriented,
> Jim, like a man fresh from the country.

> KIRK
> Iowa?

> EDITH
> *(dead serious)*
> Further away than that.

> KIRK
> "When night proceeds to fall, all men
> become strangers ... "

> EDITH
> It's true. Who said it, I don't recognize it.

(CONTINUED)

76 *CONTINUED:—2*

KIRK

Wellman 9. An obscure poet. Someday
people will call his work the most
beautiful ever known in the galaxy.

EDITH

That's a lot of territory.

KIRK

There's a lot of territory *out* there.

EDITH

Now you sound like what I tell my
people on the street corners.

KIRK

What you say is true.
(beat)
Ouch, it's my own fault.

EDITH

We could always get them stretched.

Kirk's face goes through changes. She has said
something very important, but we don't know what.
He pulls her close, buries his head in her bosom, and
she strokes his hair as we

LAP-DISSOLVE TO:

77 *KIRK & SPOCK—LIMBO SHOT*

against blackness. Why? Because this conversation is
as much inside their natures as out in the world. And
played in CLOSE 2-SHOT without recourse to sets or
distractions, it will illuminate their characters more
cleanly.

SPOCK

You are my Captain. It is not proper
that I express such opinions.

(CONTINUED)

KIRK
If I'm wrong I want to know.

SPOCK
That is my opinion.

KIRK
Why? It's necessary to be near her . . .
we can't possibly know the precise
moment Beckwith will find her.

SPOCK
You argue illogically, Captain. I do not
think Beckwith is what keeps you so
near this woman.

KIRK
You're wrong.

SPOCK
I do not think so, Captain.

KIRK
(rather annoyed)
Since when did you become a telepath?

SPOCK
Empathy is not telepathy. I can feel it
coming off you in waves . . . you are
getting involved.

KIRK
I just want to find Beckwith.

SPOCK
Captain, fooling me is simple. Just give
me the order, I will change my opinion.

(CONTINUED)

77 *CONTINUED:—2*

> KIRK
> *(a bit sadly)*
> But ... we talk, Mr. Spock. We sit and
> we talk about ... everything.

> SPOCK
> She is a fine person.

> KIRK
> Listen: I've been on the move since I
> was old enough to ship on as wiper in
> one of the old chemical-fuel rockets.
> It's been time, Mr. Spock; a lot of time.

> SPOCK
> *(understandingly)*
> And the women you have known have
> been casual liaisons, in the port cities
> and the pleasure planets. It is that way
> for every spacer, Captain.
> *(beat)*
> I am a Vulcan, not a neuter. I understand
> very well.

> KIRK
> But this is something else, Spock! Total
> communication. I've never known
> anything like this with *any*one!
> *(beat)*
> She *knows,* Spock. She understands—
> everything!

> SPOCK
> It can be a foolish thing, Captain. We
> are only phantoms here, things lost
> (MORE)

(CONTINUED)

> from a future that may not even exist
> again. We have not even been born yet.
> Lost things set down on an alien shore,
> Captain.

>   KIRK
> Why? Why does it have to end here—?

>   SPOCK
> You can not change the past without
> changing the future . . .

They are speaking faster now, almost atop one another's
words.

>   KIRK
> Why can't I bring her back with me?
> She isn't important here, the way she
> feels, the goodness, the things she
> believes for the world, they aren't
> ready for it—

>   SPOCK
>   *(suddenly)*
> She is going to die!

There is a shocked moment of silence.

>   SPOCK (CONT'D.)
>   *(softer)*
> I was able to repair the tricorder. Not
> well, but sufficiently to learn she will die.

>   KIRK
>   *(in shock)*
> No . . .

(CONTINUED)

77 CONTINUED:—4

SPOCK

Captain, she *has* to die.
(continues, softer)
The Guardian told us. We had
insufficient codification to interpret
the metaphors. But I have been
resonating the words again in my
mind.

KIRK

No.

SPOCK

(recites)
"He will seek that which must die, and
give it life. Stop him."

KIRK

I don't believe that . . . they didn't mean
that at all. How could her death alter
the course of history?

SPOCK

In a million ways. If she lived, she
might give birth to a child who would
become a dictator . . .

KIRK

That's all extrapolation, none of it real.
You're guessing . . .

SPOCK

. . . in a few years this planet will have a
war, a great war. What if her philosophy
spread, and it kept America out of the
war for a mere two years longer . . . and
in that time Germany perfected its

(MORE)

(CONTINUED)

atomic weapons? The outcome of the
war would be reversed.

KIRK

That's insanity.

SPOCK

History, Captain. There are spools of
records on the *Enterprise.* I have
played them all . . . . What I suggest is
just one logical extrapolation.
(beat)
She has to die; history and time
demand it.

KIRK

I don't want to think about it. Leave me
alone.

SPOCK

I will leave you alone, Captain—
(beat)
but time will not.

Their IMAGES BEGIN TO FADE into the blackness, like
a light being turned slowly down, dimmer and
dimmer, till all we see is the tormented face of Jim
Kirk, in the mid-f.g.

FRAME TO BLACK.

78 *EXT. NEW YORK STREET—NIGHT*

BLACK FRAME becomes the back of Kirk, as he walks
AWAY FROM CAMERA hand-in-hand with Edith
Keeler. Street dressed for a Saturday night, people out
on the sidewalk, cars passing, women leaning out of
upstairs windows calling their kids to come in, men
(MORE)

(CONTINUED)

78 *CONTINUED:*

sitting on stoops talking, the activity, the life of the city, consistent with the image of the times. CAMERA GOES WITH THEM. As they pass a series of shops, we begin to HEAR MUSIC from one of them, a jaunty tune of the times, played on a raggy piano, being sung by one of those girls who sang from sheet-music in the Thirties. She is singing "Please."

> *Please, lend your little ear to my pleas.*
> *Lend a ray of cheer to my pleas.*
> *Tell me that you love me, too.*
> *Please let me hold you tight in my arms.*
> *I could find delight in your charms.*
> *Ev'ry night my whole life through.* •

As they pass the down-below-street-level music shop, Edith stops, turns and cocks her head to one side. CAMERA IN CLOSE. She smiles, rocks to the music. Kirk grins.

> EDITH
> Let's go down for a minute, Jim. We
> have time before I speak, and I love
> this song.

79 2- SHOT—KIRK & EDITH

CAMERA PULLS BACK SLIGHTLY as Kirk nods agreement. Edith starts down the wrought iron stairs to the shop as Jim walks behind her. CAMERA BACK to give us FULL SHOT now. Edith slips. She starts to fall, Jim Kirk reaches out to catch her as CAMERA ZOOMS IN on his hand. Just before he could catch her arm, his hand closes, spastically.

•Copyright © 1932 by Famous Music Corp.

80 FULL SHOT—ANOTHER ANGLE

as she falls down the stairs. CAMERA ZOOMS IN on Kirk's face. He let her fall. He remembered what he was there for. CAMERA ZOOMS BACK out and for a beat we think Edith may have died. But we see she is merely lying there bruised. CAMERA ZOOMS IN AGAIN on *her* face, as she looks at Jim with his clenched hand still extended. She seems to know he let her fall, and a confused hurt expression crosses her face. CAMERA OUT AGAIN and Kirk rushes down to her, helps her up.

> KIRK
> *(means it)*
> Are you all right?

> EDITH
> *(slowly, mixed up)*
> Yes . . . I'm all right . . . Jim . . .

CAMERA HOLDS on their faces as Kirk turns away slightly and we see the torment in his expression . . . and the confusion on Edith's face.

DISSOLVE TO:

81 EXT. NEW YORK STREET—SAME SCENE AS 47— DAY

the street with the CCC Camp shop and the bread line shop, now minus the lamppost Kirk vaporized with the phaser. But there is nothing happening in front of the two shops. The cars and trucks still roll, but very few people on the sidewalks. Kirk and Spock in XTREME F.G. MOVE INTO FRAME from opposite sides, looking at each other, then turn to stare at the street opposite. They form the left and right sides of the FRAME with the sliver of scene between them.

(CONTINUED)

81 CONTINUED:

> SPOCK
> My computations could be wrong.

> KIRK
> Let's hope not.

> SPOCK
> Where is Miss Keeler?

> KIRK
> At the Free Milk Kitchen. She'll be out
> of the way for at least two hours.

As they stand there waiting, a large stake-bed TRUCK
filled with barrels thunders past. We NOTE the truck
in this SHOT.

> KIRK (CONT'D.)
> Edith told me that's the bootleg beer
> wagon.

> SPOCK
> "Bootleg?"

> KIRK
> They're in something called "The Great
> Depression." They're also undergoing
> something called "The Great
> Prohibition."

> SPOCK
> Trucks like that are prohibited?

> KIRK
> Sometimes, Mr. Spock, your tendency
> to take things literally is a pain in the
> fundament.

(CONTINUED)

SPOCK
But you said . . .

KIRK
No, not the truck, what it's carrying,
what's *in* those barrels. Beer. An
alcoholic beverage. Liquor is
prohibited.

SPOCK
Ah yes, I remember the spools
mentioning this "great experi—"
(suddenly)
There!

They BACK OUT OF FRAME so we have a FULL SHOT
of the street opposite, and CAMERA MOVES IN so we
see the brick wall and a sudden shimmering (NOT
THE TRANSPORTER MATERIALIZATION EFFECT—
ANOTHER) as Beckwith abruptly becomes sub-
stantial, standing there looking around, trying to get
oriented, still wearing his *Enterprise* garb. Then Kirk
and Spock dash INTO FRAME from XTREME CLOSEUP
so the FRAME IS BLACK for a beat as they race away
from us.

82 *REVERSE ANGLE—PAST BECKWITH—HIS POV*

as he looks across the street and sees Spock and
Kirk coming for him. He recognizes them instantly
and turns first one way, then another, to run—but
he doesn't know which way. Spock gets across the
street, but as Kirk moves to follow, just a beat
behind him, another huge bootleg beer truck in the
caravan rumbles down the street, and Kirk is cut
off. Spock reaches Beckwith, who falls back against
the brick wall, and raises a booted foot. He
(MORE)

82 *CONTINUED:*

catches Spock in the stomach with the foot, and hurls him back. Then Beckwith rushes OUT OF FRAME RIGHT as the truck passes and Kirk reaches Spock. He helps him up. CAMERA ANGLE NARROWER now.

> KIRK
> Which way?

> SPOCK
> Toward the Milk Kitchen ...

They tense, and race off down the street as we

DISSOLVE TO:

83 *INT. TENEMENT—SAME AS 74—DAY*

on the vestibule door, as it opens, and Kirk brings Edith Keeler in behind him. He is rushing her, holding her by the arm.

> EDITH
> Jim ... what *is* this?

> KIRK
> You shouldn't be out there alone.

She pulls away, stands her ground. She's wearing the cape with the sunburst, but a different dress of the period.

> EDITH
> What in the world are you *talking*
> about? You come dashing into the Milk
> Kitchen and practically *abscond* with
> me! Now, Jim, I've got responsi—

(CONTINUED)

Kirk moves to her, takes her lovely face in his hands, and if we are ever to see the inner man, James Kirk, this is the moment. Gathered here in his hands is everything that means anything to him. Kirk is deeply in love.

KIRK

Edith, do you trust me?

EDITH

Jim . . . I . . .

KIRK

No, please, *do you trust me?*

EDITH

(looks down demurely)

I trust you . . . and I love you, Jim.

A stricture of pain/pleasure crosses his face. She does not see it. He tilts her face up and stares at her for a long moment, then kisses her. She clings to him. After a long beat they move apart a bit and CAMERA COMES CLOSER.

KIRK

Edith . . .

EDITH

Do you love me, Jim? It's the first time
for me, so I don't know.

KIRK

Very much. More than anyone I've ever
known. You've become very important
to me. You can't know how important . . .

EDITH

And you're afraid, Jim, what is it?

(CONTINUED)

83 CONTINUED:—2

KIRK

It's nothing, I just want you to be —

He can't finish. She stares at him, with wonder.

84 ANOTHER ANGLE —FEATURING STAIRWELL

as Mr. Spock appears. He is carrying a burlap parcel. It contains the phaser, but we don't know it. He stops on the stairs. Kirk looks at him, and draws away from Edith. She looks, sees only a Chinese laborer. Spock watches them with silent understanding, then moves down the stairs and past them. He goes out.

KIRK

You'd better go upstairs. Please trust me
...I know you want to go back to the
mission to work, but if you would ...
please, go upstairs, get some rest, an
hour of sleep ... please. I have to go out
for a while, but I'll be right back.

EDITH
(deeply troubled)

Jim, if it's something you've done ...
some trouble ...

KIRK

Nothing, Edith. I'll be right back. I
promise. Just stay in your room ...
and keep the door locked.

EDITH
Please tell me, Jim!

He moves to the front door, opens it, starts to go.

(CONTINUED)

EDITH (CONT'D.)
(softly)
I love you, James Kirk.

CAMERA ON KIRK as he pauses, without turning, hearing her words. Then his jaw muscles tighten, and he goes out the door. HOLD ON HER staring after him.

85 EXT. STREET—ANGLE ON ALLEY—DAY

as Kirk passes, sees Spock waiting, the burlap wrapped package still in his arms. He moves into the alley as CAMERA GOES WITH him. Spock is looking at him with a silent condemnation.

KIRK
Mr. Spock . . . you can't know how it is with her . . .

He stops. A silent bit of character flow. He knows how Spock feels about all this. But he can't defend himself.

SPOCK
Are they still alive in the Transporter Chamber, Captain?

KIRK
You don't understand. You're not—

SPOCK
I am not *what*, Captain? A human, subject to the pains and pleasures of love? No, that is true. I am merely *part* human; and I am merely concerned with saving the lives of the ones who trusted us to save them.

(CONTINUED)

85 CONTINUED:

> KIRK
>
> I can't let her die! I can't.

> SPOCK
>
> Then Beckwith wins. Time is changed.

Spock starts past him. Kirk grabs his arm. The package slips out of Spock's grasp, falls, and the phaser is revealed.

> KIRK
>
> You can't use that on Beckwith. We have to bring him back ali—

He stops, his eyes widen.

> KIRK (CONT'D.)
> *(almost a whisper)*
> It wasn't *for* Beckwith, was it, Mr. Spock?

Spock stares at him. They stand there across a sudden abyss of conflicting interests. Spock says nothing. He gathers up the phaser, rewraps it and leaves the alley. CAMERA HOLDS on Kirk's expression of growing helplessness. He turns away abruptly as we

> SMASH-CUT TO:

86 BACK STREET—DEAD NIGHT—ESTABLISHING

as Mr. Spock slips through shadows. There is a rustle of cloth behind him. He carries the phaser now. He turns suddenly, and Beckwith is there. The scuffle is only a moment in duration, with the two

> (MORE)

> (CONTINUED)

of them wrestling among wooden crates and cans of refuse. Spock falls, Beckwith grabs the phaser and dashes off with it. Spock follows as CAMERA IN ARRIFLEX GOES WITH. Beckwith snaps off a shot, and Spock dives sideways to escape the lethal blast.

87 *ON SPOCK*

as he looks up from sidewalk and HEARS the SOUND of FOOTSTEPS RUNNING AWAY in the darkness. HOLD on his fixed expression which says time is growing deathly, inescapably short.

FADE OUT.

END ACT THREE

ACT FOUR

FADE IN:

EXT. NEW YORK STREET—EVENING—ESTABLISHING

CLOSE ON a hand-lettered placard that reads:

I FOUGHT AT VERDUN

as CAMERA PULLS BACK we see the sign is hung around the neck of a legless cripple, hunkered down on his stumps on a wooden push-board that rolls on roller skate wheels. He has a tray of apples and pencils beside him. His cap is pulled down far over his eyes, and the beard stubble looks as though it nests a troupe of nits. A VOICE O.S. speaks to him just as a PAIR OF LEGS MOVE INTO FRAME. All we see are the legs.

KIRK'S VOICE O.S.
Are you Trooper?

TROOPER looks up with rheumy eyes. In that face is the true meaning of the worst social era America ever faced. He is a man destroyed. The light has gone out in the eyes, the mouth speaks a silent sadness. Disillusioned. He was the drummer boy who went to war, and came back to find no one needed him. He nods up at the unseen person.

TROOPER
Good apples, fellah. Pencils? I fought at
Verdun.

KIRK'S VOICE O.S.
Someone told me to come see you.

TROOPER
(shakes his head as if to clear it)
I just sell apples and pencils.
(CONTINUED)

KIRK'S VOICE O.S.

Perhaps it's time for you to diversify
your wares.

TROOPER

Who are you?

Kirk hunkers down next to him on the filthy sidewalk.
And we see Kirk fully for the first time in this scene.
Trooper looks nervous about it.

KIRK

I'm just a Bo who needs some easy
information.

TROOPER

I don't know much 'cept there's nine
guys on this block sellin' apples. Try
them.

KIRK

There's two bucks in it for a few words.

TROOPER

I din't do nothin'. I been right here
sellin'—

KIRK

I'm not *after* you, mister, I want you to
find out something for me ... I was told
you know everything that goes on in
this neighborhood. Now, you want to
make a couple of bucks?

TROOPER
(warily)

How do I know you ain't crooked as a
hairpin?

(CONTINUED)

88 CONTINUED:—2

                    KIRK
            Take a two-dollar chance.

Trooper ponders a moment, licks his lips, nervously
nods.

                    KIRK
        A man wearing peculiar clothes.

                   TROOPER
            What kind of clothes?

Kirk looks around (without being melodramatic) and
pulls a parcel toward them. He opens it enough to
show Trooper the *Enterprise* comet insignia, the
velour material, the bright color, so stark beside
Trooper's own drab garb.

                    KIRK
        He'd be carrying a . . . weapon.

                   TROOPER
            What'dya want him for?

                    KIRK
            For about two bucks.

                   TROOPER
                Let's see it.

Kirk fishes out two crumpled dollar bills. Trooper
touches them with an outstretched hand. But doesn't
take them.

                   TROOPER
        I s'pose I gotta find out before you give
        it to me.

Kirk gives him the two crumpled balls of money.
Trooper is astonished. It is the first real life we've
seen in his face.

                              (CONTINUED)

                              KIRK
              I think I can trust a man who fought at
              Verdun.

There is disbelief and a kind of grandeur in Trooper's face as he is confronted with dignity, trust and honesty. He nods firmly as Kirk rises, the legs MOVE OUT OF FRAME and Trooper watches him go. Then, determined, he gathers his wares and, using two padded blocks of wood with hand-grips, he propels himself down the sidewalk on the roller skate platform as we

                                              DISSOLVE TO:

89 INT. EDITH'S APARTMENT—KIRK & EDITH—NIGHT

That plain little room. They are eating cake and having coffee, at that same little square table covered with oilcloth. There is MUSIC OF THE PERIOD UNDER.

                              EDITH
                          Too rich?

                              KIRK
                        (preoccupied)
                          Pardon?

                              EDITH
              The cake. Did I make it too sweet?

                              KIRK
              No, it's delicious. I've never tasted
              anything like it before.

                              EDITH
                        (surprised)
              You've never tasted angel food cake
              before?
                          (beat)
                          Jim . . . ?

                                              (CONTINUED)

89 CONTINUED:

> KIRK
> *(still distracted)*
> Uh-huh . . . ?

> EDITH
> I'd like to ask you a great many
> questions. But I'm afraid you might
> give me answers.

Kirk lays down his fork, gets up and walks to the window. He stares out at the night. She follows him in the shadowy room, stands behind him, barely touching.

> EDITH
> A skyful of stars.

> KIRK
> *(softly)*
> You'll never know how many.

> EDITH
> Are you going away, Jim?

> KIRK
> Perhaps. I don't want to.

> EDITH
> It's that Chinese fellow, isn't it?

> KIRK
> In a way. I know him. And he knows me.

Edith turns him to her. She puts her arms around him, lays her head against his chest.

> EDITH
> All my life I've belonged to other
> people. I know things will be cleaner,
> happier, I try to tell them, so they'll
> wait, so they'll hope. But now I don't
> belong to anyone. And I'm losing my
> own hope . . . Jim . . .

(CONTINUED)

He holds her away for a moment, speaks earnestly.

KIRK

You're right. There are a million
tomorrows. The one you believe in is
the best one. I know.

EDITH

How do you know, Jim?

KIRK

(helplessly)
Because I love you . . . and I know.

A KNOCK on the DOOR. They stand a moment.
Another KNOCK. Edith looks at Kirk, he nods for her
to open it. She goes to the door. It is Spock. She steps
aside. He doesn't come in, just stares at Kirk. Kirk
nods and walks past Edith. He turns for a beat to look
at her, then follows Mr. Spock out. The door closes
and we HOLD on EDITH.

90 *INT. TENEMENT—HALLWAY—SPOCK & KIRK*

CLOSE 2-SHOT in the dim hallway, one bulb glowing
far down the passage.

SPOCK

The little man without legs was here.

KIRK

Is it Beckwith time?

SPOCK

He thinks so. Good chance.

KIRK

Where is he?

SPOCK

I have the address.

(CONTINUED)

90 *CONTINUED:*

Kirk nods, and they go. Down the corridor as we

DISSOLVE TO:

91 *EXT. NEW YORK STREET—ANGLE ON ALLEY MOUTH*

REDRESS OF ALLEY SCENE 86. A group of SHADOWY
MEN wait in the corners and behind crates. Trooper
is there, as Kirk and Spock come upon the group. As
they arrive, the burly men in the shadows turn to
look and we catch their faces. The dregs. The gutter
men. The outcasts. The strongarm types one sees on
any skid row. We can almost smell the stench of sour
rye and sweat. (Redressed extras from previous
crowd scenes can be used here as the men will be
seen in shadow only.)

> TROOPER
> *(nods his head)*
> I think the guy you're lookin' for, the
> guy with them hoity-toity clothes like
> you showed me . . . we saw him duck
> back in there somewhere.

> KIRK
> Has he got the pha— the weapon?

> TROOPER
> If he has, he ain't usin' it.

> SPOCK
> *(softly, to Kirk)*
> We can't let him kill anyone—the time
> flow—

Kirk nods understanding. He motions the street thugs
back. They vanish, leaving Kirk, Spock, and Trooper
alone. Kirk fishes a dollar bill out of his vest pocket,
hands it down to the cripple.

(CONTINUED)

TROOPER
Hey, you din't haveta do that, two
bucks was enough.

KIRK
Thanks, Trooper. You take a powder.
He's ours, now.

92 ANOTHER ANGLE—FULL SHOT

as they smile briefly at each other. Then Trooper fades
away into the dark. Kirk and Spock start down
opposite sides of the alley, holding close to the walls,
half in crouch, moving stealthily.

93 WITH KIRK—HAND-HELD

CLOSE BEHIND HIM as the alley tilts and weaves in
the FRAME. Across the alley, past Kirk, we can see
Spock moving like a mountain cat, smooth as oil,
silent. Suddenly, a garbage can comes clanging with
NIGHT-SHATTERING IMPACT down on Spock, who is
sideswiped by the can, and falls beneath it. ARRIFLEX
CAREEN-PANS UP-ANGLE to the low rooftop, and
Beckwith framed against the night sky, the phaser
leveled at Kirk. Spock is struggling with the garbage
can as Kirk in f.g. looks up, sees Beckwith and realizes
he is pinned against the wall and cannot escape.
MAKE THIS DANGEROUS!

94 ANGLE FROM BECKWITH

as he fires. A blur of movement from the alley mouth
and Trooper is there, hurtling toward Kirk on his little
cart. He hits Kirk dead-center and the *Enterprise*
Captain is flung sidewise as the phaser blast lances
out. Trooper is hit, and with a SHARP, SHORT SCREAM
THAT CUTS OFF IN MID-NOTE he is gone.

95 *WITH SPOCK—HAND-HELD*

as he springs to his feet, grabs the garbage can, and with incredible strength hurls it up at Beckwith.

The can strikes Beckwith and he falls, dropping the phaser into the alley where it lands near Kirk with a rainbow of blast-lines. Kirk grabs it. Beckwith clambers to his feet and vanishes over the rooftops. Spock stands a beat, watching, then goes to Kirk, who is rising. They look down at the power-blasted spot where Trooper was vaporized. The bricks are cleft in half, the cement is sundered, and the cripple is gone. All that remains is one of the hand-pedaling devices with its raggedy grip.

> SPOCK
> Any death in this era that alters the
> sum of intelligence . . . alters time
> permanently.

> KIRK
> If he mattered in the time-flow.

They stand long in silence.

> SPOCK
> Why did he do that for you?

> KIRK
> Because I gave him two dollars.
> *(beat)*
> Mr. Spock, you know history: where is
> Verdun?

Spock does not answer. They stand in silence; a life has been taken. They stare down at the hand-grip left by Trooper and CAMERA RISES UP AWAY FROM THEM in the alley as we

DISSOLVE TO:

96 EXT. NEW YORK STREET—SAME AS 65—DAY

Edith Keeler in her blue-as-the-sky cape with its sunburst, on her little dais, talking to a tiny crowd of half a dozen men and women.

> EDITH
>
> There are great times on the way. Days of gold and nights cool and sweet-smelling. This isn't the only happiness, this world turning under us. Look up tonight, see them all out there ... see them burning, smiling ...

CAMERA PANS RIGHT to a doorway where Kirk and Spock are standing beside one another, watching Edith from concealment. CAMERA CLOSE ON THEM, the street scene in b.g. with EDITH'S VOICE UNDER.

> SPOCK
>
> She speaks as though you've talked to her.

> KIRK
>
> *(a little dead)*
>
> She doesn't know who we are.

> SPOCK
>
> Her ideas are years ahead of their time.

> KIRK
>
> Yes.

> SPOCK
>
> My race has a word for her kind of person: *liira:* open.

> KIRK
>
> Yes. That, too.

(CONTINUED)

96 CONTINUED:

SPOCK

Captain . . .

Edith finishes, the crowd leaves at once, and Kirk does not even wait for Spock to complete his sentence. He steps out where she can see him.

97 SEQUENCE—SELECT BEST ANGLES

thru (NOTE: this sequence is the heart of the climax. It is
100 *imperative* that the order of action, and the angles on closeups, be tight and specific. No camerawork has been indicated here purposely, so the pace and layout of shots can be best developed by on-set choices.)

Spock moves away so Edith will not see him.

Edith comes to the curb with a smile, waving across to Kirk.

Kirk sees Beckwith emerging from a building. Beckwith does not see Kirk. The building is between Kirk and Spock where he has now moved.

A huge beer truck—as noted previously in Scene 81—lumbers around the corner and into the street as Edith steps off the curb. She doesn't see it. Kirk and Beckwith and Spock see the truck as it bears down on Edith.

101   ANOTHER SEQUENCE—SLOW-MOTION—NO SOUND

thru as though time—which is our primary subject here—
107 were being silently stretched to the point of unbearability.

Beckwith starts toward the woman.

(CONTINUED)

101   CONTINUED:

thru   Kirk's face twists in anguish as he starts toward
107   Beckwith to stop him from saving Edith's life. He
stops, his hand closes on empty air as it did when
she fell down the stairs. He cannot stop Beckwith!
He will sacrifice everything for her.

Spock sees what is happening. He moves toward
Beckwith.

The truck slips slowly, silently toward Edith.

Spock reaches Beckwith and grabs him in a body-lock
that immobilizes him.

Kirk's mouth opens to scream. His empty hand
reaches.

Edith laughs a word at Kirk.

108   *XTREME CLOSEUP KIRK.*

109   *XTREME CLOSEUP SPOCK.*

110   *XTREME CLOSEUP EDITH.*

⎰ All
⎱ In
   Slow-
   Motion

111   *XTREME CLOSEUP THE TRUCK.*

CUT TO:

112   *CLOSE ON KIRK—NORMAL SPEED*

and HOLD HOLD HOLD on *his* face as we HEAR the
SOUND of the TRUCK SCREECHING TO A HALT. As
Kirk's face crumbles, we know what has happened.

13 *ANOTHER CLOSE ON KIRK—IN LIMBO*

SPECIAL EFFECT as his face RECEDES FROM CAMERA
back and back and back as though it were falling into
a bottomless pit, until it is barely a speck of tortured
light against a blackness that becomes, in SPECIAL
EFFECT, a

RIPPLE-DISSOLVE THRU:

14 *ANGLE IN SPACE—THE* ENTERPRISE

as the speck of light that is Kirk's face becomes a
star, one of many in an infinity of stars with the
Enterprise against it. All of this INTERCUT in RIPPLE
LAP-DISSOLVE so we get the impression of something
happening to the warp and woof of space and time.
The face of Kirk, the *Enterprise,* the stars, all
OVERLAP as we

RIPPLE-DISSOLVE TO:

15 *EXT. PLATEAU OF THE GUARDIANS*

as Kirk in EXTREME CLOSEUP emerges from the Time
Vortex CAMERA PULLS BACK to FULL FRAME
showing us his emergence from the pillar of light.
Behind him comes Mr. Spock with Beckwith in a judo-
like hold. Both Kirk and Spock are in 1930s garb,
Beckwith still in his *Enterprise* uniform. The
Guardians are there, waiting. The Time Vortex
continues to make its distinctive SOUND, indicating
it has not turned off.

1ST GUARDIAN
Time has resumed its shape.

SPOCK
What of the death of the cripple?

1ST GUARDIAN
He was negligible.

(CONTINUED)

SPOCK

But he found Beckwith for us. He *must*
have counted.

1ST GUARDIAN

He counted.

(beat)

But not enough. Not in the eternal
flow, the greater river.

Kirk, through all this, stands there as if stunned by
the hammer. His face is dead. He cannot co-ordinate.

SPOCK

Everything is the same as before?

1ST GUARDIAN

Everything.

116   CLOSER ON SPOCK & BECKWITH

with the Time Vortex behind them, fairly close.
Beckwith abruptly twists out of the grip Spock has
on him and, without a moment's hesitation, flings
himself back into the Time Vortex. Mr. Spock gives
a strange HOWL of frustration—so uncharacteristic
of him—and makes a move to follow, but at that
instant the VORTEX BECOMES SILENT, DARK. Spock
whirls on the Guardians.

SPOCK

He went back! It was all for nothing!

1ST GUARDIAN

No.

SPOCK

But he's in there, Old Earth. 1930!

(CONTINUED)

116 CONTINUED:

> 1ST GUARDIAN
>
> The Vortex cannot be set for the same
> exact time twice. He has created a
> fracture and plunged into it.

> SPOCK
>
> Then where is he? Escaped?

> 1ST GUARDIAN
>
> Not this time. He wanted Forever. The
> Vortex has given him Forever. Like the
> Möbius strip that has no end, that
> curves back on itself eternally, he is
> locked in time.

> SPOCK
>
> Forever? He cannot escape?

> 1ST GUARDIAN
>
> His Forever will be in the heart of an
> exploding sun, a nova. He has named
> his own doom . . .

117 SPECIAL EFFECT—ON BECKWITH

as he materializes in the exploding, fiery heart of a
supernova. We see him appear, scream in incredible anguish
and then vanish . . . then reappear alive, scream as he dies
again . . . and then vanish once more . . . reappear . . . scream
. . . die . . . over and over and over as we

FADE TO BLACK
and
FADE OUT.

END ACT FOUR

EPILOGUE

FADE IN:

118 INT. KIRK'S CABIN—ESTABLISHING

as Kirk stares out at the stars through a port. (If there is no port in the cabin, dammit, *build one*! This is absolutely essential to this scene, and the tone of the climax!) He is now dressed in *Enterprise* uniform.

> SPOCK'S VOICE O.S.
> Co-ordinates from the bridge, Captain.

Kirk does not turn around. Spock moves INTO FRAME behind him.

> SPOCK
> Jim . . .

Kirk holds a beat, then slowly turns. The deadness in his eyes there, then a small change in expression tells us he is startled.

> KIRK
> Mr. Spock . . . that's the first time you've ever called me anything but Captain.

> SPOCK
> *(gently)*
> On my world the nights are very long.
> The sound of the silver birds against
> the sky is very sweet. My people know
> there is always time enough for
> everything. You could come with me
> for a rest. You would feel comfortable
> there.

> KIRK
> *(hopelessly)*
> All the time in the world . . .

(CONTINUED)

118 CONTINUED:

> SPOCK
> And filled with tomorrows.
> *(beat)*
> But can you tell me something I need
> to understand? Something that defies
> all logic I know?

Kirk looks at him desolately.

> SPOCK (CONT'D.)
> I would not intrude, but it . . . troubles
> me . . . I believe that is the phrase . . . it
> troubles me deeply.

Kirk makes a motion with his hand that signifies, "Go
ahead and ask."

> SPOCK (CONT'D.)
> You could not stop Beckwith, I
> understand that.
> *(beat)*
> But . . . Beckwith . . . amoral, evil, a killer.
> Selfish and capable of anything. Why—

> KIRK
> *(interrupts)*
> Why did he try to save her, at risk of
> his own life?

> SPOCK
> Yes.

Kirk is silent for several beats, then:

> KIRK
> We look at our race, this parade of men
> and women, and the unbelievable
> harm and cruelty they do.
> (MORE)

(CONTINUED)

118 CONTINUED:—2

>(beat)
>And we sigh, and we say, "Perhaps our time is past, let the sharks or the cockroaches take over."
>(beat)
>And then, without knowing why, without even thinking of it, the worst among us does the great thing, the noble deed, that spark of impossible human godliness.
>(beat)
>And we say, "Perhaps the human race is entitled to a little more sufferance. Let them keep trying to reach the dream."

SPOCK
(softly, understands)
Evil can come from Good, and Good from Evil.
>(beat)
>But the little man ...Trooper ...

KIRK
(a bitter smile)
He was negligible. He fought at Verdun, and he was negligible. And *she* ...

SPOCK
No, *she* was not negligible.

KIRK
(simply; groping for understanding)
But ... I loved her ...

SPOCK
No woman was ever loved as much, Jim. Because no woman was ever offered the universe for love.

(CONTINUED)

118   *CONTINUED:—3*

Kirk looks at him. There is understanding in his face. A sadness he will never ever lose, because his loss is so great. But through friendship, caring, Spock has shown him understanding. His smile is in no way happy, but it shows resignation. He nods at Spock, and Spock goes. We HOLD several BEATS on Kirk staring out at the star-flecked distance as the SOUND of FULL-AHEAD ALARMS RINGS through the *Enterprise* and the CAMERA MOVES SMOOTHLY IN PAST KIRK to FULL FRAME on the stars.

DISSOLVE TO:

EXT. SPACE—USS ENTERPRISE *(STOCK)*

119   as the ship speeds off into the darkness and we HOLD on the stars once more. The stars, like Kirk's love—eternal.

FADE TO BLACK:
and
FADE OUT.

THE END

APPENDIX

2nd Revised Final Draft 12/1/66

FADE IN:

1   *ESTABLISHING SHOT—INT. McCOY'S LAB—*
     ENTERPRISE

CLOSE ON ALIEN CREATURE. It is a small creature.
It is silver-blue, with a lot of hair, with bright, beady
little eyes, maybe even with antenna. Something like
a Yorkshire Terrier with a big furry head and a
scrawny hairless blue body. It looks alien, but not
outlandish. (Cast it to suit yourself.) The hands of
DOC McCOY are in the frame, taking a blood sample
of the little dingo. We HEAR the VOICE OF CAPTAIN
JAMES KIRK OVER:

> VOICE OF KIRK (OVER)
> Ship's log: star-date 3134.6. What began
> as a routine mapping expedition has
> turned into the darkest enigma of all
> our flights.

CAMERA PULLS BACK to show McCoy with MR.
SPOCK and two ENTERPRISE CREWMEMBERS (male
and female optional). The dingo is wired in to the
metabolic panel on the wall. They are all intent on
what's happening to it.

> McCoy
> It's growing younger. Little by little.
> Reversing the aging process.

The blood sample has been fed into whatever
instrument McCoy utilizes for this purpose. The
Crewmember hands it back.

> McCoy
> There's poison here. It wasn't present
> when we took this pup for specimen
> on Spahfohn. The radiation's doing it.

                                              CUT TO:

2   *INT.* ENTERPRISE *BRIDGE—CAPT KIRK—(MEASURE)*

CLOSE ON KIRK as CAMERA PULLS BACK to show us WHAT HE SEES in the view-screen. A strange silvery planet under a wan and dying red ember of a sun.

> VOICE OF KIRK (OVER)
> The magnetic radiation that has drawn us here to this desolate Rim of the Galaxy ... the radiation that has somehow set our chronometers to running backward ... is having a strange effect on all of us ...

There is an O.S. BLEEP from an intercom.

3   *INTERCUT—THE INTERCOM*

as it flashes for Kirk's attention.

4   *KIRK—MED. CLOSE*

as he flips the switch and the face of Spock appears on the intercom screen by his control chair.

> KIRK
> Yes, Mr. Spock?

> SPOCK
> Dr. McCoy has taken samples from each of the zoological specimens. They are growing younger.

> KIRK
> Conclusion?

> SPOCK
> So are we.

(CONTINUED)

4 CONTINUED:

Kirk pauses a beat in perplexity. Troubled, deeply troubled. Strange things are happening.

>KIRK
>
>What is it that can reverse machinery *and* human beings?

>SPOCK
>
>Was that rhetorical, Captain?

>KIRK
>
>Unless you have some facts for an answer.

>SPOCK
>
>Do you believe in magic, Captain? Alchemy? The power of the supernatural?

>KIRK
>
>No.

>SPOCK
>
>Then I have no answer. There aren't any in science, not for this. It's the radiation, of course, but more than that—

5 FULL SHOT—THE BRIDGE—TILT/ANGLE

as a HIGH KEENING WHINE erupts in the chamber, the very air is suffused with a crimson glow, the banks of equipment begin running wild, fire breaks out in a shower of sparks on one panel, the ship rocks and bucks and SOUND PHASES UP AND DOWN the sonic scale.

(CONTINUED)

5   CONTINUED:

>   SULU
>   (from controls)
>   Radiation intensity just jumped,
>   Captain! Bang, we've got overload!

>   KIRK
>   (sharply)
>   Mr. Sulu, lay-in that parking orbit! Let's
>   not get any deeper into this radiation ...

6   SERIES OF SHOTS—HAND-HELD & TILT/ANGLE

thru   MED. CLOSE on Kirk even as he delivers the preceding
9   line. The ship rocks and bucks so violently, suddenly,
    that Kirk is thrown out of his control chair.

                                        SMASH-CUT TO:
    ANGLE ON BRIDGE as other crewmembers are tossed
    around like loose peas. The SCENE GOES RED again,
    eerily.

                                        SMASH-CUT TO:
    TILT/ANGLE IN CORRIDOR as the ship heaves and
    people are dumped, crashing into one another. Red
    haze.

                                        SMASH-CUT TO:
    INT. McCOY'S LAB as the shock wave hits and flasks
    shatter on the shelves, racks of equipment tumble
    and crash. McCoy and Spock are thrown against one
    another and both of them are thrown against the
    specimen table.

10 XTREME CLOSE SHOT—McCOY & BEAST
    as the red effulgence fills the room with more of the
    radiation. McCoy is shoved against the little beast
    they were examining, and with the speed of a
    raccoon, the alien creature strikes, in panic. It sinks
    its tiny fangs into McCoy's hand.

11 *CLOSE UP ON McCOY*

as he screams, his eyes squinch shut in pain, and he
pulls his hand away from the creature, suddenly
thrusting it against his mouth to stop the pain. But
we see on the back of the hand, in that fleshy area
just behind and between the thumb and first finger,
three tiny flaming red dots where the beast has
bitten.

McCOY
(strangled)
The poison . . .

12 *WIDER SHOT—FAVORING SPOCK*

as the *Enterprise* stabilizes. The red glow is still there.
McCoy stumbles, begins rocking back and forth as
though he is in terrible anguish. Spock tries to help
him, but McCoy turns away. His back is to us, and he
is twisted over as though shot in the stomach. Then
he straightens up sharply, and as Spock moves toward
him again he suddenly grabs a long-necked retort
from a table and swings it in a whistling arc, crashing
it against Spock's temple. Spock is hurled backward
and goes slamming into a bulkhead, hits and falls face
forward. The two *Enterprise* Crewmen, who have, for
the most part stayed in the b.g. or moved to assist
Spock, now go for McCoy. They grab him from either
side, and with startling agility he pulls his arms free
and clubs them together. They go down and McCoy
turns SUDDENLY TO FACE CAMERA as CAMERA
ZOOMS IN on his face:

He has been changed. Not Jekyll-Hyde. More subtle
than that. Spots of color, flaming in his cheeks, his
eyes quite mad, whirling discs dilated and dark. A very
indefinable *something* wrong that tells us very simply
and directly that the poison is in his system

(MORE)

(CONTINUED)

12 CONTINUED:

and he has gone berserk. He STARES INTO CAMERA several beats, to give us a good look, then PLUNGES INTO CAMERA and

                                      FRAME TO BLACK:

13 ANGLE IN CORRIDOR—McCOY

as BLACK FRAME becomes McCoy RUNNING AWAY FROM CAMERA down the corridor. ALARMS SOUND OVER AND OVER.

14 REVERSE ANGLE—CORRIDOR—McCOY

as he comes DASHING TOWARD CAMERA and CAMERA PANS WITH him as he turns sharply and the door before him sighs open, and he rushes inside. We HEAR Sulu's VOICE OVER intership comm system:

                    VOICE OF SULU
                       (filter)
           Security Alert! Find and restrain Dr.
            McCoy at once. Security Alert!
               (repeats this over and over
                  as action proceeds)

CAMERA HOLDS on the door through which McCoy has vanished as it sighs shut. Then CAMERA TILTS UP SLIGHTLY to read the plate near the door: TRANSPORTER CHAMBER. CAMERA HOLDS a beat on the plate and then very smoothly PANS LEFT to SHOOT DOWN CORRIDOR as we see, at the other end, Kirk and Spock and SEVERAL OTHER CREWMEMBERS of the Security Force as they plunge toward us. CAMERA PULLS BACK as they come abreast of the Transporter Chamber. One of the SECURITY MEN points to the door with anxious words ad lib that he has seen McCoy enter. The door slides open for them and they rush in as CAMERA FOLLOWS.

15 FULL SHOT—INT. TRANSPORTER CHAMBER

as we see the TRANSPORTER CHIEF lying unconscious by his machinery. And on the beaming stage, the last tell-tale flickers and sparkles of the TRANSPORTER EFFECT that tells us McCoy has gone. CAMERA IN CLOSE on Spock and Kirk in 2-SHOT.

KIRK
He's beamed down . . .
(scared)
. . . there.

SPOCK
He'll be dead in two hours.

CAMERA HOLDS CLOSE on their faces locked in horror as we

FADE OUT.

END OF PROLOGUE

ACT ONE

FADE IN:

16 EXT. PLANET—ESTABLISHING—DAY

CLOSE on booted tracks as CAMERA ANGLE WIDENS
to show us a rocky defile, obviously on an alien world.
The tracks lead out of the rocky defile. A burnt-out sun
hangs dolorously in the cadaverous sky. A dead world,
even from what little we see here . . . as if some
cosmic god had flicked an ash and it had grown into
a planet. We HOLD on the SCENE for a BEAT as we
HEAR the VOICE of KIRK OVER:

> KIRK'S VOICE (OVER)
> Ship's log: star-date 3134.6. The deadly
> radiation that drew us to this desolate
> Rim of the Galaxy, has thrown the
> *Enterprise* into chaos.

As these line are SPOKEN OVER we see the tell-tale
shimmering of the TRANSPORTER EFFECT as Kirk,
Spock, Yeoman Janice Rand and two enlisted crewmen
appear. VOICE OVER CONTINUES:

> KIRK'S VOICE (OVER)
> Somewhere on this nameless ash of a
> world, Dr. McCoy is wandering, the
> poison in his blood giving him less
> than two hours to live. We are
> transporting down with an antidote.
> *(beat)*
> Can we track him down in time?

As the preceding lines are SPOKEN OVER we see
Spock indicating tracks to Kirk, pointing in the
direction they vanish. They move forward as VOICE
OVER CONTINUES and we:

LAP-DISSOLVE THRU:

17 *FULL SHOTS—THE SCENES*

thru
19 the Patrol moving through random sets of alien terrain (whatever is most economical to convey feeling of covering distance on this planet, without exorbitant set-ups) as VOICE OVER CONTINUES as indicated above.

CONTINUE LAP-DISSOLVES

THRU TO:

20 *EXT. PLANET—ANOTHER ANGLE—MED. CLOSE SHOT*

PAST Yeoman Janice Rand in f.g. as she turns her head sharply to look just PAST CAMERA. A tricorder, a simple black case, hangs over her shoulder. A HUM grows stronger from tricorder.

RAND

Captain: there's the source of the
radiation.

CAMERA PULLS BACK RAPIDLY to show Kirk, Spock and the rest just behind her, and as CAMERA FILLS we see mountains that rise up into the sky, till they become vague and whispy.

SPOCK

The tracks . . . straight for the
mountains.

CAMERA MOVES BACK IN and TO THE LEFT to come in CLOSER on Kirk, and past him, as if they were miniatures right over his shoulder, the mountains, with a strange glittering on one far, distant peak.

KIRK

(almost dreamily)

Mr. Spock: do you see a great city up
there?

(CONTINUED)

20 CONTINUED:

SPOCK'S VOICE O.S.
It is there, Captain.

KIRK
Like a city on the edge of forever.

CAMERA HOLD as Kirk moves away and the others
move with him. CAMERA HOLD on the gleaming city,
seen almost in opaque dimness as we

DISSOLVE TO:

21 PLATEAU OF THE GUARDIAN—LATER DAY—CLOSE
SHOT

ON KIRK as he climbs up the last of what is obviously
a mountain pass. The stones are a peculiar silvery
material, with buried shimmers of light in them. As
Kirk climbs up onto the plateau, CAMERA GOES
WITH HIM as the ANGLE OPENS to show us bracing
rock walls and niches all around us.

22 THE PLATEAU—ESTABLISHING SHOT—KIRK'S POV

PANNING SHOT from Kirk's immediate right,
around the bowl of the plateau. Gray sky past the rock
prominences, light and eerie mist that gives
the entire area an ethereal look, niches up in the rock
walls, boulders of the same bright substance here and
there, and on a higher peak but still quite far-off—the
city, glittering like a hypersensitive's dream. And as the
CAMERA PANS AROUND we see, for the first time, THE
GUARDIAN OF FOREVER. The shot continues a beat
and then CAMERA ZOOMS IN on "him." For that beat,
he had looked almost like another sparkling rock in
the stone walls. But as CAMERA CLOSES in the
ZOOM we see "he" is something quite different:

(MORE)

(CONTINUED)

22 *CONTINUED:*

The GUARDIAN OF FOREVER is pure thought. Resting in a shallow bowl on a pedestal, he looks like a globe of flickering light . . . like a shimmering handful of fog . . . like something totally alien and omnipresent. (Construction of the Guardian should combine a minimum of expense with a maximum of ingenuity.)

23 *CLOSING SHOT—KIRK & SPOCK*

as they move toward the Guardian. Spock moves in behind Kirk and the others follow, fanning out. They move closer, awed (for it *is* an awesome presence).

> SPOCK
> *(softly)*
> It's alive.

> KIRK
> *(with wonder)*
> The power, Mr. Spock. Can you feel the power coming from it?

There is the SOUND of a deep, sepulchral VOICE OVER. A voice that rings out in the rocky enclosure, seeming to come from nowhere and everywhere at once. It is the VOICE of the GUARDIAN.

> GUARDIAN
> *(a voice of power)*
> I am the Guardian of Forever. Welcome.

> KIRK
> You live in the city?

> GUARDIAN
> Once. Before we became pure energy.
> A time before your sun burned hot in
> space. Before your race was born.

(CONTINUED)

23 *CONTINUED:*

> SPOCK
>
> This place is dead, empty. Why do you
> stay?

As the Guardian speaks, movement within the fog,
light, mist, the substance of "him," changes, glows,
dims, sparkles, changes color . . . whatever EFFECT
has been opted for.

> GUARDIAN
>
> Because I am the last of my kind.

> KIRK
>
> The last?

> GUARDIAN
>
> The city is empty. Built to last even
> after I am gone.

> KIRK
>
> We followed some sort of radiation to
> this planet . . . it damaged our vessel—

> GUARDIAN
>
> You wandered into the time-flow. This
> world is the center of the Universe.

> KIRK
>
> The center? I don't—?

24 *CLOSER SHOT—ON GUARDIAN*

as his form shimmers and pulses.

> GUARDIAN
>
> Only on this world do the million
> pulse-flows of time and space merge.
> Only here do the flux lines of Forever
> meet.
>
> (MORE)

(CONTINUED)

24 *CONTINUED:*

> *(beat)*
>
> Only here can exist the gateway to the past, where the Time Vortex of the Ancients can work.
>
> *(beat)*
>
> My race was set to watch the Time Vortex, so many hundred of centuries ago that even I do not have clear memories of it.

KIRK

> The gateway to the past? A time machine?

GUARDIAN

> Not a machine. A creation, a vortex.

Kirk is about to ask what he means but Spock logical—cuts in.

25 *ON SPOCK*

SPOCK

> Have you seen another man, dressed as we are?

GUARDIAN

> What I see has already been, or is yet to be. No. No other like you.

> > > CUT TO:

26 *ROCKY NICHE—CLOSE PAST McCOY*

past him, hidden in a shadowy crevice, listening to Kirk and Spock talking to the Guardian. There is a flagrant madness in McCoy's face. The feverish color of the poison coursing through his veins can be seen in his cheeks. He sweats. His eyes are bright and wild.

(MORE)

> > > (CONTINUED)

26 *CONTINUED:*

He is a man totally out of his senses. He looks around himself, for a way out, but we see he is in a cul-de-sac. The only way out is past the *Enterprise* patrol. KIRK'S VOICE CARRIES.

> KIRK
>
> There are legends in space. About you.
> About this place.

> GUARDIAN
>
> You are the first visitors I have had in
> twice two hundred thousand years.

27 *ANGLE PAST KIRK IN F.G.*

to the Guardian, the mist rising, the light changing. Kirk approaches another step. We can see something in him we have never seen before: wonder, absolute all-consuming wonder. He has found a key to the secrets of the universe that compel him. He is being filled to the top with amazement, and he leans forward almost like a child.

> KIRK
>
> I always thought stories about time
> machines were the drunk-stuff of lab
> technicians when they'd had too much
> pure grain to drink.

> GUARDIAN
>
> The Vortex of Time is real. Look!

Kirk looks and his eyes open wide; delight and amazement and confusion and *belief* there.

28 *THE TIME VORTEX—ESTABLISHING*

Set in a tall, narrow rocky crevice, it rises up, different

(MORE)

(CONTINUED)

to each who see it. A pillar of flame, a shaft of light, a roiling brightness of smoke, whatever wonder you care to make of it, the obvious aspects are light, height and insubstantiality. Construct it as you choose.

> GUARDIAN O.S.
> Pure matter. Built by a science man will not understand for a hundred thousand times the span of years he has already existed.

29 PAST GUARDIANS TO KIRK

and the others near him, wondering, listening.

> KIRK
> *(awed)*
> And it's possible to go back ... and forward ... in time ...?

> GUARDIAN
> All time, all space. They meet in this brightness, the Vortex.

> SPOCK
> *(very scientific)*
> Can you give us a demonstration? Is that possible?

The Guardian's answer is oddly tinged with weariness and pleasure.

> GUARDIAN
> Time is weary for the craftsman who cannot demonstrate his craft. It would give me pleasure to show you the past.

> KIRK
> Can you show us the past of any world?

(CONTINUED)

29 *CONTINUED:*

GUARDIAN
I can even show you the past of your
own planet ... Old Earth.

KIRK
(softly)
The past of Old Earth ... please...

The pillar of light blazes and as Kirk turns to look, the CAMERA SHOOTS PAST HIM. In a moment there is movement in the light ... a thickening ... a roiling like oil ... like quicksilver mixed with smoke ... and a scene begins to take FORM IN THE VORTEX. (NOTE: this, and other scenes in Vortex will be MATTE INSERTS.)

30 *CLOSE ON VORTEX—FEATURING MATTE INSERTS (STOCK)*

A *scene* of primordial times; great saurians; a woolly mammoth; steaming prehistoric jungle; reality!

It FADES OUT to be replaced by:

A *scene* in the days of the Clipper ships; something typical of the period; reality!

It FADES OUT to be replaced by:

A *scene* of NYC STREET in the time of the Depression, 1930-32.

(NOTE: At Director's discretion, INTERCUTS of the Earthmen marveling at this demonstration may be inserted.)

NOTE: The indicated sequence of stock shots is merely offered as a pattern. *Any* stock will suffice, reeled in sequence so that shot 34 occurs at just the time when the Vortex is showing Old Earth in the

(MORE)

(CONTINUED)

30 CONTINUED:

Depression, 1930s. Facilitation is at the discretion of Production.

31 PAST McCOY TO VORTEX

as he watches in his madness with as much rapt attention as Kirk and his patrol. But the cunning is there, the arched brow and the faintly smiling mouth. The animal has sensed an avenue of escape, as we HEAR KIRK SAY:

KIRK
Could we go back to Old Earth?

32 ANGLE ON GUARDIANS

SHOT FROM TILT rising up, almost Messianic in tone, something reverential as they speak about their religion—time.

GUARDIAN
Yes, but it is not wise. If passage back is
effected, the voyager may add a new
factor to the past, and thus change
time, alter everything that happened
from that point to the present . . . all
through the universe.

33 SPOCK AND GUARDIAN PAST HIM

fascinated by the concepts, not the magic of it all.

SPOCK
Then time is not a constant. It isn't
rigid?

GUARDIAN
Time is elastic. It will revert to its
original shape when changes are
(MORE)

(CONTINUED)

33 CONTINUED:

               minor. But when the change is life or
               death—when the sum of intelligence
               alters the balance—then the change can
               become permanent ... and terrible.

                              SPOCK

               Like changing the flow of a river.

                          GUARDIAN

               A river, a wind, a flow, elastic. It makes
               no difference how you imagine it to
               yourself.

                             KIRK

               How long has it been since anyone
               went—

                          GUARDIAN

               For nine hundred thousand years no
               one has gone back.

                              SPOCK
                          (to Kirk)

               I understand now why our
               chronometers turned backwards.

The Time Vortex has been running through dialogue,
now draws near 1930. While CAMERA DOES *NOT*
dwell on it, whatever shot we enter, we should see
the scene of the Depression back there, to remind
us it's on.

                             KIRK

               They've created a zone of no-time
               here.

                              SPOCK

               But if this is true ... if time does not
               move at its normal rate here ... how
               long have you been here to get as old
               as you are ...

34 FULL SHOT—THE SCENE—HAND-HELD

But they have no time to ponder an answer, for at
that moment McCoy breaks from cover and makes a
long run toward the Time Vortex. He is halfway there
before they realize what is happening. Kirk and Spock
plunge forward to stop him. Spock gets to him first
but McCoy slams Spock across the jaw and keeps
going. He grabs Yeoman Janice Rand as a shield and
roughhouses her in front of him, ever closer to the
Vortex. She half-turns and elbows him; he leaves her
and Kirk reaches him just as he closes on the Vortex.
Kirk sees he is going for the Vortex (from which the
1930s scene is gone, but which still flickers and
glows so we know it is in operation) and makes a
flying dive for him. But McCoy does a little dance-
step of broken-field maneuvering and flings himself
forward.

35 ANGLE ON McCOY

as he dives headfirst into the Vortex. There is the
SOUND of a LOUD WHOOOOOSH! as space rushes to
fill the vacuum where he has been. Then the Vortex
is as it was before. McCoy is gone. Into the past of
Old Earth.

FADE OUT

END OF ACT ONE.

AFTERWORDS

Peter David
D.C. Fontana
David Gerrold
DeForest Kelley
Walter Koenig
Leonard Nimoy
Melinda Snodgrass
George Takei

PETER DAVID is the author of more than two dozen novels (including *Star Trek: The N Generation* titles such as *Q-In-Law, Strike Zone, Vendetta, Rock And A Hard Place,* and *Imza* He was the writer on DC Comics's *Star Trek* for years, but is now best known as the fek intellect behind *The Incredible Hulk* and *Aquaman* and the weekly *But I Digress* colum *Comics Buyer's Guide.*

D. C. FONTANA started out as Gene Roddenberry's secretary. When she began selling excel scripts to such other shows as *Bonanza,* Roddenberry lured her back to pen such episode the original series as "Charlie X," "Tomorrow is Yesterday," and "Journey to Babel." She beca story editor on the original series, 1967 and 1968; Associate Producer of the *Star Trek* anima series, 1974; and Associate Producer of *Star Trek: The Next Generation* in its first year. She wr books, stories, essays, and award-winning teleplays. She is married to SFX wizard Dennis Skot

DAVID GERROLD will be the first to tell you he got his start with Gene Roddenberry and original *ST* series, and was both Gene's and the show's staunchest supporter for decades. wrote two hooks about *ST ... The World of Star Trek* and *The Trouble With Tribbles.* If the of that latter volume sounds familiar, it is because the episode of the original series bearing the only neck-and-neck contender with "City" for Most Popular Episode. He has written mov excellent novels, won a Hugo and a Nebula this year, and has been affiliated with virtually ev incarnation of the *ST* concept. When you say *Trek,* you're saying Gerrold.

DEFOREST KELLEY was already an established feature film star when he was cast as Dr. "Bon McCoy in the original series. He is a classically-trained actor, and among the films in which appeared are *Warlock* and *Johnny Reno.* He is universally considered the nicest person of the original cast members. Anyone who says less is automatically a jerk.

WALTER KOENIG has been a novelist, screenwriter, noted acting coach, lecturer, and actor. credits are extensive, but he appears here due to his assaying of the Chekov character on original *Trek.* He appeared in all of the *ST* feature films and, most recently, created a mini-ser for comics, *Raver.* He writes very well indeed.

LEONARD NIMOY was Mr. Spock. Sometimes he says he was *not* Spock; and sometimes he s he *was* Spock. In either case, he has been a friend for thirty years, and the author of "City" owes h considerable weight of favors. He likes Indian cuisine.

MELINDA M. SNODGRASS served as Executive Script Consultant on *ST: The Next Generati* She adapted George R. R. Martin's award-winning *Sandkings* for the new *Outer Limits* seri Screenwriter, novelist, short story expert, and asst. editor of the *Wild Cards* anthology seri She lived in the *ST* production cauldron.

GEORGE TAKEI played Sulu on the original series. He has been a potent Los Angeles politico, hav sat on the Board of Directors of the Southern California Rapid Transit District, having spearhea numerous urban development programs, and having cleverly used his celebrity from *Trek* and m other series to better the condition of life for all Angelenos. He is held in much affection by ot actors, by those who worked on the series, and by the rest of us who are privileged to know hi

PETER DAVID

One grows up.

It's inevitable (unless you're Peter Pan, or Jeffty) and as the years pass, you discover that the world is not as black and white as you once thought. That many things are possible. And that just because something is different doesn't make it bad.

I thought the original script for "City" sucked.

I thought this because, the first time I learned of it, I was a snot-nosed kid whose entire view of the creative process behind *Star Trek* was predicated on the concept that if it was on the air, it was good, and if it wasn't, then it must be bad because it wasn't good enough to get on the air.

So when I read about how "City" had undergone massive rewrites to make it good enough to ride the television waves, I thought, "Wow . . . it must really have sucked." Furthermore, the publicized reasons as to what made it unacceptable were appalling. A Starfleet officer selling drugs? How ridiculous! Kirk ready to let the universe shift into an unfamiliar, parallel line, out of love for a woman? Preposterous!

Boy oh boy oh boy. What a sucky, sucky script. The fact that it had won the Writers Guild and Hugo Awards merely confirmed for me that the rest of the world was composed of purblind nitwits who didn't understand that if it wasn't good enough to air on *Star Trek* in its original form, then it wasn't good, period.

And then, some years later, when I'd had a chance to grow up a bit, I happened to buy the Roger Elwood collection that featured the original script.

And I understood.

With a vengeance.

In the words of Yogi Berra, "You can observe a lot by watching." Watch the story, the original story of Sister Edith Keeler, unfolding, and you will observe a master craftsman at work, producing a story of infinitely deeper meanings, shadings and complexities than what aired.

To a degree, we see a theme present in "City" that recurs in some of Ellison's most renowned work, and yet it's not exactly the happiest of themes: those who are the best, the brightest, the most vibrant and alive . . . they don't survive. The perpetually unaging Jeffty — the embodiment of perpetual childhood — is battered, bruised and ultimately killed. The Harlequin, shouting defiance, is brainwashed into an obsequious supporter of The Way Things Are. Beth O'Neill, in order to survive life in the city, sacrifices her soul to become one of the grim, faceless beings who observe man's inhumanity without lifting a finger to stop it.

And Sister Edith Keeler, well, jeez . . . this woman doesn't just have society or the unspoken dark gods hiding in the city's shadows arrayed against her. Fate itself, the cogs of time, crush her in their unyielding motions. It's a somewhat fatalistic view of the universe — this woman must die, is meant to die, has *got* to die, or else matters cannot proceed. "City" presents a paradox of what's right and what's wrong, and the answer we get is that it just . . . is.

This is the core of the script, and it's put forward far more forcefully in this version than in what aired. For example:

Beckwith, the drug-pushing, murderous Starfleet officer.

For all the claims that *Star Trek* is genuine, realistic science fiction, nowhere is this more brought into question than in the dismissal of the notion that a Starfleet officer would ever behave in the manner we see Beckwith engaging in.

If we parallel Starfleet to the modern-day navy, well, let's see what we've got: Can you envision a modern-day navy officer reshaping a society into Nazism? Or ordering his officers to fight and die, one at a time, in a gladiatorial arena? Or battling, *mano a mano,* another officer to defend his place in a society built upon a corrupted version of the Constitution?

Suddenly Beckwith's actions don't seem too extraordinary at all. Not a whit, not a smidgen. But in a series which sought to explore infinite possibilities, Beckwith was just a tad *too* possible to make it on the air.

With the loss of Beckwith, we also lose one of the most morally complex and debatable aspects of the story. Here was a man who was a drug pusher and a murderer. Yet from Starfleet the worst he would have gotten was being tossed in the stockade, since the only thing you get executed for in the 23rd century is popping by Talos IV, the planet of the telepathic buttheads.

Yet, indisputably, Beckwith's greatest crime is that he altered history. You can argue that he got what he deserved because he's a total shit, but good lord, this guy's reincarnating in the heart of a sun forever. An infinity of torture with no hope of parole — it is, by design, living hell. The enormity of his punishment must be matched by the enormity of the crime. By interfering in the grand, fatalistic cosmic scheme of things — by getting out a magic marker and drawing a mustache on God's grand design — we presume that that is the reason that he receives the extreme punishment of literally and figuratively burning forever, unto eternity.

Except the deed that got him into this fix was *the one selfless action* we ever see him take. He was trying to save Edith Keeler. For a moment, the qualities that first made him an officer emerged, and that moment doomed him.

Even when the guy tried to do something that, in some way, redeemed him, it turned out to be the greatest sin yet. Talk about damned if you do, damned if you don't.

But the aired version did away with moral grayness and cosmic injustice by pumping McCoy full of uppers and sending him through the portal to perform an action that was perfectly in character, with no shades of right or wrong.

Nor were the hero's actions allowed to have any gray areas to them, and in that, we have an even greater loss of what "The City on the Edge of Forever" was really saying. Because it can always be argued that Beckwith wasn't really that important; that he was merely the MacGuffin. That the real story was Kirk and Spock and Edith Keeler, and just changing the catalyst wasn't as vital as maintaining the integrity of the original concept.

And that's where the greatest injustice occurred. The thing that I, as the aforementioned snot-nosed kid, couldn't understand.

In the aired version, Kirk sacrifices the woman he loves so that time can be restored.

In the words of Harry Anderson: "Well, we weren't expecting that now, were we?"

It's the predictable way. It's the safe way. It's the way that you can presume it's going to go, because you know that Joan Collins isn't going to be on next week, but Kirk and Spock and the rest of the *Enterprise* crew are.

That's the one-dimensional portrayal of a hero. He always does what's right. Because of course, Edith Keeler *must* die. The universe of the Federation *cannot* be sacrificed. Edith dying is right. Kirk is the hero. So Kirk must let her die. Q.E.D.

But not the Kirk of Ellison's script. Because this Kirk is real. This Kirk is frustrated. This Kirk agonizes over the cosmic unfairness of the situation. His pain goes beyond loving her: "She isn't important here, the way she feels, the goodness, the things she believes for the world, they aren't ready for it." He sees her as significant to the spiritual welfare of humanity in whatever time she's in, and cannot comprehend, cannot accept, that she is simply to be cast aside, crushed, lost.

And because it's so wrong to him, this Kirk refuses to be a party to it. When the crunch comes down, Kirk reacts instinctively and cannot force himself to be Fate's Triggerman. Kirk is willing to shoot craps with the cosmos because he cannot bring himself to accept the fatalistic situation into which he's been thrust.

Out of character? Not at all. Perfectly in keeping with the Kirk we saw who played fast and loose with the rules time and time again because he had a strong moral center. And in this case, his moral center shouted, "No! I will not accept this predestination! I will not sacrifice this gentle, loving woman on the altar of inevitability! I won't!"

Was it the right thing to do? Was it the wrong thing? It's difficult to say. But this we can say beyond question: It was the human thing to do.

Which is why he needed Spock.

Because whereas Kirk fought for the moral center of the universe, Spock was the intellectual, logical center. And not only was Spock willing to be Fate's Triggerman, he even produced a weapon to do the job should fate — or his captain — screw it up.

Whereas in the aired version, Spock primarily served as comedy relief and dispenser of information — with an occasional, stark "Edith Keeler must die!" — while making it very clear that the final decision was going to be on Kirk's shoulders; in the original, Spock is the one with his priorities in order. Ellison anticipated Spock's "The need of the many outweigh the need of the few, or the one" in *Wrath of Khan* by a good couple of decades.

Spock doesn't have to worry about doing the human thing, because he's not human. Rarely has his alien demeanor been quite so coldly, fully realized. This is the chilling, almost callous Spock of "Where No Man Has Gone Before" — a character who is much harder to like than the one we were subsequently given. And never has he been less likable than here, where he makes it clear that he's going to do whatever it takes to restore his preferred time line. When have you ever seen a situation where one of the ostensible heroes is ready, willing and able to take a life that the "villain" wants to save?

In a burst of overwhelming humanity, Kirk could not find it in himself to allow Edith Keeler to be condemned to death. So Spock did it for him. He took his captain off the hook, seized the initiative and saved the day when Kirk's humanity would not let he himself do the job. Kirk never expresses any appreciation for what Spock has done. Maybe he doesn't understand. Maybe the man of action is embarrassed at his own inaction. Maybe he's pissed at Spock's letting Edith die. But Spock, in his closing speech, makes it clear that he understands Kirk; nor does he endeavor to judge or issue recriminations. We simply have the eloquent observation that "No woman was ever offered the universe for love."

And that element was excised. No examination of Kirk's human hesitations or Spock's alien single-mindedness. No great romantic ideal. The aired version gave the impression that Kirk had two choices, but in fact he only had one. He wasn't allowed to do the thing that the script hinged upon. When we see the aired episode, we feel for Kirk when he stops McCoy. We share his loss. It's a poignant moment. But that's it; it's over. Business as usual. "Let's get the hell out of here." There's none of the carryover that would have given the aired episode that extra depth.

The point has been lost, the meaning obscured in the overwhelming compulsion to play it safe. The last time anyone took real chances with Kirk's character was "The Enemy Within," revealing Kirk's rape fantasies of Janice Rand. Now *that* was daring . . . and unduplicated.

(Speaking of Rand, the roles that female crewmembers play

between the unaired and aired scripts is intriguing. Granted that time considerations might have prompted them to lose scenes 30 to 40 anyway, but nevertheless I find it interesting that Ellison's script portrays Yeoman Rand left behind to hold the fort; by the time the episode aired, Rand was gone and we were left with Uhura, whose contribution was limited to almost saying "Captain, I'm frightened.")

We see, with the rewriting of Ellison's script, that limits were set early-on as to just how far and how realistic *Star Trek* would be allowed to be in its themes; just how human (or alien) the characters would be allowed to be perceived.

Now, it is easily argued — and not without merit — that *Star Trek* was Gene Roddenberry's baby, and he had final say. Fair enough. If Roddenberry felt it wasn't what he wanted to see on his show, that was his right.

However, that perception has changed over the years — mutated even — to the point where representatives of Gene Roddenberry now make efforts to distance televised *Star Trek* from anything else that could taint the purity of the program. "Not Gene" = "Sucky." In other words, the perception that I held as a snot-nosed kid is now, in many instances, policy.

Richard Arnold, who for years was Roddenberry's public face, repeatedly made a distinction between *Star Trek* fact and *Star Trek* fiction, prompting fans to observe, "God, and they tell *us* to get a life!"

Although Arnold's involvement with the television series was minimal, he had major sway for several years over the licensed *Star Trek* novels and comics. On the one hand stating that such published fare was not official *Star Trek* (despite the hefty licensing fees paid to ensure that "official" designation), and had no bearing on *Star Trek* fact. Arnold would, on the other hand, pore over the manuscripts to make sure that they met with his standards. Standards that included such fiats as that Kirk was no longer interested in pursuing romantic relationships (despite his long sexually active history); that the words "Terran" and "civilian" could not be used (although they were in the "Next Generation" series); and my personal favorite, the ludicrously self-contradicting, "This proposed storyline is like a combination of several other *Star Trek* episodes; it's not at all like *Star Trek*."

Why the novels and comics are required absolutely to toe the line (a line which keeps moving) when, according to Arnold, they have no relevance to real *Star Trek,* well . . . we've never gotten an adequate explanation on that.

Arnold, before Paramount canned him, pursuant to Roddenberry's death, never ever copped to any opinions and declarations coming from him, swearing instead they all originated with Gene Roddenberry who, Arnold maintained, read every manuscript that came in. This was a patently ludicrous assertion that was persistently denied by all other concerned parties, including Paramount officials.

The reason all of this is germane is that Arnold made some public comments about "City" in an extensive interview. His first comments were about novelists, but he could just as easily be discussing "City" . . . and then he goes on to do so:

" . . . the books that the fans jump up and down (about), and praise and cheer about how wonderful they are . . . they should have seen the original versions of them. And yet, do the authors say, 'Well, this really isn't entirely my story . . . the entire ending of this book was suggested to us through the *Star Trek* offices because the ending that we had for it didn't work, but, no, I'm happy to sign it for you and take all the royalties — which we don't get a penny of. That's painful, when you see — especially when I go to conventions and see onstage somebody going on and on about this wonderful book they've written, and I know damn well that half the suggestions came from Gene . . . that made it work in the *Star Trek* format. And, again, any author's going to disavow that, too . . . they're going to completely disagree with it . . . 'It was all my own idea, sure.'

"Harlan's taken accolades for 'City' for 25 years, and at the same time, behind Gene's back, bitched and complained about it. He's perfectly happy to take the royalties . . . he's perfectly happy to be 'the author of "The City on the Edge of Forever"' . . . and I love Harlan dearly, and if this ever gets back to him, believe me I'm going to get a phone call from him . . . 'cause he and I have spoken many times over the years, and he has given me some very strong advice, about this sort of thing, not dealing with this sort of thing. But at the same time, he's been very public, too. And Gene's kept his tongue all this time, because Gene knows that if you're going to continue to work with people, that you've got to stay on good terms with them."
(Richard Arnold interview copyright © 1991 by Tim Lynch)

If you've read the introductory essay to this book, you have seen the evidence that Arnold toadyingly got it all backwards . . . on purpose. It was Ellison who was restrained in his comments, and Roddenberry who lied endlessly.

Since Arnold states elsewhere in the interview that he has never been and never will be a writer, the first part of the above commentary smacks of extreme jealousy over those more talented receiving justly due accolades. The list of popular books with Paramount-dictated endings is never spelled out, possibly because they don't exist; and possibly because, from the time Arnold first got a firmer grip on the novels, readers began to complain about a downswing in quality.

As for the rest of the diatribe, Arnold essentially accuses Harlan Ellison — one of the most highly principled individuals in the industry, if not the country — of being a hypocrite. What he fails to mention is that Ellison has stated repeatedly over the years that, yes, he is the author of "The City on the Edge of Forever" . . . and that the aired version is markedly different from the script that he wrote. Ellison has stuck meticulously to the truth, something that not everyone can claim.

For you see, some of us actually are suckers enough to believe in the concept that *Star Trek* put forward called IDIC — Infinite Diversity in Infinite Combination. Taking joy in the many varieties and points of view that the universe has to offer, and treating them all with respect. Or perhaps some of us have quite simply managed to wipe that ignoble snot from our noses and appreciate the grander and infinitely more complex shadings that *truly* talented people can bring to a shared universe.

Whereas others still have their olfactory senses hopelessly plugged up, going nicely with the blinders on their eyes and the bile in their words. For people like that, who will never be able to fully appreciate the remarkable achievement that the original script of "City" presents — but instead will only perceive that it, along with other unaired stories, is "not real" and therefore not good enough — mere fiction, if you will — well, they are to be pitied, much like Ron Moody at the end of "The Twelve Chairs," flailing about and feigning epilepsy to get a few coins.

If nothing else, you can all toss coins to Richard Arnold next time he appears at conventions, so that he can buy a copy of this book . . . and hate it. At the very least, perhaps he might be able to purchase a package of Kleenex™.

D.C. Fontana

Whenever I am asked what *Star Trek* episodes are my favorites, I always reply "The City on the Edge of Forever" and "The Trouble with Tribbles." Both stories are unique in that they show sides of Captain James T. Kirk that were seldom displayed on the show — a sense of humor and a fine appreciation for the ridiculous ("Tribbles") and a genuine growth of love and poignant loss ("City"). In all the episodes that had Jim Kirk involved with a young lady, only "The City on the Edge of Forever" portrays a romance with a woman of admirable human qualities, purpose, and intelligence as well as beauty; and it is a romance which Kirk knows is doomed.

The production story of "The City on the Edge of Forever" began in the spring of 1966 when Gene Roddenberry was given the go-ahead on the series from NBC. He had decided that he would approach some of the top science fiction writers who were also experienced screen and television writers to write episodes of *Star Trek*. Among them were Theodore Sturgeon, Richard Matheson, Jerome Bixby, Jerry Sohl, Robert Bloch — and Harlan Ellison.

Harlan's idea in rough was the discovery of a planet where all time meets and an adventure which takes Kirk and Spock back through time to Earth of the Depression era. It was to be a genuine and poignant love story for Kirk.

The idea was approved, and Harlan went to work on the story outline. The writing of the outline seemed to take a long time. Producers don't like to badger writers about delivery. Most of them are also writers, and they understand the reluctance of writers to face the blank page or computer screen. Besides, it was not uncommon then for a writer to be juggling two or three assignments at the same time, having one in outline, one in first draft, and one in final draft. Other stories came in. Then scripts. Weeks went by. No Ellison.

Finally the outline for "The City on the Edge of Forever" was delivered, and it was received with glad cries of enthusiasm from Gene Roddenberry, Desilu and NBC. Harlan received a prompt go-ahead for a first-draft script. The series was deep into production by then, and Roddenberry wanted "The City on the Edge of Forever" scheduled soon. But — no script.

Granted, Harlan was going through an emotionally intense and difficult period — the breakup of one of the shortest marriages on record. On the other hand, we needed the script. Desperate measures were called for. Roddenberry set aside a desk in the assistant directors' room and asked Harlan to come in and work on the script in the studio. Every day. Please.

Harlan arrived with his manual typewriter and a record player and set up shop. There are some stories told that Roddenberry had to lock the door of that office to keep him working — but Harlan got out the window. The stories say Roddenberry had the windows nailed shut — and Harlan *still* got out. Well, they are just stories. Harlan did spend time visiting the set, but that's considered necessary research for a writer. When a show hasn't been on the air yet, freelance writers must have an opportunity to study the actors' speech patterns and delivery, the little gestures and nuances each one brings to his or her role, and — most of all — the character relationships which are being built episode by episode. The script for "The City on the Edge of Forever" began to emerge page by page, and finally it was done.

By then it was fall, and changes had taken place on the staff of the show. Gene Roddenberry had moved up to the position of Executive Producer, and Gene L. Coon had come aboard as Producer. John D. F. Black had departed as story editor to write a movie at Universal, and Steve Carabatsos replaced him. I had left the position of Roddenberry's executive secretary to write freelance, so I wasn't there when Harlan was asked to do revisions on the script and turn in his final draft.

When he did, things were still in flux. Grace Lee Whitney had completed her thirteen-show contract, and the character of Yeoman Janice Rand shipped off the *Enterprise.*

DeForest Kelley's role had become more important because his warm and gently humorous portrayal of Dr. McCoy balanced the logical Spock and the volatile, action-oriented Kirk. Roddenberry decided he would not renew Steve Carabatsos's contract and offered me the opportunity to become *Star Trek*'s story editor if I could do a good rewrite on a troubled script. The complete overhaul of the script which became "This Side of Paradise" landed me the job of story editor at the beginning of December, 1966. I reported the first day and walked right into a hornet's nest of trouble with "The City on the Edge of Forever" at the heart of it.

Harlan's script was brilliant. Always a master of words, his language conjured the images of the desolate planet "as if some cosmic god had flicked an ash and it had grown into a world," the enigmatic Guardian of Forever, and the Time Vortex. The streets of 1930 Earth were described artfully — deep in the Depression, peopled by characters like Verdun veteran Trooper and the vivacious Edith Keeler who could see beyond this moment into a hopeful future. What man wouldn't lose his heart to her (except for Mister Spock, of course)?

If "The City on the Edge of Forever" had been written for an anthology such as *Outer Limits,* undoubtedly it would have been shot almost without change. As written, it stands shoulder to shoulder with Harlan's bleak study of future warfare, "Soldier," and his twisting, turning, character-rich "Demon with a Glass Hand."

Unfortunately, it was not best suited to a series format. As the reader readily can see, the plot problem (the change in history) is brought about by characters who are strangers to the audience, LeBeque and Beckwith. The result of Beckwith's meddling with the past is that the *USS Enterprise* is now the *Condor,* a raider ship with a crew of renegades. Once this situation is established, it is seen again only once, in a flash cut, leaving the audience to wonder how the few defenders in the transporter room are doing while Kirk and Spock are in the past. It is almost the end of the second act before Kirk and Spock see Edith Keeler — and at that moment, Spock realizes Edith is the focal point of the time change because of clues the Guardian of Forever gave them. Kirk does not meet Edith face to face until Act Three, so their personal relationship is short (though no less deep). Kirk loves her despite the fact he knows she must die. He loves her despite the even more cruel fact that he knows he *cannot* lift a hand to save her. At the climax of the story, it is Beckwith who reaches out to save Edith and Spock who stops him while Kirk looks on in his grief.

While it was masterfully written, full of passion and emotion, in Gene Roddenberry's opinion, the script wasn't *Star Trek* enough. It would have to be rewritten. At that time, the rumor had not yet emerged that the reason it had to be rewritten was because "Harlan had Scotty pushing drugs on the *Enterprise.*" That came later, and possibly it came because Roddenberry felt he had to justify the rewrite. I know the explanation has been heard at a number of *Star Trek* conventions over the years. Well, the addictive Jewels of Sound were interesting "drugs" all right; but as the reader can see, Scotty isn't even in the script!

In the *Star Trek* offices, however, the immediate question was — who would rewrite "The City on the Edge of Forever"? Now the story can be told because Harlan has mellowed over the years. Used to be, his temper burned at such a low firing point and with such high explosivity that it devastated buildings for ten square miles around ground zero when it went off. (You've heard of the "H Bomb"?) There are still places on the Paramount lot where nothing will grow. Now, however, it's maybe only three square miles around that are leveled — and I live at least six miles from Harlan.

So who did the rewrite? Gene Coon took the first crack at it. As I recall, primarily he came up with structural changes, eliminating LeBeque and Beckwith and substituting McCoy as the catalyst. The pirates disappeared. In fact, the entire ship vanished because of the tampering with history. Kirk met Edith sooner, and dialogue and some relationships were changed. I believe it was Gene Coon whose delightful sense of humor spawned Kirk's explanation that Spock's ears got that way when he had a childhood accident — he got his head caught in a mechanical rice picker. Harlan hated it. He thought Steve Carabatsos had written it. No one offered to change that idea in Harlan's mind.

Then Gene Roddenberry and Gene Coon turned to me and said, "You're it. You try a rewrite." Talk about being tossed a live grenade! Harlan was a friend — and not only a friend. He was a writer I deeply admired, one who stood ten feet tall as a master of his art. The very notion of rewriting him scared me witless. On the other hand (said the coward in me), if I rewrote it, I'd do it with respect and love of the original work. I gave it my best shot.

The Jewels of Sound were gone, of course. I invented cordrazine to put McCoy into a temporary madness. I tried to build the relationship of love between Edith and Kirk gently and meaningfully so her death would be the most wrenching personal moment Kirk would ever know. And I inserted the running joke of Spock's tricorder which grew larger and more complicated with mechanical additions each time it was seen. The tricorder was Spock's instrument for discovering the focus of the history change — Edith — as well as the how and when of her death. Naturally, he was hampered by the fact that the tools he needed hadn't been invented yet. Thus the octopuslike appearance of the contraption and its continual growth. Harlan liked this draft a little better, but not much. He thought the characterization and dialogue showed sensitivity, but it wasn't his script. He thought Gene Coon wrote it. We kept our mouths shut. (Remember those places on the lot where grass still doesn't grow?)

Gene Roddenberry decided to rewrite it himself, and it was his version which became the shooting script. Harlan's general structure was there, as were his major characters and the main conflict of the story. What Roddenberry did was make it "more *Star Trek.*" You will notice that every writer who worked on the rewrite was trying very hard to please Harlan, allowing him to read each draft and comment on it. It was a sign of the respect *Star Trek* had for writers. That doesn't happen now — on any show.

Casting was lucky as the charming and lovely Joan Collins took the role of Edith Keeler. The directing chore fell to Joe Pevney, who had exhibited a special sensitivity and understanding of *Star Trek* and its characters.

As the episode approached production, there was a glitch in the art direction. *Star Trek*'s art director, Matt Jefferies, fell ill with the flu just as "City" was going into preparation. The department head, Roland (Bud) Brooks, stepped in to avoid any delay. He read the script, came up with set sketches, and got the carpenters going on the planet set. When Matt returned, he went down to the stage to look at it, and his mouth dropped.

"What the hell is that?"

He was looking at a gray planet surface on which were scattered broken Grecian columns, tumbled walls and statues. Bud explained they were the ruins, as called for in the script. Matt couldn't recall any ruins. Bud opened the script to the planet description and said, "Oops."

As he tells the story, he'd had two drinks with dinner the night he read the script and was puzzled by a description of "rune stones" covering the landscape. He had flipped through his dictionary and come to ruins before he got to runes. Deciding it must have been a typo, he had proceeded to design the ruined stones of the planet. (We never did figure out why the Guardian of Forever looked like a lopsided donut.)

The episode, which aired April 6, 1967, almost a full year after its birth, was a good *Star Trek*. It had humor, danger, and a deeply poignant love story. It turned out to be one of the most popular episodes of all time with both original Trekkers and with the youngest of the breed. But it wasn't Harlan's. It was Harlan, filtered through Coon, Fontana and, most of all, Roddenberry. For myself, I missed Trooper — a beautifully drawn portrait of a worn and despairing veteran of the Great War; I missed the Jewels of Sound — and the marvelous idea that sound could be an addictive narcotic; I missed the glittering city that is the source of the title; I missed the magic of Harlan's words.

Harlan had the last word. He always does. He submitted his draft of the script to the Writers' Guild of America for its annual award consideration. For the television awards, contending scripts are read by a number of writer judges who do not know the author of the piece. The film is never seen. Scripts which are nominated in each category are then read by a blue ribbon panel of writer judges and voted upon. In 1968, Harlan won the Writers Guild of America award for "Best Episodic Drama." Writers judging other writers declared his script the best of all contenders for that year. They read his words — and the spell of them captured them all.

Read the script again, and fall under the enchantment yourself.

David Gerrold

The Steamroller of Lies

This book is not about Harlan Ellison.

It *should* be about Harlan Ellison. It has his name on the cover and it has one hell of a television script by Harlan Ellison inside but, unfortunately, this book is really about Gene Roddenberry, because Gene Roddenberry was the one who made it necessary.

For years, Roddenberry stood up in front of audiences and said with bland composure that he had to rewrite Harlan Ellison's script for the "The City on the Edge of Forever" episode of *Star Trek* because Harlan had Scotty dealing drugs. That's not the truth, you can see that for yourself, but Gene continued the falsehood in numerous speeches and interviews. He said it again and again, even after Harlan called him on each embarrassing occasion and asked him not to.

I witnessed more than one of these conversations between Harlan and Gene. When confronted, Gene acknowledged that Harlan was correct and promised that he wouldn't say it again. Yet, at the very next convention he attended, he repeated the lie. I saw him do it. Did he forget what he had promised?

That's why this book is about Gene Roddenberry. It's Harlan Ellison's long overdue refutation of the falsehood.

I can understand why Harlan feels the need to set the record straight. Every time that Gene Roddenberry repeated the lie, he was implying that Harlan Ellison did not understand *Star Trek* or that he did not do his job properly. He was insulting Harlan's professional credential. At the very least, it was an inappropriate thing for Gene Roddenberry to say. At worst, well — it was unkind and unprofessional.

If there's one thing that I have learned from Harlan — and also from Gene, albeit in an entirely different way — it is this: *You are your word.* Harlan Ellison understands this; I'm not sure that Gene Roddenberry ever did; but the difference between speaking a commitment and *living* it is the difference between eating the menu and eating the meal.

Maybe telling the truth isn't important if you're only a television producer, or worse — a television producer's lawyer; but if you're a writer, it's *all* you have. A writer is a servant of the truth. He's a channel for enlightenment. If he's anything less than that, he's a fraud, a charlatan, a phony, a waster of trees and time. Anything less than a total commitment to accuracy as a way of life is the murder of integrity and trust.

What I'm talking about here — *authenticity* — is apparently an alien experience for too many people. As individuals, we've been blinded, conned, manipulated, trashed, beaten up, beaten down, and hammered into insensibility by the publicity mills, the hype, the grind, the weight of peer group pressure, and ultimately even our own belief systems. We end up believing what we want to believe instead of seeing what is really so. Goebbels had it right — if you tell a big enough lie and you tell it loud enough and long enough, people will accept it as truth. It all depends on how well you package it. This is the essence of American discourse in the '90s:

Say anything. He who can lie the most sincerely will win the affection of the public.

And when someone does stand up to object, "Hey, wait a minute — the clothes have no emperor," he too becomes a target. The steamroller of lies will aim itself at him, too.

Everyone who has a vested interest in having you believe that there really is an emperor inside all that taffeta will do everything they can to discredit and destroy any person who still believes in accuracy enough to stand up and say, "Uh, excuse me — ? That's not the way I saw it and I was there." Even goodhearted people will unknowingly add their voices to the chorus of falsehoods because it's more fun to believe the glamorous lie than the dirty truth; but the cost of that easy acceptance is such a complete and total destruction of our respect for authenticity that, as a society, we now act as if we have the right to vote on reality.

The one place where we really do have a vote — *where it really matters* — is in our interactions with other human beings. Samuel R. Delany said it. Drama occurs in the space between two people. It goes beyond that. All of life occurs in the space between us. All we really have is each other — and it's in our commitment to each other that we make the kind of difference that really *can* change the world. But when we lose our commitment to accuracy, honesty, and justice, we lose our ability to make a difference, because we also lose our vision of *what is possible.*

Harlan Ellison's strength, the essential reason why he has dominated the conversation of this community for so many years, is that he is a man who refuses to let his vision be muddied by the convenient little lies of politeness and tact, because those little lies lead directly to the bigger lies of greed and venality. Harlan stands up against the steamroller of lies again and again and again. I think it is this singular commitment to honesty that makes him one of the most important voices in the literature of amazement.

A great deal of the most passionate and inventive and imaginative writing in the genre was done during the '60s and early '70s. Some of the best was done by Harlan. Much of the rest was done by people who were inspired or angered by Harlan's furious calls to glory. Whether you agreed or disagreed, you could not ignore the fires that were burning. Old visions were being vaporized. New ones were being forged. There was a lot of heat and fury — but there was a lot of illumination as well. It was an exciting time to be a writer; it was a great time to be learning one's craft — because there were so many options to explore.

Curiously, this was also the moment in time when *Star Trek* began to assert its influence on the genre. In one respect at least, that influence has been a pernicious one: the allure of catching some of *Star Trek*'s fame and glory and wealth has caused too many good writers to lower not only their standards, but their goals as well. Science fiction used to be a dangerous literature. Now, it is a very commercial genre, and whatever dangers might still lurk within seem to have been safely sanitized for the marketplace. The real crime is that the lobotomy has been self performed.

I suspect that only a small part of Harlan's disdain for *Star Trek* is the result of his own experience with the steamroller of lies that follows in its wake; the larger part must surely come from realizing that *Star Trek* is also a series of broken promises and missed opportunities to expand the range of what is possible in the genre.

You see, Harlan Ellison is a writer.

I'm going to have to explain this.

I'm only a storyteller. Harlan Ellison is a writer.

I tell stories for a living. I write about people who have problems and what they do to solve those problems and what they learn in the process. I try to make the people and the situations interesting and understandable. I try to keep the language as clear as possible because I'm terrified of looking silly in print. Only occasionally do I succumb to temptation and try to get my prose airborne — usually, the next morning, my head hurts and I'm embarrassed by the stylistic excesses committed to paper.

But Harlan Ellison is a writer. And that's a whole other kind of critter than a mere storyteller.

Language pours from his typewriter in a torrent of words. Visions explode like anger-filled hand grenades. Liquid images flow onto the pages, neon-streaked, high-voltage, screaming charges of emotion, vibrating with pain and horror and rage. Harlan writes with words as clean as surgical-grade stainless steel, as hard as lunar diamonds, as bright as a roaring solar flare, as precise as a neurosurgical laser, and as deadly as a monofilament wire tightening around your neck. At his very best — when his most exquisitely crafted work shatters through the bland oatmeal of your everyday existence into the pulsating wet heart of your conscious self — Harlan writes of emotions so rare and precious and altogether human that in the act of reading, the reader transcends his own limitations, and is expanded to a new level of receptivity to the universe around him.

Do you see what I mean about the difference between writers and storytellers?

Harlan Ellison is a passionate human being. He cares. He feels. He reacts. He acts. He writes. He demands the truth — from himself and from everybody who dares to enter his space. He's not idealistic. He simply demands that the world live up to its own standards — or stop professing them. And he puts all of that passion into his work. Where better?

But even that is not sufficient for Harlan.

There is one area in Harlan's life, in which he is so demanding that his behavior is punishingly brutal. It has destroyed four marriages and an uncountable number of friendships. There are people who cannot keep up with Harlan and who cannot tolerate his near-fanatical dedication for perfection in this single arena. In my entire life, I have never met any human being who has demanded so much of himself, who has challenged himself so consistently and with such persistence as Harlan Ellison. Whatever else Harlan Ellison may be — and the stories are legion — the one brutal drive that motivates this man is the need to do better.

He is self-educated on a scale that is nothing less than astonishing. His knowledge of music, literature, art, comics, science fiction, contemporary culture, history, and trivia is second to none. You may be surprised to read this, but his growth as a compassionate man is no less.

Look, I know that Harlan Ellison has a thermonuclear reputation, and yes, it's fairly earned; but that's merely the public perception of Harlan. The real Harlan is a little old Jewish man with the cutest little pot belly, who shlumps around the house in his bathrobe and slippers, muttering about finding a bottle of seltzer water. The real Harlan Ellison is a man who takes every death as a personal insult.

He can't stand to see people suffering unnecessary pain. I am tempted to insert an artful tangent here, discussing Harlan's perception of necessary pain — the art of revenge — but most of that is performance and perception. In practice, Harlan limits most of his revenge to simply telling his side of the story and letting you make up your own mind. This book, for example. The point is that the real Harlan Ellison is a very human being, a combination of both the best and the worst that a human can be; but his best is beyond simple description — and even his worst is still terrific.

When you have a couple of spare centuries, read through Harlan's body of work in the order in which it was written. You will be able to watch a man grow, expand, transcend, challenge, renew, rededicate, and recommit himself over and over and over again. Reading his work is hard, painful work sometimes. Disturbing, annoying, frustrating — the nightmares and fantasies that he puts in your head are inescapable. He shoves timebombs down your throat; 15-kiloton time bombs that go off days, weeks, months later. I don't know how history is going to judge Harlan; it may be that he is a special phenomenon unique to the twentieth century, but I hope not. Some of these screams of rage deserve to echo for a long, long time.

Gene Roddenberry, on the other hand, was a TV producer. (A TV producer is an ordinary human being who has made the mistake of falling asleep next to a big green pod filled with money. When he awakes again, he has been transformed into an alien thing that feeds on power, talent, and the blood of the innocent. Now, some people I know have argued with me about this, saying that a TV producer is nowhere near as bad as a lawyer, but TV producers are one of the leading causes of lawyers in Los Angeles. You don't need to be a rocket scientist to figure that one out.)

At his best, Gene Roddenberry was an inspiring speaker. He knew how to say all of the right things. He knew how to speak to a crowd or an individual with equal grace. He knew what you wanted to hear and that was what he told you. He made you want to believe again.

At his worst — well, he was a producer, the American version of a feudal lord. Despite whatever assertions for truth and justice a feudal lord might make, he's still a lord. He might believe he's acting justly, but the way the system is constituted encourages acts of abuse, if not by the lord himself, then certainly by those who act in his name. The lord doesn't have to drive the steamroller; there are lots of peasants working in the fields who will happily do that job for him, without regard to whose home or livelihood they're rumbling over.

The real issue here is not "The City on the Edge of Forever." That's just a side battle in a much larger war. The real issue is the challenge of *Star Trek* and the underlying commitment of the storyteller. It is clear from reading this script that Harlan Ellison wanted to do more than just another hour of forgettable television. He wanted to do something powerful and unique.

As science fiction, *Star Trek* ranges from pretty bland to pretty silly with occasional forays to pretty godawful. I do not say this as a blanket condemnation. *Star Trek* is a television show. It is a commercial enterprise (pun intended). When a camel flies, you don't judge it by the same standards as an eagle. (The good news about *Star Trek* is that it has raised the standard of acceptable mediocrity. If this is the lowest common denominator, then maybe we're not doing too badly. The *bad* news is that so many fans of the show never think to raise their sights any higher.)

To put it simply, *Star Trek* is the McDonald's of science fiction; it's fastfood storytelling. Every problem is like every other problem. They all get solved in an hour. Nobody ever gets hurt, and nobody needs to care. You give up an hour of your time and you don't really have to get involved. It's all plastic.

This is why "The City on the Edge of Forever" is such an extraordinary episode. It is the one story in which the problem is never solved; the pain goes on forever. Whether you are reading Harlan's script or watching the produced version, the impact of Edith Keeler's death is a devastating blow. Kirk will never be the same. Neither will the audience. Kirk will age a century in a single moment; he can never again have the same adventurous innocence. The last scenes of "The City on the Edge of Forever" are a promise. "Don't ever relax. Nothing is certain. Not in this universe — and not on this TV show."

Unfortunately, it's a broken promise. Never again did *Star Trek* startle its audience so brilliantly. When we came back again next week, here was Kirk, no different than before. Edith Keeler was never mentioned. She might never have existed.

This is the difference between Harlan Ellison's view of writing and Gene Roddenberry's. When Harlan tells a story, it's about an important event in a person's life; it assaults that person's sensibilities, shatters him, forces him to reinvent himself, and ultimately leaves him forever transformed. A Harlan Ellison story is a challenge to festering complacency.

Gene Roddenberry's view of the job seemed to be much less ambitious: get the Captain laid and clean up the mess before the last commercial. Nobody gets permanently hurt. Our people are the best and the brightest; our people are perfect; they don't have problems. Everything is wonderful. Everybody is loyal. Nobody ever argues with the Captain.

The Captain is always right. Everybody stays in his place. And is happy. Forever.

I guess so, but if our people don't have any problems to solve, they're really not very interesting, are they? They certainly aren't human. They're just ... nice to look at.

But that's not storytelling. That's cowardice. That's a failure to use the tool. A television show like *Star Trek* is an opportunity to make a difference — to demonstrate that human beings can rise above adversity, that life as it is lived is not necessarily the way that life has to be, to evoke the best from ourselves and demonstrate that we as a species are committed to challenging ourselves against whatever horrors the universe can throw against us. A television show like *Star Trek* shouldn't be polite. It should be unafraid and passionate. It should startle and disturb and leave your view of the universe shaken. It should expand your vision of what's possible in the world.

Most of all, a show like *Star Trek* should be a writer's dream assignment — it should be a place where a writer can come in and tell that story that he's always wanted to tell, a place where he can take that thing that sticks in his craw and lay it out for all the world to see. When a writer cares, when he is committed to truth, and passionate about life, then he is willing to wrestle with the devil himself if the result will be a story that makes a difference.

It's about keeping the promise.

Anything less is like having your imagination gummed to death by tribbles.

If there is only one reason to fault Gene Roddenberry, this is it — his failure to allow *Star Trek*'s writers to be the very best that they aspired to be.

The loss is *Star Trek*'s. And ours.

DeForest Kelley

I am certain, I have no doubt: most of you are familiar with *Star Trek*'s "The City on the Edge of Forever." You should also know that it was my favorite episode, as well as the runaway favorite of *Star Trek* viewers, as noted in a poll conducted prior to a recent *Star Trek* marathon.

I had a feeling about that show. After you've done as many scripts as those of us who work steadily in film and tv have done, you can feel the electrical charge in the really top-notch ones. I knew it was going to be a winner, and I'm proud to have been a part of it. It's one of the few times I wished that I had been playing Kirk's role.

In fact, during the filming, I became convinced that McCoy should *also* fall for the lovely Edith Keeler (played by Joan Collins). I felt it would add to the intrigue, should McCoy as well as Kirk come under the spell of her decency, humanity, and beauty — both inner and outer.

I suggested it to Joe Pevney, our director. I thought a good spot to indicate the attraction would be when Edith comes to McCoy's room where he's recuperating. McCoy, at this point, is up and feeling better. She's on her way out, just prior to meeting Kirk — moments before her death.

As she goes to the door to leave, she turns and looks at McCoy and smiles. McCoy meets her look and returns her smile as he says, "You have the biggest eyes I've ever seen!" She pauses, looks at him, smiles, exits. Close on McCoy. He's nuts for her. Pevney shot it. It was never seen.

Now . . . about my association with Harlan: I am not sure just when or where I first met this bundle of energy. Was it on *The Tomorrow Show* antagonizing Tom Snyder, our host, in brilliant verbal battle — or was it on a *Star Trek* convention stage, taking on the whole audience while projecting humor, charm, intelligence, and yes, always that in-dwelling anger that somehow manages to sneak past its security guard? I *am* sure when I first *saw* him. It was in the commissary of the old Desilu Studio during the first season of *Star Trek* while having lunch with a friend. My attention was drawn to a very animated, rather noisy conversation between a handsome young man and a lovely young girl. I asked my luncheon partner who they were. He glanced over to their table in the middle of the room and said, "Oh, that's Harlan Ellison, the writer," and went back to his lunch. I took another look — just in time to see him push a dish of ice cream in his date's face. I said with disbelief, "Harlan Ellison just pushed a dish of ice cream in her face." As my friend looked up, the lovely young woman very deliberately shoved *her* dish of ice cream into *his* face. My friend said: "That's Ellison!"

I later learned that this was a carefully prearranged gag Harlan and the starlet — who was in that week's episode, and whom Harlan had been dating — had set up to amuse the cast and crew during the lunch break.

That *is* Ellison — and this screenplay is Ellison at his best. All of these emotions are pounding throughout this script that he so desperately wanted produced ... all of the fire and anger rage as he races through one exciting moment after another — and then, quite suddenly, when we take a deep breath, he delivers some of the most touching, heartbreaking scenes ever to grace the pages of a film script. Harlan's wonderful, irreverent feel for a scene is rare among writers. This is the story behind the story of "City."

It has been a choppy history and, like Harlan himself, a legendary topic of controversy. But at last, apparently, much of the story we did not know is before us. It makes one wonder.

Read it. *You'll love it!*

Walter Koenig

At the time *Star Trek IV* was released, Harlan and I had yet another heated exchange in what has become a vast catalogue of heated exchanges. So indigenous to our mental set and so inevitable in our lives is this mutual contentiousness, that I am convinced the first stooped and knuckle-dragging primates to turn their backs on Tyrannosaurus Rex and start throwing rocks at each other were progenitors of the clans, Ellison and Koenig.

The Jungian battle presently addressed occurred in 1986 and was fought out over the phone. Expletives of a most incendiary kind were followed by telephone carriage abuse that rivaled the impact suffered by crashed automobiles in traffic school films.

Histrionics notwithstanding, to this point, the fight was still a thing easily forgotten and dispatched with time. But then Harlan committed the cardinal sin; he took it public, wrote about it — to be sure, not as the basis of a treatise, only in passing — and used my name making sure which of us looked like the good guy. (Well, I guess I can't blame him for that.)

It was then I swore I would never ever speak to him again. I swore it and I swore it with nostrils flaring and veins popping, with legs locked and fists raised to Heaven, with epic oaths and pledges made to the devil. I swore it and I swore it and, of course, here I am writing this afterword, my resolve as insubstantial as RediWhip™, as cotton candy, as dandelion puffs. Why? Because in the end, no matter what the transgression (real or imagined) homage must be paid the artist.

Harlan Ellison can really piss me off, but when he writes of Edith Keeler's idealism, Captain Kirk's pure love and the tragedy of being Trooper, I begin to suspect, against all reason, that I, alone, am ignoble and the sole cause of the endless disputes between us.

There is in "The City on the Edge of Forever" a profound sensitivity that taps into what is good in man while never letting us forget that we are also by nature a callous, selfish, indifferent breed and that only through monumental struggle and much personal sacrifice can we achieve the best of which we are capable.

It is a story that is both despairing and uplifting. It makes us ashamed and it makes us proud and because of that, time portals and Guardians and the twenty-third century notwithstanding, it is about life, our life, life in North Hollywood, California and Beacon, New York and Kaukauna, Wisconsin and Culpeper, Virginia.

The test of any work of art is the uniqueness of its creator's vision and the universality of his message. Harlan Ellison, the sonofabitch, is a master craftsman who marches to his own drummer but never fails to teach us the steps.

How often have we read a story and said what a terrific film script could be made from it. The book you hold in your hands is a film script that reads like a terrific story. If you loved the TV episode, you have to love this tome even more. And if you didn't like the TV episode, you still have to love this work.

He's done it again, the mother____!

Leonard Nimoy

In our business, that of producing movies and television shows, there is a commonly repeated saying that is, sadly, too often true: "Success has many fathers. Failure is an orphan."

Clearly "The City on the Edge of Forever" was a resounding success. I remember well the day I read the draft of the script submitted by Harlan Ellison. I found myself holding my breath and turning pages without knowing it, as this wonderful story unfolded. Some *Star Trek* scripts were actually unreadable. Harlan's was unstoppable. You couldn't put it down. No matter what happened later, the unalterable fact is: Harlan Ellison delivered a piece that had creative love pouring out of every page.

And if you don't know by now that Harlan Ellison and Gene Roddenberry were engaged in a blood battle over this project ever since its inception, then you have been living on some strange planet devoid of intelligence and communication.

The fact is that "The City on the Edge of Forever" lives. And I have always been deeply grateful to Harlan for his energy, his passion, his talent and this gift to *Star Trek*.

Melinda M. Snodgrass

Star Trek is almost thirty years old, and there are going to be hundreds, nay thousands, of words devoted to its impact, its genius; words of wisdom from its actors, past and present; and of course hosannas sung to its creator. As I look over this list I notice the one glaring omission — where are the writers?

Kirk would never have been so charming, nor Picard so turgid — excuse me, wise — without the writers. But writers do more than merely put words in the mouths of the attractive mynah birds. In the field of science fiction they create entire cultures (evidence D.C. Fontana's remarkable work in creating Spock and Vulcan society), and if they're any good at their craft they look at the collections of traits and quirks which define "character" on your average television show, and they try to find the guts of these people.

Guts are messy, and writers root about in them because we're trying to understand humanity, its condition, and ultimately ourselves. This is terrifying to the pablum of television that demands life be simple and comfortable, and problems which are solvable in 22 or 47 minutes.

"The City on the Edge of Forever" is not a comfortable script. There is nobility and sacrifice, but there is also pain and imperfection on these pages. No wonder Gene Roddenberry wanted it rewritten.

I came aboard *Star Trek: The Next Generation*, and within weeks discovered I was bound in a creative straitjacket. The directive had come down from on high — my people are perfect. Star Fleet is perfect. The Federation is perfect. Only the little fuzzy-wuzzies possess flaws, and our mission is to seek them out and set them straight.

Most of my Wailing Wall generation (Richard Manning, Hans Beimler, Ira Behr) grew up on Classic *Trek*. We would look back, and fantasize about how wonderful it must have been on the old show. Imperfect people, passionate scripts...

And then I read "City," and realized it had all been a shuck. Gene was already protecting his place in history, although perhaps not as desperately as he would by 1988. Heaven forbid there should be immorality, and out and out dishonesty on the blessed *Enterprise*. Perish the thought that Spock and Kirk could *fight*, and yet still remain friends. In Gene's universe, love is established by people standing around telling each other how much they love each other, and never doing a damn thing about it.

Please note I am discussing love here, not sex. In addition to the mantras of "Picard is the Captain, keep him strong," and "My people are perfect," we often received the directive to "LET THEM FUCK!"

Read "City" again. This is about love. Not fucking.

Like Harlan, I came into the insane world of Hollywood through the emotionally sustaining but economically unsatisfying world of books. There, a writer's words are his coin, and his spirit, and no one touches them. Editors can suggest, but a writer can refuse to accept their guidance; in publishing we're permitted to starve on our principles. Not so in Hollywood. You're a high-paid typist, your words are worthless, your vision unimportant. You take the high ground, and they come through with a bulldozer and remove it. If they don't like a script, they'll "polish" (piss on) it, and make it their own.

Being invited to write this afterword meant a great deal to me. I, too, have a script in my closet which was destroyed. Unfortunately the filmed version of "Ensigns of Command" does not bear comparison with even the watered-down film version of "City." I think that is a testament to the power and passion of Harlan Ellison's work.

A final note. For those of you vid kids who bought this book because it was *Trek,* and TV, and so cool, and who have never read a word of Harlan Ellison's prose — *Go Buy Some and Read It!*

Because ultimately books are better.

George Takei

Before reading the manuscript of Harlan's original "The City on the Edge of Forever," I thought I would jump through the "time portal" of my own to refresh my memory of the version we had filmed back in 1966.

I threw the cassette into the VCR and snuggled down with a hot cup of tea. It opened with the familiar soaring music and the good old *Enterprise* dependably whooshing by — it was all so comfy. Then, the jolt. It wasn't, however, the action of the first scene where the bridge was being violently shaken by a time disturbance. I had expected that. The shock was in how bloomingly young we all looked back then. Oh, so very young.

But the action quickly grabbed me away from the warm fuzzies of nostalgia. This was gripping drama. Yes, it was one of our best episodes. Sure, some of it was dated — Uhura's whispering "Captain, I'm afraid" — a line that could hardly be written for a woman today, though perhaps it could be said by a man now — a measure of the times.

Another time warp — Joan Collins as the personification of

purest virtue. Time — that's what this story was about — past, present and future deconstructed by Harlan's fertile imagination into a mind-play fable. Intriguing concept, tight drama and stimulating science fiction.

So, what was Harlan's big beef about his script being debased? This was great television. With that, I began reading the original manuscript.

Immediately, the differences become apparent. The images are soaringly elegant and striking science fiction. The Guardians of Forever — the tall, petrified, ancient keepers of the Time Vortex — resonate mysticism and the quality of legend. How awesome, in the truest sense of the word, it would have been to have seen these immensely dignified science fiction figures realized cinematically.

Even the language of the stage directions and descriptions is compelling poetry. The sun of this alien planet is described as "a burnt out ember . . . hanging dolorously in the cadaverous sky."

There is a real villain here, not our good Doctor McCoy temporarily crazed. The odious act of drug dealing is still today, as it was in the 1960s, and as it will always be, an agonizingly real societal cancer. The evil is pure, constant and absolute, as is the goodness.

And in Harlan's original, the play and the balance between evil and good, death and life, is made more intriguingly ambiguous in the larger context of history. The aching tragedy and personal pain of Verdun (absent in the filmed version) is dramatically poignant in the longer perspective of time. The vast, epic scope of Harlan's original gives "The City on the Edge of Forever" the resonance of legend.

This manuscript truly tantalizes the mind. Yes, I can understand Harlan's frustration. Yes, I would love to have seen this original filmed. This is one of the intriguing "what ifs?" of life — but time has played out this plot differently — just as in his story.

Harlan, you rascal, you master manipulator — you've done it again. You've placed a clear mirror in front of a tarnished mirror. Is that expression I see reflected on your face one of frustration, or a Cheshire Cat grin?

...AS WE WENT TO PRESS.

TV Guide, 1 July, 1995.

70 **Halting the Tanks** (June 5, 1989) After six weeks of pro-democracy demonstrations by students and workers, the Chinese government ordered the Army to retake Tiananmen Square. As a convoy of tanks rolled into the city, a lone man carrying groceries stepped in front of the lead tank, stopping the column. This intrepid act, seen worldwide, was a potent symbol of individual will.

69 **Terrorists at the Olympics** (September 5, 1972) In the middle of the night, Arab guerillas stole into the athletes' compound at the Munich Olympics, killing two Israelis and taking nine hostage. After negotiations failed, West German police made a rescue attempt that resulted in a tragic firefight in which all the hostages died. Pressed into service to cover the 23-hour crisis, ABC Sports announcer Jim McKay somberly reported, "They're all gone."

68 *Star Trek's* **"City on the Edge of Forever"** (April 6, 1967) In the original series' most provocative episode, Captain Kirk and Mr. Spock pursue Dr. McCoy through a time portal to Depression-era New York, where Kirk falls for a social worker (played by a radiant Joan Collins). But Kirk faces a torturous dilemma: If she does not die young, her subsequent activities will result in the Nazis winning World War II. So, as a truck barrels toward the woman, Kirk restrains McCoy from saving her. "Do you know what you've just done, Jim?" asks the horrified doctor. "He knows, Doctor," says Spock, his Vulcan reserve cracking. "He knows."

A Visit to Neverland (March 7, 1955) Fueled by a sprinkle of fairy dust, NBC's *Producers' Showcase* reached the pinnacle of live television with a lavish mounting of the musical *Peter Pan*. Custom-built machinery was shipped in from England to make the flying as convincing as possible. In the case of Mary Martin, they probably could have saved on the special effects. She was so effervescent and evocative as Peter, it seemed she could soar at will. The production was such a huge critical and popular success that NBC reprised it twice more live—in 1956 and 1960.

WITNESS
Martin's daughter, Heller Halliday DeMeritt, played a maid in the NBC special. "Mother was Peter Pan," she says. "I can still hear her laughing in that role."

TV GUIDE JUNE 29, 1996

TV GUIDE SPECIAL ISSUE

100 MOST MEMORABLE MOMENTS IN TV HISTORY

To the Reader:

Isn't it odd...everyone from Roddenberry on down knew how to "improve" my poor, wretched efforts...but NOT ONE of all the shows THEY wrote <u>without</u> me became one of the 100 most memorable moments in TV history.

At last, after 30 years, I rest my case.

6 July 96

In a career spanning 40 years, Harlan Ellison has been honored by professional organizations and won more awards for his over 1,700 pieces of published work than any other living fantasist. Included among his numerous distinctions are the Hugo Award (8 $1/2$ times!), the Nebula Award (3 times), the Edgar Allan Poe Award of the Mystery Writers of America (2), the World Fantasy Lifetime Achievement award, and the Silver Pen for Journalism by P.E.N. (the international writer's union).

Harlan Ellison has become as notorious for his creative approaches and commitment to researching and promoting his topics as he has for his writing. *The Washington Post* has described him as "one of the great living American short story writers."

White Wolf Publishing will release 31 backlist titles by the multiple-award winning author. The first of the 20-volume series, *Edgeworks 1*, is already available. For the first time in years, fans of Harlan Ellison's writings will be able to acquire works which have become difficult to find in any form other than expensive collector editions.

The following is an excerpt from
Edgeworks 2: The Collected Ellison

SPIDER KISS
by Harlan Ellison
chapter one

First there was only the empty golden circle of the hot spot, blazing against the silk curtains. That, and in another vein, the animal murmuring of the audience, mostly teen-age girls with tight sweaters and mouths open-crammed by gum. For what seemed the longest time that was the portrait: cut from primordial materials in an expectant arena. There was a tension so intense it could be felt as warmth on the neck, uncontrollable twitches in the lips and eyes, the nervous shifting of small hands *from* nowhere *to* nowhere.

The curtains gave a vagrant rustle and from three parts of the orchestra and four parts of the balcony came piercing, wind-up-a-chimney shrieks of pleasure and torment. Behind the velvet ropes, overflow crowds pressed body on body to get a neck-straining view of the stage. Just those purple and yellow draperies, the golden coin of the spotlight beam. The scene was laid with a simple, but forceful, altogether impressive sense of dramatics.

In the pit, the orchestra began warming its sounds, and the jungle murmur of the anxious crowd rose a decibel. There would be no Master of Ceremonies to start festivities, no prefatory acts — the Tumbling Turellos; Wally French & Sadie, the educated dachshund; Ivor Harrig with mime and merriment; The DeLaney

Sisters — there would only be that golden spotlight, a blast of sound, and the curtains would part. This was one man's show, as it had been one man's show for two weeks. This was The Palace, and it had been invaded.

Two weeks before they had made The Palace alter all its precedents. The screaming, feral teen-age girls with their eyes like wine-soaked jewels, their mouths hungry, their adolescent bodies rigged and trussed erotically. They had booed and hissed the other acts from the stage before they could gain a hearing. They had stamped and clamored so outrageously, the booker and stage manager had decided — in the absence of the manager — to cut straight through to the feature attraction, the draw-card that had brought an audience rivaled only by the gates of Garland, Belafonte and in days past, Martin & Lewis.

They had set the other acts aside, hoping this demonstration was only an opening day phenomenon. But it had been two weeks, with SRO at every performance, and the other acts had been paid off, told a profusion of sorrys, and the headliner had lengthened his stint to fill the space. He seemed, in fact, suffused with an inner electricity that allowed him to perform for hours without fatigue. The Palace had regretfully acquiesced…they had been conquered, and knew it.

Now, as the golden moon-face contracted, centering at the overlapping folds of the curtains, the orchestra burst into song. A peculiar song; as though barely adaptable to full brass and strings, it was a repetitive melody, underslung with a constant mechanical piano-drum beat, simple and even nagging. Immature but demanding, infectious.

The audience exploded.

Screams burst from every corner of the theatre, and in the first twenty-seven rows of the orchestra, girls leaped from seats as though spastic, lanceted with emotional fire. A senseless, building fury consumed The Palace, and beat at the walls, reverberated out onto Seventh Avenue. The love affair was about to be consummated — again.

The curtains withdrew smoothly, the golden circle of light fell liquidly to the stage, hung in the black mouth of no scenery, no cyclorama, nothing, and the orchestra beat to a crescendoing final riff.

Silence...

The hushed intake of a thousand, three thousand, too many thousand breaths...

The muscle-straining expectancy as bodies pressed upward toward the empty space soon to be filled...

The spotlight snapped off...

Darkness...

Then back to life and he was *there!*

If the insanity that had ruled seventy-six seconds before was great, what was now loosed could only be called Armageddon. Seats clanged up against the backs of chairs, a Perdition's chorus of screams, wails, shrieks, moans and obscenities crashed and thundered like the waves on the Cliff at Entretat. Hands reached fervently, feverishly, beseechingly upward. Girls bit their fists as their eyes started from their heads. Girls spread their hands against their breasts and clutched them with terrible hunger. Girls fell back into their seats, reduced to tears, reduced to jelly, reduced to emotional orgasms of terrifying intensity.

While he stood quietly, almost humbly, watching.

His name was intoned, extolled, cast out, drawn in, repeated, repeated repeated repeated till it became a chant of such erotic power it seemed to draw all light and sound to it. A vortex of emotionalism. With him at its center, both exploding and imploding waves of animal hunger.

He was of them, yet not of them. With them, yet above them.

He stood tall and slim, his legs apart, accentuating the narrowness of his hips, his broad shoulders, the lean desperation of his face, the auburn shock of hair, so meticulously combed with its cavalier forelock drooping onto his forehead.

A guardian of unnamed treasures.

Then he began to play. His hands moved over the frets of the guitar slung across his chest, and a guttural, sensuous syncopation fought with the noise of the crowd...fought...lost momentarily...lost again...crowd swell...then began to mount in insistence...till the crowd went under slowly slowly...till he was singing high and loud and with a mounting joy that caught even the self-drugged adolescents who had not come to listen, merely to worship.

His song was a pointless thing; filled with pastel inanities; don't ever leave me because I've got a sad dog heart that'll follow you where'er you go, no, don't leave me 'cause my sad dog heart cries just for you for you, ju-ust fo-o-o-or you...

But there was a subtext to the song. Something dark and roiling, an oil stain on a wet street, a rainbow of dark colors that moved almost as though alive, verging into colors that had no names, disturbing colors for which there were only psychiatric parallels. Green is the dead baby image...

The running line of what could be sensed but not heard was ominous, threatening, sensuously compelling in ways that spoke to skin and nerve-ends. It was like the moment one receives the biopsy report. It was like the feeble sound an unwatered plant makes in the instant before all reserve moisture dries from the tap root and the green turns to brown. It was like the sigh of anguish from the victim of voodoo at the instant the final pin is jammed into the ju-ju doll half a continent away. It was like the cry of a mother brought to see the tiny, crushed form lying beneath the blanket on a busy intersection. It was like the kiss of a spider.

And the great animal that was his audience, his vacuous, demanding, insensate, vicious audience, purred. Ripples of contentment washed the crowd. Almost mystically the surface of mass hysteria was smoothed, quieted, molded by his singing into a glossy plane of attention and silence. Girls who had been facially and bodily contorted by his appearance, who had thrown themselves forward in a spasm of adoration, now settled back demurely, seated and attentive.

He went on, singing, gently strumming the guitar, making idle movements of foot and hip and head — yet nothing overly suggestive, nothing that would rouse the sleeping beast out there. His movements, his voice, the chords he chose to pull from his guitar — all combined to lull the herd. His performance was as much a casting of hypnotic trances as it was a demonstration of musical ability. Like some advanced breed of snake charmer he piped at them, and their eyes became glassy, their limbs limp; they stared and absorbed and wanted, but were silent, all waiting.

And he *could* sing. Granted his material was that semi-obscene and witless conglomerate of rhythmics known as rockabilly — half thump-thump of rock n' roll, half twang and formalized beat of hillbilly — he *moved* his people with it. His voice was low and strong, sure on the subterranean notes that bespoke passion, winging on the sharp, high notes demanding gentleness. His was a good voice, free from affectation, based solidly in the sounds of the delta, the back hills, the wanderlusts of the people.

It came through. And they listened.

Until he was sure he had wrung everything from the song; then he finished. A soft rise to a lingering C-sharp, held till it was flensed clean, and a final chord. Then silence. A quick-phrased reporter from *Time* had once compared the hushed silence following the song to the silence when Lincoln completed his Gettysburg Address. Compared it and found it wanting, diseased, laughable, sexually stimulating, dangerous. Nonetheless, there it was. A long instant without time or tempo. Deepest silence. The silence of a limestone cave, the silence of deafness, the silence of the floor of the Maracot Deep. No one spoke, no one screamed, and if there was a girl in that audience who breathed — she did it self-consciously, inadvertently, quietly.

It lasted a score of heartbeats, while he stood in the spotlight, head down, wasted, empty, humble.

Then the holocaust broke once more.

The realization that they had actually felt honest emotion burst upon the constantly self-conscious teen-agers, and they quickly covered their embarrassment with the protective cloak of crowd behavior. They screamed.

The sound rose up again, a cyclonic twisting outward, reaching even those beyond the sight of the stage (where the most demonstrative always clustered), sweeping all sanity before it. Carrying its incoherent message of attack and depravity with it like a crimson banner.

The noise lasted only until he struck the first four notes of the next song.

Then...the somnambulistic state once more.

He sang.

Sang for the better part of an hour and a half, ranging widely in interpretation, though restricted by arrangement and subject matter and the idiom of his music. His songs were the tormented and feeble pleadings of the confused teen-ager for understanding in a time when understanding is the one commodity that cannot be found pre-packed in aluminum foil. His songs were not honest, nor were they particularly meaningful, but they mirrored the frustrations of that alien community known as the teens.

There was identification, if nothing else.

The lean boy with the auburn hair, gently moving his hips in rhythm to his own music, unaided by the full string orchestra in the pit, unaided by the lush trappings of The Palace, was spellbinding the third largest audience in the theatre's history.

Here he was, a twenty-two-year-old singer with a faint Kentucky accent, dictator of emotions to a horde of worshipful post-adolescents. Humble, handsome, heroic in fact. He did nothing but sing, step about the stage with little relation to terpsichore, and strum a Gibson guitar with steel strings.

Yet he ruled. Unquestionably, his was a magnetism not easily denied. His singing was clear and strong, and he *reached*. He held them. Tightly, passionately, expertly.

Stag Preston was doing the one thing in this world he *could* do in public.

From the wings he was being watched by a pair of dark eyes. The man slouched against the flats, a cigarette dangling from a corner of his mouth, burning but forgotten. He was easily as slim as the singer, hut there was lacking the wiry command inherent in every line and muscle of Stag Preston's body. Rather, this man was quick-looking. Almost feral. His eyes were set back under thin but dark eyebrows, and he watched the entire scene. He was shorter than Preston, no more than five feet seven, and his clothes hung on him with good style, unlike the clinging form of Preston's flamboyantly fitted garb.

Sheldon Morgenstern, publicity man, ace flakmerchant of the Stem, bodyguard and handmaiden to the hottest talent in the game, inveterate chainsmoker and decrier of the human soul, stood silently watching his meal ticket.

There was a singular lack of expression on his tanned, planed face. But his eyes, though dark, were a-swim with flickers of emotion.

The ash lengthened on his cigarette, as he drew deeply, split among its gray folds and dropped, dusting his jacket front. He swiped at the debris absently. The cigarette burned on, unnoticed. *Sing, kid,* he thought. *Yeah, sing.*

Behind him, the many nameless busymen who always infest backstages stood silently, listening to Stag Preston. Though their expressions were not those of the girls out front, still they were being *reached*, they were being *held* by this boy in his modern jester's motley. It was that way with anyone who listened to Stag Preston.

He was that peculiar phenomenon, the natural talent. He was uniquely Stag Preston, with no touches of Sinatra or Presley or Darin in him. He was an electric thing on a stage, a commanding personality that instantly communicated itself.

That was one-tenth the reason he had become the most valuable musical property in the business, inside four years. Just one-tenth.

Four years.

Shelly Morgenstern lipped the butt from his mouth and ground it underheel, shaking another from the pack without conscious effort. He lit it and the brief lighter flame made the stage manager wince: smoking was prohibited in the wings, so close to the highly flammable scenery. But this was *his* PR man, and godlings could ignore mere mortal rules.

Four years.

Shelly Morgenstern stared at the tilted, arched body as it

made a one-step, two-step in slightest beat to the guitar's music. Stag Preston had it, all right. There was no question about it. He was Destiny's Tot. Up from nowhere, with a handful of doubloons. Nothing to sell save that which no one else had to sell. A voice, a manner, a look, a pair of hands that could innocently warp forth innocuous backgrounds to subtle oral pornography. That was all he had, yet when those components were joined and bathed by a spotlight, or trapped and grooved on an LP...he was more. Lautrec had once said, "One should never meet the artist; the work is always so much better than the creator." That, Shelly Morgenstern mused, was more true of Stag Preston than it had ever been of anyone.

Four years.

Shelly Morgenstern watched as Stag Preston finished his final number. There would be no curtain call. Stag would announce a "little private show" around back in the alley under his dressing room window, and the stampede would start out of the theatre. That, they had found, was the only way to cleanse the theatre of its prepared-to-stay-an-eternity-with-peanut-butter-sandwiches horde. The turnover had been slow till they had employed the old Martin-Lewis dodge to empty the theatre. How they followed him; they loved him; how they ached to touch his lean, hardrock body. It was sick, Shelly was certain of that, all arguments about Vallee and Sinatra and Valentino be damned. It was sick, and four years before, *he* had been steering for a poker game. Just that long ago he had been a hungry kid with too much moxie, too much hair, and no place to go.

Four years.

Shelly Morgenstern corrected himself. That wasn't so, no place to go. The kid would have made it somehow; he had been too hungry, too anxious, too much on the grab to ever settle for a fink's life in Louisville. If it hadn't been Colonel Jack Freeport and Shelly Morgenstern, he would have done it another way. Yet it was phenomenal the way he had clawed his way up; even Jack Freeport — a tooth and nail career money-maker — had been amazed at the drive and verve with which the kid had pushed himself in so short a time. Amazed, a little frightened, but altogether impressed.

Four years.

Shelly Morgenstern stared at the advancing face of Stag Preston as it came offstage. One of the "gopher" flunkies waited with outstretched arm, presenting the ceremonial towel. The towel into which Stag Preston would wipe all that semi-holy Stag Preston sweat... which could easily be sold for twenty dollars to any of the screeching, drunk-with-adoration infants now jamming into the alley. The god sweated, yeah, it was true. But all the better. Don't put him completely out of reach. Put him just a handhold away, with the characteristic humbleness of all the new teen-aged idols. A god, yet a man.

Stag Preston stopped directly in front of Shelly Morgenstern, his face buried in the towel. When he pulled it away the dark, penetrating eyes stared directly into the shorter man's face. It was a good face, Stag Preston's face, though under the eyes and in the cruel set of mouth, the Stygian darknesses under the cheeks, there was the hint of something too mature, too desperate.

Now, as Stag shoved the towel under his shirt, wiping his moist armpit, the change would take place. *Watch the remarkable, magical transformation,* folks, Shelly thought. *Watch as Sheldon Morgenstern, whose father was a cantor and whose mother had wanted her son to become a CPA, subtly undergoes a sea-change from publicity man for the great Stag Preston to pimp for the great, horny Stag Preston. Watch closely, folks, the degradation is faster than the eye.*

"Shelly..."

Here it comes. "See one, Stag?"

The smile. The *Motion Picture/Look/Life/Teen Magazine*-famous smile guaranteed to contain 100% unadulterated sex appeal combined with bullshit. The smile, and, "A cutie, Shel. A little redhead down front with a ponytail. She's got a sign says Stag Preston We Love You. Can't miss her. She'll be out in the alley. G'wan and round her up for me, how's about, Shel." There was no question in it; it was an order, despite the lisping, gentle Kentucky voice.

Sure, Stag. "Sure Stag."

Stag Preston made his way to the dressing room, and Sheldon Morgenstern made his way to the stage door. He paused to dump the old cigarette, light a fresh one, and open the huge metal door.

There they were. Growling, clamoring, straining for a sight of God on Earth. He watched them with the pitying scrutiny of a compassionate butcher, and found the little redhead. Stag had a good eye, there was no taking that away from him. She was too large in the chest for a kid her age, and the hair was a bit too brassy, but that was invariably the way Stag liked them.

He moved out into the crowd, reached her and tapped her shoulder. "Miss?" The wide, green eyes turned up to him, registered nothing.

"Miss, Stag would like to meet you." He said it with no feeling, with, in fact, a definite absence of inflection in hopes she might be scared off. But they never were. Any of them.

Her breath went in like a train through a tunnel, fast and sharp and leaving emptiness behind it. "*Stag?* Me?"

He nodded. No encouragement, no deterrent.

She said something to a girl beside her, a fat girl with pimples (why did the best-looking ones always come with their comparison-friends, so they looked that much better?), and gave her the Stag Preston We Love You sign. Then she turned, with Roman candles in her eyes, and followed Shelly Morgenstern into the theatre.

Four years, he thought. Four years, and how did it all start? Was it that request from the Kentucky State Fair for Colonel Jack Freeport to judge the talent contest?

Had it started then, when they'd met Stag in Louisville? Or did it go further back, much further Back to the days when Shelly had been trying to break away from the orthodox enslavement of his home, when he had discovered he could no longer believe in the terrible God of his father, and worshipped more easily at the heavenly throne of Success (and Money is his profit)? Did it go back to Jack Freeport, who needed more, more, more of everything...to rebuild a name that had been shattered as far back as the burning of Atlanta? Had it begun with hungers, or with simple supply-and-demand?

He knew how it had started.

And as he walked the little redhead into the lion's mouth, he thought about it...about the four years.

Well tell it, then. Tell it, but make it quick.

We've still got three shows to do.

harlan ellison
edgeworks

2: **SPIDER KISS**

STALKING THE NIGHTMA

ou think *city on the edge of forever was cool?*
ait'll you get your hands on these!

Edgeworks: The collected Ellison

h a r l a n   E l l i s o n

E d g e w o r k s

ITE WOLF PUBLISHING RELEASES 20
LUMES OF THE COLLECTED FICTION,
AYS, TELEPLAYS AND COLUMNS OF THE
TER *THE WASHINGTON POST* CALLS
" OF THE GREAT LIVING AMERICAN
RT STORY WRITERS. THESE HANDSOME
LUMES CONTAIN COMPLETELY REVISED,
DATED AND EXPANDED MANUSCRIPTS AS
L AS AN ORIGINAL INTRODUCTION BY
AUTHOR IN EVERY VOLUME! THE
HOR WHO HAS WON MORE AWARDS FOR
AGINATIVE LITERATURE THAN ANY
IER LIVING FANTASIST WILL UNLEASH
NTROLLED CHAOS WITH 31 RAZOR-
RP EDGEWORKS.

Shadow

From a Great Height

Night Vigil

Xenogenesis: An Essay

Rock God

Ernest and the Machine God

Pennies, Off a Dead Man's Eyes

The Words in Spock's Mouth: An Essay

RAISE FOR HARLAN ELLISON:

masterful storyteller whose goal is to leave you with a bittersweet taste — like a jalapeño-
d cinnamon bear."
—Playboy

times, Ellison's writing is so willful, so bizarre, that one is not sure whether to be offended or
ressed. It has chutzpah....it is always brilliant, always full of emotional power. His skills are as
p as ever, his wit as mordant, his eye for details telling...for Harlan Ellison, the magic hasn't
e away."
—*Washington Post Book World*

Mr. Ellison has some of the spellbinding quality of a great nonstop talker, with a cultural warehouse
a mind."
—*New York Times Book Review*